Human Nature

ROYAL INSTITUTE OF PHILOSOPHY SUPPLEMENT: 70

EDITED BY

Constantine Sandis
and
M.J. Cain

CAMBRIDGE
UNIVERSITY PRESS

PUBLISHED BY THE PRESS SYNDICATE OF THE UNIVERSITY OF CAMBRIDGE
The Pitt Building, Trumpington Street, Cambridge, CB2 1RP,
United Kingdom

CAMBRIDGE UNIVERSITY PRESS
The Edinburgh Building, Cambridge CB2 8RU, United Kingdom
32 Avenue of the Americas, New York, NY 10013–2473, USA
477 Williamstown Road, Port Melbourne, VIC 3207, Australia
C/Orense, 4, planta 13, 28020 Madrid, Spain
Lower Ground Floor, Nautica Building, The Water Club, Beach Road,
Granger Bay, 8005 Cape Town, South Africa

Printed in the United Kingdom at the University Press, Cambridge
Typeset by Techset Composition Ltd, Salisbury, UK

A catalogue record for this book is available from the British Library

ISBN 9781107651975
ISSN 1358-2461

Contents

Notes on Contributors

Stephen J. Boulter
>Stephen J. Boulter is Senior Lecturer in Philosophy at Oxford Brookes University and the author of *The Rediscovery of Common Sense Philosophy* (Palgrave, 2007).

M.J. Cain
>M.J. Cain is Programme Lead for Philosophy and Religion at Oxford Brookes University. He is the author of *Fodor: Language, Mind and Philosophy* (Polity, 2002) and several articles in the philosophy of language and mind. He is currently completing a volume on the philosophy of cognitive science.

Beverley Clack
>Beverley Clack is Professor in the Philosophy of Religion at Oxford Brookes University. Her publications include *Feminist Philosophy of Religion: Critical Readings*, co-edited with Pamela Sue Anderson (Routledge, 2004), *Sex and Death: A Reappraisal of Human Mortality* (Polity, 2002), *Misogyny in the Western Philosophical Tradition* (Macmillan, 1999), and *The Philosophy of Religion*, co-authored with Brian R. Clack in 1998 (fully revised 2nd edition, Polity, 2008).

John Cottingham
>John Cottingham is Professor Emeritus of Philosophy at the University of Reading, Professorial Research Fellow at Heythrop College, University of London, an Honorary Fellow of St John's College, Oxford, and editor of the international philosophical journal *Ratio*. His recent titles include *On the Meaning of Life* (Routledge, 2003), The *Spiritual Dimension* (CUP, 2005), *Cartesian Reflections* (OUP, 2008), and *Why Believe?* (Continuum, 2009).

Tim J. Crow
>Tim J. Crow was Head of the Division of Psychiatry at the Clinical Research Centre at Northwick Park from 1974 to 1994 and subsequently a member of the External Staff of the Medical Research Council and Honorary Director of the SANE Prince of Wales Centre for Research on Schizophrenia and Depression in the Department of Psychiatry at the

University of Oxford. He has written on the nature and causation of psychosis, in particular on its relation to the evolution of language. He edited *The Speciation of Modern Homo Sapiens* (OUP, 2002).

Hans-Johann Glock

Hans-Johann Glock is Professor of Philosophy at the University of Zurich (Switzerland), and Visiting Professor at the University of Reading (UK). He is the author of *A Wittgenstein Dictionary* (Blackwell, 1996), *Quine and Davidson on language, thought and reality* (CUP, 2003), *La mente de los animals* (KRK, 2009), and *What is Analytic Philosophy?* (CUP, 2008), as well as the editor of numerous volumes including *The Rise of Analytic Philosophy* (Blackwell, 1997), *Wittgenstein: a Critical Reader* (Blackwell, 2001), and *Strawson and Kant* (OUP, 2003).

P.M.S. Hacker

P.M.S. Hacker is an Emeritus Research Fellow at St John's College, Oxford. His most important works are his four volume Commentary on Wittgenstein's *Philosophical Investigations* (Blackwell, 1980–1996), the first two volumes co-authored with G.P. Baker, *Wittgenstein's Place in Twentieth Century Philosophy* (Blackwell, 1996), *Philosophical Foundations of Neuroscience* (Blackwell, 2003), co-authored with Max Bennett, *Human Nature: The Categorial Framework* (Wiley-Blackwell, 2007), and its sequel, *The Cognitive and Cogitative Powers of Man* (Wiley-Blackwell, forthcoming).

Wolfram Hinzen

Wolfram Hinzen is Professor of philosophy at Durham University, and author of *Mind Design and Minimal Syntax* (OUP, 2006) and *An Essay on Names and Truth* (OUP, 2007).

Rosalind Hursthouse

Rosalind Hursthouse is Professor of Philosophy at the University of Auckland, New Zealand. She is the author of *On Virtue Ethics* (OUP, 1999) and of various articles in the same area, including some on Aristotle.

P.J.E. Kail

P.J.E. Kail is University Lecturer in the History of Modern Philosophy at Oxford University and Tutor and Official Fellow in Philosophy at St. Peter's College. He has published on Hume, Hutcheson, Malebranche, Berkeley and Nietzsche. His book *Projection and Realism in Hume's Philosophy* was published in 2007 by OUP.

Sarah Patterson

Sarah Patterson is took a BA at Oxford and a PhD at MIT. She taught at Michigan, Harvard and Tufts before coming to Birkbeck College, University of London, where she is Senior Lecturer in philosophy. She has published papers in early modern philosophy, philosophy of mind and philosophy of psychology, and is working on a book on Descartes's philosophy of mind.

Richard Samuels

Richard Samuels Professor of Philosophy at the Ohio State University. His research focuses primarily on topics in the philosophy of mind and foundations of cognitive science.

Preface

The study of human nature has always been of central importance to philosophy. Indeed, some understanding of what it is to be human has been central to the work of some of the greatest philosophical thinkers including Plato, Aristotle, Aquinas, Hobbes, Descartes, Locke, Hume, Rousseau, Mill, Nietzsche, Freud, and Marx. In more recent years writers as diverse as Steven Pinker, Ian McEwan, Philip Pullman, Simon Baron-Cohen, Mary Midgley, Jesse Prinz, and Edward O. Wilson have all expounded their views on related issues with much passion. Questions such as 'what is human nature?', 'is there such a thing as an exclusively human nature?', 'through what methods might we best discover more about our nature?', and 'to what extent are our actions and beliefs constrained by it?' are of central importance not only to philosophy and science, but also to our general understanding of ourselves as people who belong to the human species.

The essays collected in this volume collectively address key issues and taboos surrounding the theme of human nature by bringing together philosophers working in a multitude of areas including the philosophy of cognitive science, evolutionary psychology, the philosophy of biology, psychoanalysis, ethics and moral psychology, developmental psychology, the philosophy of mind and action, the philosophy of psychology, the philosophy of religion, and the history of philosophy. Most of the work included in this volume was presented at the 32nd Royal Institute of Philosophy conference, which took place at Oxford Brookes University on June 15–17, 2010, with Human Nature as its theme. The two exceptions are the papers by Rosalind Hursthouse and Sarah Patterson, both of whom were unable to be present. The conference also included talks by John Dupré and Kim Sterelny that had already been committed to other publications.

We would like to thank all of the contributors and participators for their work and involvement. Thanks also to Mollie Ashley, James Garvey, Martin Groves, Diana Jarman, Jim Hyndman, and Stan Thomas for their organisational assistance. We would also like to thank The Analysis Trust, Cambridge University Press, Gazelle Book Services, Oxford Brookes University, Palgrave Macmillan, Polity Press, the Royal Institute of

Preface

Philosophy, and Wiley-Blackwell for generous support. Particular thanks is due to Nicola Marshall and her team at Cambridge University Press, for so efficiently guiding us through production and making the whole process enjoyable. Last but not least we owe special thanks to our conference co-organiser Dan O' Brien.

CS & MJC
Oxford, September 2011

Science and Human Nature

RICHARD SAMUELS

There is a puzzling tension in contemporary scientific attitudes towards human nature. On the one hand, evolutionary biologists correctly maintain that the traditional essentialist conception of human nature is untenable; and moreover that this is *obviously* so in the light of quite general and exceedingly well-known evolutionary considerations.[1] On this view, talk of human nature is just an expression of pre-Darwinian superstition.[2] On the other hand, talk of human nature abounds in certain regions of the sciences, especially in linguistics, psychology and cognitive science. Further, it is very frequently most common amongst those cognitive-behavioral scientists who should be most familiar with the sorts of facts that putatively undermine the very notion of human nature: sociobiologists, evolutionary psychologists, and more generally, theorists working on the evolution of mind and culture.

Faced with such a tension, three main kinds of response come readily to mind. A first possibility would be to charge one party with ignorance or idiocy. Perhaps students of human behavior and cognition are, for example, just too stupid or ignorant to recognize the implications of well known, general facts about evolution. But this is highly implausible – not to mention uncharitable. Whatever else is going on here, the problem is surely not one of silliness. A second possible response would be to adopt a deflationary attitude towards talk of human nature. Perhaps all talk of human nature is mere rhetorical flourish – just filigree to decorate more sober views. No doubt there is something to this. Talk of human nature sounds grand and exciting, and connects one's views to historically deep and influential intellectual traditions. But it's hard to believe that this is the whole story. For it makes little sense of the fact that people *argue* for the existence of human nature,[3] or propose that a

---

[1]   D. Hull, 'On human nature', *PSA: Proceedings of the Biennial Meeting of the Philosophy of Science Association* **2** (1986), 3–13.
[2]   M. T. Ghiselin, *Metaphysics and the origins of species* (Albany: State University of New York Press, 1997).
[3]   See, for example, E.O. Wilson, *On Human Nature* (Cambridge MA: Harvard University Press, 1979); J. Tooby & L. Cosmides, 'On the universality of human nature and the uniqueness of the individual: The role of

---

doi:10.1017/S1358246112000021   © The Royal Institute of Philosophy and the contributors 2012
Royal Institute of Philosophy Supplement **70** 2012
                                                                            1

Richard Samuels

central *goal* of science should be to develop a theory of human nature.[4]

This brings us to the third option. Perhaps the notion of human nature at play within the cognitive and behavioral sciences is not the traditional essentialist one targeted by evolutionary critiques, but some more sensible alternative – or *replacement* – notion. This is, I maintain, the most plausible option. Yet if this is what's going on, then it is not at all obvious what the relevant notion of human nature is supposed to be. With this in mind, the overarching issue that I address here is: What could contemporary cognitive and behavioral scientists *sensibly* have in mind when they make claims about human nature? More precisely, I focus on a three subsidiary issues:

1)   What notion of human nature is implicit in the practices of cognitive science? (Roughly equivalently: What sort of phenomena do cognitive scientists purport to characterize when providing a theory of human nature?)
2)   Does this notion of human nature evade the standard biological objections to traditional human nature essentialism?
3)   Is the notion of human nature that figures in the cognitive and behavioral sciences sufficiently similar to the traditional one to merit the honorific 'human nature'? In particular, does it play an appropriately large number of the theoretical roles traditionally played by the notion of human nature?

If the answer to 1) yields affirmative answers to both 2) and 3), then we have a *prima facie* attractive replacement notion of human nature. And as luck would have it, there is such a notion. Or so I will argue.

It would perhaps be useful to summarize my responses to these questions. Indeed it might be useful to do so twice over: once with an eye to the content of the claims that I make, and once with an eye to the history of the notion of human nature. First, the non-historical summary: With regard to the first of the above questions, I defend a version of what might be called *causal essentialism* about human nature – roughly, human nature is a suite of mechanisms that underlie the manifestation of species-typical cognitive and

---

genetics and adaptation', *Journal of Personality*, **58** (1990) 17–67; and S. Pinker, *The Blank Slate: The Modern Denial of Human Nature.* (New York: Viking, 2002).

[4]   See, for example, N. Chomsky 'Human Nature: Justice vs. Power'. In N. Chomsky & M. Foucault *The Chomsky-Foucault Debate On Human Nature* (New York: New Press, 1971, 1–67).

behavioral regularities. In response to 2), I argue that this causal essentialist conception of human nature does not succumb to the evolutionary critique; and in response to 3) I argue that it does much – though not all – of the work traditionally expected of the notion of human nature. But, I argue further that it is implausible to suppose that anything could perform all the roles traditionally expected of human nature.

Now for the more historical summary: The connection between a science of the mind and human nature is not a novel one. Rather cognitive scientific interest in human nature is an extension of the intellectual tradition that runs through David Hume. Hume was, of course, amongst the more influential, pre-Darwinian advocates of a science of the human mind; and for Hume, the science of the mind *just was* the science of human nature: an empirical discipline that sought to identify the principles and mechanisms responsible for human psychological phenomena. Though Hume was never very explicit regarding what precisely he meant by 'human nature', the notion played various theoretical roles in his research. Moreover, these roles differed in important respects from the one assumed by contemporary, evolutionary critiques of human nature. Specifically, Hume never assumed that the notion of human nature played the taxonomic function in defining what it is to be human. The working hypothesis of the present paper is that contemporary cognitive scientists are, at least in this regard, the intellectual descendants of Hume. Though most disagree – often vehemently – with the details of Hume's own theory of the mind, they readily accept his characterization of the goals of the science of the mind; and so construed, the Humean notion of human nature comes along for the theoretical ride.

Here's the game plan. In section 1, I sketch some of the central theoretical roles that the notion of human nature has traditionally been intended to play. In section 2, I briefly rehearse the standard biological objections to the traditional essentialist conception of human nature. In section 3, I discuss one proposed reconfiguration of the notion of human nature: Edouard Machery's nomological conception of human nature. Though this conception fairs quite well in capturing many of the traditional theoretical roles of human nature, there are some central roles that it will not readily play. Specifically, it will not play the traditional taxonomic and causal-explanatory roles of human nature. In view of this, in section 4, I defend an alternative *casual essentialist* conception of human nature. If we are looking for a conception of human nature that accommodates the maximal number of traditional theoretical functions and yet remains compatible with the evolutionary facts, then this view is preferable. Or so I maintain. In section 5, I conclude by addressing an objection to the proposal, and by spelling out the Humean character of contemporary notions of human nature.

1. The Theoretical Roles of Human Nature

In order to address the above issues, we need first to get clearer on the various theoretical roles that human nature – and theories thereof – have traditionally been intended to play within scientific enterprises.[5]

1.1 Organizing Role

A first major theoretical function for human nature is organizational in character. It is to delimit an area of scientific enquiry, and more-over, to do so by specifying a distinctive *object* of empirical enquiry. In short: some regions of science are to be demarcated, at least in part, by the fact that they are concerned with human nature.

Hume's philosophy nicely illustrates this function. In setting out the project of his *Treatise*, Hume makes quite clear that human nature is to comprise a distinctive object of enquiry for his new science of Man; and though Hume maintained that *all* the sciences were to some degree related to aspects of human nature, what made the science of Man distinctive was that it, and it alone, had human nature *per se* as its object.[6] The *goal* of this fledgling enquiry was to provide an account of human nature. Moreover, the methods for at-taining this end were for Hume resolutely empirical in character. Thus on Hume's view, human nature was an empirically discoverable phenomenon – a part of nature in much the same way as animals, plants and planets are.

It seems that this Humean attitude towards human nature is very much in evidence today. If one surveys the writings of theoretically oriented cognitive scientists, one finds much the same sentiment. Thus, for example, Chomsky asks whether

---

[5] Though human nature has often been expected to play a central role in moral theory, I will discuss this here. The main reason for this is that I am concerned with the status of human nature in the sciences; and in such con-texts, little or no moral work is expected of human nature.

[6] D. Hume, *A Treatise of Human Nature* edited by L. A. Selby-Bigge, 2nd ed. revised by P.H. Nidditch (Oxford: Clarendon Press, 1975).

[T]he concept of human nature ...might not provide for biology the next peak to try to scale, after having...already answered to the satisfaction of some the question of what is life.[7]

For Chomsky, then, as for Hume, the concept of human nature is to play an organizing role in the sciences: to pick out – albeit in rough-and-ready fashion – a set of phenomena that will form a focus of empirical enquiry for some region of science.

1.2 Descriptive functions

A second role that theories of human nature have traditionally been taken to play is a descriptive one. They are supposed to characterize *what human beings are like*. Historically, this has often been taken to involve describing properties that are presumed to be unique to human beings, and moreover, universally possessed by us. On such a view, a fondness for cooking Beef Wellington, though unique to humans, would not be an aspect of human nature since it is not a universal characteristic. Conversely, possessing lungs, though universal, would not count as an aspect of human nature since many non-human organisms also possess lungs. On the traditional view, then, the task of saying what human beings are like becomes the task of specifying a set of properties possessed by all and only humans. As we will see in section 2, this characterization of human nature's descriptive function will require modification. But for now, let it stand.

1.3 Causal explanatory functions

A third central function of human nature is causal-explanatory. Human nature – and theories thereof – are supposed to contribute to the *causal explanation* of reliably occurring features of humanity. So, for example, if the capacity for language-use is a reliably occurring feature of human beings, then aspects of human nature will be expected to figure in the causal explanation of the fact that we exhibit this capacity.

As we will see later on, there are different ways in which human nature might contribute to the causal explanation of species-typical regularities. But on the standard conception of natures – one variously associated with Aristotle, Locke and others – it is assumed that human nature is, in some sense, an underlying – 'hidden' or

[7]   Op. cit. note 4.

Richard Samuels

unobservable – entity that explains more readily observable, reliably occurring features of human beings.[8] That is, the fact that humans have the same nature is supposed to contribute to the causal explanation of generalizations that hold amongst human beings.

1.4 Taxonomic function

A fourth function that is commonly attributed to human nature is a taxonomic one. A theory of human nature should specify *what it is* for something to be a human being. That is, it should provide necessary and sufficient conditions for kind membership. On this view, widely regarded as deriving from Aristotelian philosophy,[9] human nature is in some sense *definitional* of kind membership, and as such, has a certain modal status. It is not merely that, as a matter of fact, all and only humans possess a human nature. Rather, for something to be a human being, it *must* as a matter of metaphysical necessity possess a human nature.

1.5 Invariances

The fifth and final assumption about the role of human nature that I discuss here is that it is supposed to set limits on human flexibility. That is, human nature is presumed to be, in some sense, *hard to change*. This idea is not readily articulated with precision; and clearly takes a variety of forms. On the strongest reading of this idea, aspects of human nature are supposed to be *impossible* to change.[10] But something weaker is often intended. Perhaps human

---

[8]   Louise M. Antony, '"Human Nature" and Its Role in Feminist Theory' In Janet A. Kourany (ed.) *Philosophy in a Feminist Voice: Critiques and Reconstructions*, (Princeton: Princeton University Press, 1998, 63–91).

[9]   Op. cit. note 8.

[10]   Two points are in order. First, the precise modal status of such impossibility claims is unclear – e.g. whether they are supposed to be expressions of nomological, metaphysical or logical impossibility. Second, however else the claim is intended, it is clearly distinct from the idea that human nature is definitional of being human. The mere fact that one's membership of a kind is defined by one's nature does not imply that one's nature is hard to change. It just means that if one's nature changes, then so too does one's kind membership (and vice versa).

nature can be changed; but it is hard to do so, and when done tends incur costs – e.g. slow, laborious efforts, curtailment of freedom, or social disruption.

2. Traditional Human Nature Essentialism

As already noted, the notion of human nature is closely intertwined with the idea that human beings share a common essence. Indeed, if human nature were a shared essence, then it would play the previously enumerated roles. But the idea that we share a common essence – at least in the traditional sense – is untenable, and for very familiar reasons. In what follows I briefly rehearse the view and its central problems. The lessons to be learned from this will help guide us in identifying a replacement notion.

2.1 The View

Essentialism about human nature is not an isolated thesis, but an instance of other more general forms of essentialism that are familiar from metaphysics and from the philosophy of science. Perhaps the most general thesis that is relevant here is what is sometimes called *kind essentialism*. This is primarily a thesis about what it is for something to be a genuine or *natural* kind as opposed to, say, a merely arbitrary class of entities. On one very typical rendition, kind essentialists maintain the following.

K is a natural kind if and only if:

E1. All and only the members of a kind share a common essence.
E2. The essence is a property, or a set of properties, that all (and only) the members of a kind *must* have.
E3. The properties that comprise a kind's essence are intrinsic properties.
E4. A kind's essence causes the other properties associated with that kind.[11]

Some philosophers of science argue that this conception of natural kinds applies to certain regions of science. For instance, Brian Ellis has argued that chemical kinds plausibly satisfy the above

---

[11] M. Ereshefsky 'Natural kinds in biology' In E. Craig (ed.) *Routledge Encyclopedia of Philosophy* (New York: Routledge, 2009).

Richard Samuels

conditions.[12] For example, perhaps having the atomic number 30 is the essence of zinc in precisely the above sense. But the particular variant of kind essentialism most relevant to the present discussion is not essentialism about chemical kinds, but about *species*. To be an essentialist about species is to maintain that for each species, there is an essence or nature that satisfies conditions E1–E4. Essentialism about human nature is just an instance of this thesis. Thus, to endorse a traditional essentialist view of human nature is to maintain that humans have an essence or a nature: that all and only human beings possess a set of intrinsic properties that define membership of the kind and cause other properties reliably associated with the kind.

Notice that *if* essentialism about human beings were true, then human nature could play its traditional theoretical roles. According to traditional essentialism, essences are definitive of kind membership and figure in causal explanation of properties associated with the kind. Further, a theory of such a nature would obviously need to describe unique, universal characteristics of human beings; and if there were such natures, then plausibly they could be objects for scientific enquiry, in much the same way as the 'essence' of zinc and other chemical elements are. The problem is that we are excellent reasons to suppose that traditional essentialism about species – and about human nature, in particular – is false.

2.2 Two Objections from Biology

The main difficulties with traditional species essentialism are exceedingly well known; so I won't make heavy weather of them here. (For more detailed elaborations, see Hull, 1986; Ghiselin, 1997.) They can be divided into two, related objections.

2.2.1 The Descriptive Objection
The first targets the traditional descriptive function of human nature. As a matter of empirical fact, it seems highly unlikely that we will succeed in identifying many, unique universal properties of humanity (still less ones that are intrinsic and causally central). First, it seems that to the extent that there are properties possessed by *all*

---

[12]   B. Ellis, 'Essentialism and Natural Kinds'. In S. Psillos & M. Curd (Eds.) *The Routledge Companion to Philosophy of Science* (New York: Routledge, 2008, 139–148).

human beings, they are shared by non-human organisms as well. Second, though there are a great many properties that are unique to humans, they almost invariably fail to be universal. This is plausibly true for many of the characteristics that have historically been proposed as aspects of human nature – e.g. the capacity for language, for moral judgment and for rational foresight. Such characteristics are in some sense species-typical; but they clearly admit of exceptions.[13] In which case, it would seem that if a theory of human nature is supposed to describe unique, universal properties, then there is little or nothing for it to describe.

2.2.2 A Moral

In addition to providing a reason to reject the traditional human nature essentialism, the above consideration also yields a moral for how best to construe the descriptive function of a theory of human nature. By broad acknowledgment, a theory of human nature is supposed to describe *what humans are like*. For traditional essentialists, this seems to consist in specifying unique, universal characteristics. But if the above objection is correct, then we ought not to expect a theory of human nature to do this. In which case, the task of describing what we are like needs to be glossed in some alternative way.

How? One alternative that I find attractive is this: We should think of a theory of human nature as, amongst other things, providing a kind of *field guide* to humanity.[14] To a first approximation, field guides function to describe what some species of organism *is like*. Moreover, they do so in such a way as to render kinds members readily identifiable; and this amongst other things involves describing typical (and readily observable) morphological and behavioral features. But they don't achieve this end by describing unique, universal characteristics. On the contrary, they seldom contain such descriptions. Instead they make reference to characteristics not possessed by other species, but that are hardly ever strictly universal. Moreover, they contain descriptions of lots of typical features that are not unique to that species. No doubt a theory of human nature should not be oriented so much towards the goal of identification; and nor (for this reason) need it focus on describing features that

---

[13]   Of course, there are a *huge* number of characteristics that are unique to humans that no-one thinks are aspects of human nature because they are socio-historically local. Playing for the Dallas Cowboys, scoring an 800 on one's GRE's, or having a fondness for cooking Chateau Briand are characteristics of this sort.

[14]   This idea was suggested in discussion with Paul Griffiths.

are readily observable. So, a theory of human nature should differ from typical field guides in being theoretically deeper: less concerned with superficial, readily observable regularities. Nevertheless, in describing what we are like, a theory of human nature should capture aspects of human beings that are in some sense species-typical as opposed to unique and universal.[15]

2.2.3 The Taxonomic Objection

The second, and perhaps more serious problem for traditional species essentialism focuses on the presumed taxonomic function of essences or natures. It can be framed as a tension between the assumption that kinds are individuated by their causally relevant, intrinsic properties, and the assumption that species are individuated at least in part by genealogical relations: roughly, by their locations on phylogenetic trees. This second assumption is deeply entrenched in contemporary biological theory. Yet species essentialism of the sort outline above violates this assumption in at least two ways. First, if species essentialism were true, it would be possible for organisms to be members of the same species and yet genealogically unrelated.[16] Yet this is incompatible with the genealogical assumption about species individuation, and so flies in the face of how evolutionary biologists individuate species. Second, if species are individuated genealogically, it is possible for two organisms to vary enormously in both genetic and phenotypic properties, and yet be members of the same species because they bear the appropriate genealogical relations to each other. Suppose for example, that humans evolve dramatically – undergo massive phenotypic and genetic modification. By genealogical criteria, human beings now and them could be members of the same species. Not so, on the essentialist picture.

---

[15] Recently Griffiths has stressed the importance of regularities that do not concern *similarities* between conspecifics but reliably occurring *differences* – e.g. sexual dimorphisms, and systematic behavioral or morphological variation that is a function of, say, climate. Though I see no serious problem with accommodating such regularities into an account of human nature, for the sake of simplicity, I will not to focus on them here.

[16] Imagine an atom-for-atom duplicate of President Obama that inhabits a planet far, far away. If species essentialism were true, then this Twin Obama must be a human being since it is intrinsically indistinguishable from Obama. Moreover, this would be so even if Twin Obama were entirely genealogically unrelated to Obama and other humans.

2.3 The Austerity Objection

There is another, rather different problem with traditional essential-ism about human nature. Though human nature essentialism is an instance of species essentialism, it is also an instance of a more generic essentialism about natural kinds. Yet this conception of natural kinds is highly problematic; and once one sees that this is so, it is utterly unclear why one should suppose that traditional essences should be at all important to the task of understanding human beings – or any other natural kind, for that matter.

2.3.1 The Objection

The notion of a natural kind has had a notoriously checkered intellectual history; and for much of the twentieth century was considered little more than an artifact of an ancient and outmoded metaphysics. But in recent decades, the notion has regained some philosophical respectability, in large measure because it has proven useful in understanding some central aspects of contemporary scientific practice.[17] Most importantly, all sciences mark a distinction between a) those kinds that are objects of systematic enquiry, and over which inductive generalizations and causal explanations range; and b) kinds that are not apt to play these roles.[18] The notion of a natural kind appears to capture just such a distinction; and it is largely for this reason that it has regained an air of respectability. In view of this, if one's theory of natural kinds fails to capture this distinction, then it fails to satisfy a central desideratum for such a theory.

Now a major problem with traditional kind essentialism – i.e. a theory that endorses E1–E4 – is that it is manifestly too *restrictive* to permit the notion of a natural kind to capture the above distinction between scientifically 'respectable' kinds and the rest. Perhaps, as noted earlier, traditional essentialism holds of some scientific categories – such as the elements of the periodic table. But it clearly does not apply more broadly to the kinds that figure in scientific practice:

- Many scientific kinds are not characterizable in terms of their intrinsic properties at all. This is true of many biological

[17]   R. Boyd, 'Realism, Anti-Foundationalism and the Enthusiasm for Natural Kinds', *Philosophical Studies* **61** (1991) 127–148.

[18]   E. Machery, 'Concepts are not a Natural Kind', *Philosophy of Science*, **72** (2005), 444–467.

kinds; but it is also true of many of the kinds in psychology, materials science and arguably physics.

- Even if we allow essences to contain relational properties – i.e. we reject E3 – the modified view is still overly restrictive since it implies both that for each natural kind there is a set of necessary and sufficient conditions on kind membership (i.e. E2) *and* that these conditions are also the causally central properties of kind members (i.e. E4). Yet it is doubtful that natural kind membership is always defined by its causally most central characteristics. This is plausibly true of kinds, such as cell and neuron.

- Finally, as Richard Boyd noted long ago, there is not the slightest reason to suppose that all the (presumed) natural kinds that figure in science can be defined by sets of individually necessary and jointly sufficient conditions (i.e. E2). Boyd's parade case is biological species; but the point is almost certainly true of many other natural kinds as well, including the kinds of psychology, anatomy and ecology.

In short: Not only is traditional essentialism bad biology, it is also bad general philosophy of science.

2.3.2 Another Moral
Again, there is a lesson to be learned from the failure of traditional essentialism. If one seeks a theory that captures the broad distinction between the explanatory kinds of science and other kinds, then traditional essentialism won't fit the bill. But if this is so, then it is obscure why a theory of human nature – or of anything else for that matter – should place much stock in the traditional conception of essences. For it is only within the theoretical framework provided by traditional kind essentialism that traditional essences make theoretical sense. In view of this, we would do well to locate an account of human nature within some alternative, more plausible account of natural kinds. I return to this issue in section 4, when I present a positive proposal regarding how to construe the notion of human nature.

3. The Nomological Conception of Human Nature

We have already seen that an important moral of the demise of traditional human nature essentialism is that a theory of human nature ought not to be expected to describe unique, universal features of humanity. More plausible is the idea that its descriptive role is discharged when it specifies species-typical regularities. In recent work, Eduoard Machery has gone a step further and argued that the commitment to human nature *just is* the commitment to the existence of such regularities. Thus, for example, Machery and Barrett (2006) assert that a commitment to the existence of human nature is a commitment merely to the fact that:

> [T]here are generalizable statements that we can make about humans: that there are some properties that, characteristically and for the most part, humans posses.[19]

Still more recently, Machery has endorsed what he calls 'the nomological conception' of human nature.[20] On this view, human nature is what we might call a *nomological nature*: a set of species-typical, lawful regularities; or equivalently, a set of properties that humans reliably, though need not invariably, instantiate. Further, he maintains that the relevant properties are ones that result from the evolution of our species.

Notice that the nomological conception of human nature is, in a number of respects, less demanding than traditional human nature essentialism. First, regularities need only be species-typical as opposed to strictly universal. This is an acknowledgement of the fact that few, if any, scientifically interesting regularities apply literally to all humans. Second, the nomological conception of human nature does not restrict the class of regularities to those ones that are unique to humans. Thus lots of regularities might hold of other organisms as well as humans and yet still be aspects of human nature. Third, the nomological conception is consistent with the idea that human nature can change over time. In particular, it is consistent with the idea that human beings might evolve in such a way that many – even all – extant regularities cease to be regularities that apply to humans.

What are we to make of the relatively undemanding character of the nomological conception? An obvious virtue is that it insulates the notion of human nature from standard biological objections. If a commitment to human nature does not imply the existence of unique and universal intrinsic properties, then the fact that there are no such properties – and, hence, that species membership cannot be defined by the possession of such properties – is no objection. But in order to assess the adequacy of the nomological

[19] E. Machery & C. Barrett, 'Debunking Adapting Minds', *Philosophy of Science* **73** (2005), 232–246.
[20] E. Machery, 'A Plea for Human Nature', *Philosophical Psychology*, **21** (2008), 321–330.

conception, there are two further issues to consider: a) Do human beings possess a nomological nature? b) To what extent can nomological natures play the theoretical roles that human nature has traditionally been expected to play?

3.1 Do Human Beings have a Nomological Nature?

Scientists have intensively studied many different kinds of organisms, including such 'model' organisms as the bacterium *Escherichia coli*, the sea slug *Aplysia*, the *Drosophila* fruit fly, the freshwater zebrafish, and the common house mice, *Mus musculus*. As a matter of fact, whenever scientists have engaged in such intensive research, they have almost invariably uncovered a wide array of regularities that hold largely – though seldom invariably – across the species. In the nomological sense, then, such species have a nature; and though it is (of course) an empirical issue, there is excellent reason to suppose that human beings are exactly similar in this regard. This is because there are many disciplines that have generated substantial numbers of species-typical generalizations about human beings. Research on human anatomy and physiology is, for example, replete with such generalizations. But so are those sciences more intimately concerned with mind and behavior – such as, neuroscience, behavioral ecology and psychology. According to the nomological conception, all such regularities comprise aspects of our nature.

Since we are concerned primarily with the notion of human nature as it figures in contemporary cognitive-behavioral science, it would be useful briefly to highlight the above general point with some plausible candidates from the domain of psychology. Start with some readily observable – 'superficial' – examples chosen more-or-less at random. Human beings speak languages. We engage in pair bonding. We make moral judgments; and we engage in means-ends reasoning. We experience emotions, such as anger and fear; and we have thoughts about the world. Little or no systematic research is required to recognize these as robust features of our psychology – no doubt subject to plenty of exceptions, but robust all the same.

Now for some examples, again chosen more-or-less at random, whose discovery required more systematic empirical research:

- In the study of perceptual categorization, human beings exhibit typicality effects. Roughly, the extent to which something is a *typical* instance of some category (e.g. *birds*) correlates with a host of independent psychological measures, such as speed of response, accuracy of categorization judgments, order of recall, and so on.[21]

- In the study of memory, power laws of learning and forgetting are widespread.[22] Roughly, much data concerning remembering and forgetting – how quick, how reliable etc. – can be fit by power functions. Similarly, it is a robust finding that statistical and semantic associations influence reaction times in recall tasks.

- In the study of concept acquisition, there is good reason to suppose that concept acquisition in childhood exhibits certain regularities. For example, the concept ONE is acquired prior to the concept FOUR (if indeed the latter is ever acquired); and the concept BELIEF is typically possessed prior to the age of 5.[23]

- As a final example, the study of human perception has uncovered an enormous range of trans-cultural regularities. So, for example, in the domain of vision, there are many psychophysical findings that are extraordinarily robust.[24]

This is, of course, a vanishingly small sample of the sorts of regularities to have been identified by psychologists and cognitive scientists. Moreover, they are ones that remain open to empirical enquiry; and it may turn out that not all of them really are species-typical.[25] Nonetheless, it is plausible that they are; and to that extent, it is plausible that our psychology exhibits the sorts of regularities that according to the nomological conception constitute human nature. In any case, from hereon I will suppose that this is so.

---

[21] G. Murphy, *The Big Book of Concepts* (Cambridge, MA: MIT Press, 2004).
[22] J. R. Anderson & L. J. Schooler, 'The adaptive nature of memory'. In E. Tulving and F. I. M. Craik (Eds.) *Handbook of Memory*, 557–570. (New York: Oxford University Press, 2000).
[23] See, for example, Susan Carey *The Origin of Concepts* (New York: Oxford University Press, 2009).
[24] See, for example, G. A. Gescheider, *Psychophysics: The Fundamentals* (Mahwah: Laurence Erlbaum Associates Inc., 1997).
[25] The Muller-Lyer illusion illustrates this point. Though widely assumed to result from species-typical perceptual biases, it is in fact quite sensitive to developmental- environmental conditions. For discussion see R. McCauley and J. Henrich, 'Susceptibility to the Muller-Lyer Illusion, Theory-Neutral Observation, and the Diachronic Penetrability of the Visual Input System' *Philosophical Psychology* **19** (1) (2006) 1–23.

Richard Samuels

3.2. Can nomological natures play the traditional roles of Human Nature?

So, there are good reasons to suppose that humans have a nomological nature. But is this something that deserves the honorific 'human nature'? Specifically, to what extent will it play the theoretical roles traditionally assigned to human nature?

Let's start with the good news. First, nomological natures can readily play the organizational role of delimiting areas of enquiry. On the present view, human anatomy, human psychology, and so on can be viewed as largely concerned with the study – discovery, confirmation and explanation – of species-typical regularities.

Second, if Machery is right, a theory of human nature can play the role of describing what humans are like. On the present proposal, this descriptive function is not performed by specifying unique, universal features of human beings. On the contrary, the nomological conception of human nature is largely motivated by the assumption that there are few, if any, interesting generalizations of this sort. Rather, saying what we are like will involve articulating a range of species-typical generalizations. No doubt many of these will also hold for other organisms. But it is presumably the case that some of them will be unique to us. To that extent, a theory of human nature will on the present view describe features that are both species-typical and unique.

Third, the nomological conception provides, pretty much for free, a sense in which human nature is fixed. More-or-less by definition, laws of nature exhibit fixity in the sense that they are in some sense *counterfactually robust*. This is because, in contrast to accidental generalizations, lawful generalizations project to counterfactual scenarios. But if this is so, and if as the nomological conception maintains, human nature *just is* a set of lawful regularities, then human nature must exhibit fixity, at least in the sense that it is counterfactually robust. Of course, this might not – and presumably doesn't – capture all that theorists have meant when saying that human nature is fixed. So, for example, it won't capture that idea that human nature is strictly impossible to alter; and nor will it capture the idea that efforts to change our nature – 'to meddle with nature' – will come to no good. But it is *far* from clear that a replacement notion of human nature – one that seeks scientific respectability – should seek to capture such ideas.

Now for the less good news. There are two traditional aspects of human nature that nomological natures do not readily play. Moreover, they are perhaps the two most central theoretical functions

16

of human nature. First, nomological natures will not play the taxonomic function that human nature has been expected to play.
There are two reasons for this:

- On the nomological conception, it is doubtful that possessing
  a human nature is even extensionally equivalent with being
  human. In other words, it is doubtful that all and only *actual*
  humans satisfy the relevant range of regularities. Given the
  ceterus paribus character of generalizations about human
  beings, it is almost certain that many humans will fail to
  satisfy many of the regularities that (putatively) comprise
  human nature. Thus, for example, some humans (e.g. aphasics)
  fail to satisfy some of the regularities regarding language comprehension and production; some fail to satisfy various regularities regarding perceptual capacities (e.g. visual agnosics);
  and some humans fail to satisfy robust regularities regarding
  memory (e.g. amnesiacs). Thus on the nomological conception
  possessing a human nature will not even be extensionally equivalent with being human.
- On the nomological conception, human nature will lack the
  modal properties required for defining kind membership.
  Even if, contrary to fact, all and only humans satisfied the relevant regularities, it would still be the case that something *could*
  be human and yet fail to possess the relevant nomological
  nature. So, for example, humans might evolve in such a way
  that many of the extant generalizations no longer hold.

Of course, the present points come as no surprise to Machery.
Indeed, the nomological conception is deliberately engineered to
have these properties since it is in part by rejecting the assumption
that human nature plays a taxonomic role that the proposal seeks to
evade the standard biological objections to human nature. For all
that, this does mark an important divergence from the traditional
conception of human nature.

The second central role of human nature that the nomological
account does not readily accommodate is its causal-explanatory function. As noted in section 1, natures have traditionally been expected
to play of the role of underlying – 'hidden' or unobservable – entities
that figure in the causal explanation of regularities involving the kind.
To use a well-worn example, the essence of water – e.g. its molecular
structure – is according to traditional essentialists expected to contribute to the explanation of various water-involving regularities –
e.g. that water boils at 100 degrees at sea level. Similarly, human
nature is supposed to be an underlying causal factor that figures in

17

Richard Samuels

the explanation of regularities involving human beings. But, if human nature *just is* the set of human-typical regularities, then it clearly cannot be the *cause* of these regularities, underlying or otherwise. In which case, on the nomological conception, human nature cannot play its traditional causal-explanatory function.

Again, Machery is fully aware of the implications of his view. As he puts it:

> [I]t is important to see that the nomological notion of human nature inverts the Aristotelian relation between nature and generalization. For Aristotle, the fact that humans have the same nature explains why many generalizations can be made about them ... For me, on the contrary, the fact that many generalizations can be made about humans explain in which sense there is a human nature.[26]

This is not, of course, to claim that, on the nomological conception, human nature can do *no* explanatory work. One obvious possibility, for example, is that the regularities that comprise a nomological nature can figure in DN (or statistical nomological) explanations. Another possibility, recently suggested by Machery,[27] is that human nature, construed nomologically, might figure in explanatory sketches of a certain kind. Roughly put, by asserting that something is part of human nature, one implicates that it is a product of a particular kind of cause – viz. that it can be explained evolutionarily and that a purely non-evolutionary (cultural/social) explanation would be wrong.

So, on the nomological conception human nature can do *some* explanatory work. Moreover, I would not wish to deny that it is work that is *worth* doing. For all that, it is important to be clear that from the vantage of traditional conceptions of human nature such explanatory work is *ersatz*. Natures are supposed to be underlying structures that play a central role in the explanation of an entity's more superficial properties; and *this* is not something that the nomological conception can give us. If we seek a replacement for the traditional essentialist conception of human nature, we would do well to look further afield – to seek a conception on which human nature can play its customary causal-explanatory function.

[26] Op. cit. note 20, 323.
[27] 'Virtues of the Nomological Notion of Human Nature' presented at *The International Society for the History, Philosophy and Social Studies of Biology*, Utah 2011.

4. What Next? Causal Essentialism About Human Nature

The traditional essentialists conception of human nature is incompatible with the biological facts; and the nomological conception won't perform two of the most central theoretical roles traditionally assigned to human nature. We can do better. In this section I argue for a version of what we might call *causal essentialism* about human nature. As with the nomological conception, it is compatible with the evolutionary facts and enables human nature to play its traditional organizing, descriptive, and fixity-specifying functions. But in contrast to the nomological conception, it also allows us to endorse a traditional conception of human nature's causal-explanatory function. What it will *not* plausibly do is play both the traditional causal explanatory role *and* the taxonomic function of human nature. But as I hope to make clear, nothing can do this consonant with the biological facts. To the extent that we seek a replacement conception of human nature, then, it is no criticism of the present causal essentialist proposal that it cannot do this.

4.1 Casual Essentialism (1st Pass)

According to *traditional* kind essentialism, a kind's essence is a set of intrinsic properties that must be possessed by all and only members of the kind, and which causes the instantiation of other properties associated with the kind. One common relaxation of these commitments is to give up the assumption that essences must be intrinsic. This yields a version of kind essentialism that allows essences to consist of relational properties; and in the context of debate over species this is associated with a view that is sometimes called *relational* essentialism.[28] Still, both traditional and relational essentialism demand that essences both a) individuate their kinds and b) cause the instantiation of properties associated with the kind. That is, they both posit what are sometimes called *taxonomic* essences.[29]

[28]   Paul Griffiths, 'Squaring the circle: Natural kinds with historical essences'. In R. A. Wilson (Ed.), *Species: New interdisciplinary essays* (Cambridge, MA: MIT Press, 1999, 209–228).

[29]   S. A. Gelman, 'Psychological essentialism in children', *Trends in Cognitive Sciences* **8** (2004) 404–409. D. Walsh, 'Evolutionary essentialism' *The British Journal for the Philosophy of Science* **57** (2006) 425–448.

But there is another *causal* conception of essences that relaxes the traditional notion even further by giving up the demand that essences are kind individuating. According to this *causal essentialist view*, essences are entities – mechanisms, processes, and structures – that cause many of the more superficial properties and regularities reliably associated with the kind.[30] In which case, the causal essentialist about human nature maintains that human nature should be identified with a suite of mechanisms, processes, and structures that causally explain many of the more superficial properties and regularities reliably associated with humanity.[31]

Notice that the distinction between taxonomic and causal essences suggests a way of avoiding the standard biological objections to human nature essentialism. Recall: what the objections purport to show is that essences cannot play the traditional descriptive and taxonomic functions of human nature since there are no properties that are necessarily possessed by all and only members of the kind. But this is no objection at all, if, as the causal essentialist maintains, (causal) essences need not be shared by all kind members. Specifically, on a causal essentialist conception of human nature, when cognitive and behavioral scientists profess an interest in human nature they are in no way committed to the assumption that there is some common nature that all and only humans share. Rather, they are concerned with is the existence of empirically discoverable causal mechanisms (processes, structures and constraints etc.) that explain the characteristic properties and regularities associated with human beings – especially those concerning behavior and cognition. Thus the biological objections have no force against causal essentialism about human nature.

---

[30] Some maintain that this causal conception of essences and not the taxonomic one is the more traditional. For example, Walsh (2006) argues that Aristotle has a causal conception of essences was a causal as opposed to taxonomic one. I do not propose to dispute the issue here.

[31] As I use the terms, all taxonomic essences are causal essences but not *vice versa*. For in addition to figuring in causal explanations, a taxonomic essence is, as a matter of metaphysical necessity, possessed by all and only the member of the kind. In contrast, causal essences need not even be possessed by all members of the kind, let alone be individuative of the kind. They may, for example, be lacking in deviant, abnormal or borderline members of the kind. In terms of the essentialist commitments outlined in section 2.1, the point may be put as follows: Taxonomic essences must satisfy conditions E2 and E4, whilst causal essences need only satisfy E4.

4.2 Developing the View: Homeostatic Property Clusters

Clearly the above formulation of causal essentialism requires elaboration; and though there are, no doubt, many ways to do this, a possibility that I find attractive recruits Richard Boyd's well-known *homeostatic property cluster* account of natural kinds. In what follows I first say what the HPC account is, and then apply it to the case of human nature.

4.2.1 HCP Kinds
The HPC account is arguably the most popular extant account of natural kinds to have emerged from recent philosophy of science.[32] Boyd and others have developed the account over a number of decades; and I do not propose to go into the fine-grained details here. For our purposes, the following sketch will do. Let us say that a kind K is a natural kind if:

> *H1.* It is associated with a contingently co-varying property cluster – a range of properties that tend to be co-instantiated by instances of the kind, but need not be genuine necessary conditions for membership.
> *H2.* There is some set of empirically discoverable causal mechanisms, processes, structures and constraints – a *causal essence*, if you will – that causally explains the co-variation of these various symptoms.
> *H3.* To the extent that there is any real definition of what it is for something to be a member of the kind, it is not the symptoms, as such, but the causal essence that defines membership. More precisely, to the extent that natural kinds have definitions, it is the presence of a causal essence producing aspects of the property cluster that defines kind membership.

Consider an illness such as influenza. Influenza is, on the homeostatic cluster view, a plausible candidate for natural kind status. First, it is associated with a range of characteristic symptoms – coughing, elevated body temperature, and so on – even though these symptoms do

---

[32]   For more extensive characterizations of the homeostatic cluster view see: R. Boyd 'What Realism Implies and What It Does Not', *Dialectica* **43** (1990) 5–29; R. Boyd, 'Realism, Anti-Foundationalism and the Enthusiasm for Natural Kinds', *Philosophical Studies* **61** (1991) 127–148; and R. Boyd 'Homeostasis, Species, and Higher Taxa'. In R. Wilson (ed.) *Species: New Interdisciplinary Essays* (Cambridge, Massachusetts: MIT Press, 1999, 141–186).

not *define* what it is to have flu. Second, there is a causal mechanism – roughly, the presence of the flu virus – whose operation explains the occurrence of the symptoms. Finally, to the extent that influenza has a definition, it is the presence of the virus – or better, the presence of the virus producing some of the symptoms – but not the symptoms as such, that make it the case that one has flu.

4.2.2 HCP Kinds applied to Human Nature
How might the idea of HPC kinds be applied to the notion of human nature? Traditional essentialists recruit a general theory of natural kinds in order to provide an account of human nature as an intrinsic taxonomic essence. But as we have seen the general theory of natural kinds is problematic; and there is good reason to suppose that it doesn't apply to species – and to human beings in particular – since we do not possess an intrinsic taxonomic essence. In response, I propose that if we wish to preserve the connection between talk of natures, and the theory of natural kinds, we would do well to opt for a better general account of natural kinds – the HPC view – and that we should identify human nature with whatever it is that plays a role most similar to the one played by taxonomic essences within the traditional essentialist framework. Within the HPC approach, it is obvious what this should be. Human nature should be identified with a set of empirically discoverable causal mechanisms, processes, structures and constraints that causally explain the co-variation of the various properties – especially psychological properties – associated with being human. In other words, we should identify human nature with this causal essence.

Two further issues require our immediate attention. First, an HPC view of human nature presupposes the existence of an appropriate property cluster: a set of psychological properties that reliably co-vary with each other. But does such a cluster exist? Presumably the answer is 'Yes'. Indeed, this follows with minimal addition from our earlier discussion of the nomological conception of human nature. On the nomological conception, human nature is a set of species-typical psychological regularities; and as noted, there are excellent reasons to suppose that human beings have a nature in this sense. But the regularities assumed by the nomological conception *just are* the reliable instantiation and co-variation of various psychological properties. In which case, if we have reason to suppose that human beings conform to robust psychological regularities, then we also have reason to suppose that human beings exhibit a property cluster of precisely the sort required by the HPC conception of natural kinds. Indeed, the presumed cluster *just is* a nomological nature of the sort that Machery has in mind. The idea that we have a nomological nature and that there is a human nature in the causal essentialist sense are, therefore, not incompatible. Rather the latter idea presupposes the former.

The second sort of issue concerns how, on the present proposal, to think about the causal essence that is to be identified with human nature. In contrast to traditional essentialism, which assumes that essences must be intrinsic, the HPC view of natural kinds makes no such assumption about causal essences. Rather, the entities responsible for property co-variation might be relational and may operate at quite different time-scales. Consider the following crude, but useful three-way division:

- Evolutionary mechanisms: Phylogenetic processes and mechanisms that operate over evolutionary time and cause human species-typical properties. This might include, selection, drift, mutation, and many other things besides.
- Developmental mechanisms: Ontogenetic mechanisms that are responsible for the acquisition of human psychological capacities. This will include developmental biological processes and mechanisms – e.g. those involved in the development of the neural tube – but it will also involve more straightforwardly psychological mechanisms, such as conditioning, induction and other sorts of learning.
- Synchronic mechanisms: Mechanisms that are causally responsible for particular manifestations of psychological capacities. For example, seeing involves various visual processing mechanisms, speaking involves language production systems, recollecting involves memory systems, and so on.

Which of these time-scales are most relevant to the present project? If we aim to provide comprehensive explanations of species-typical regularities, then *all* of them are presumably relevant. But our current task is rather more restrictive. It is to characterize a replacement notion of human nature that fits the use of contemporary cognitive-behavioral science. And as a matter of fact cognitive-behavioral scientists are not primarily in the business of characterizing evolutionary mechanisms. Rather they are most centrally concerned with the characterization of *more proximal* cognitive and neural mechanisms: those involved in online processing and in the development of psychological states and structures. Indeed the task of characterizing such mechanisms is arguably *the* central goal of cognitive science. Further, it should be noted that this focus on proximal causes is very much in line with the traditional view of human nature's causal explanatory function. For if essences are intrinsic properties of kind members, then they must be proximal causes, if they are to be causes at all. Thus a replacement notion of human nature that fits the usage of cognitive and behavioral scientists by construing casual essences in a *proximal fashion* – i.e. as synchronic and/or ontogenetic mechanisms – fits quite well with tradition.

To summarize the discussion so far: The general conception of human nature that I have developed here is one on which human nature is a suite of empirically discoverable proximal mechanisms – a *causal essence* – that causally explains the various psychological regularities that comprise our *nomological nature*. It is now time to see how well this proposal accommodates the scientific roles traditionally assigned to human nature.

4.3 The Traditional Roles that Causal Essences Can Play

In section 1, I characterized five traditional scientific roles for human nature. The causal essentialist conception of human nature readily accommodates four of these.

First, it can function to delimit an area of enquiry. In particular, human psychology on this view would be the study of human causal mechanisms and the psychological regularities for which they are responsible. On the face of it, this fits well with what cognitive-behavioral scientists are up to.

Second, the causal essentialist conception readily accommodates the descriptive function of human nature by describing species-typical features of human beings. Indeed, it does so twice over. It must describe the species-typical regularities of the sort incorporated in a nomological nature since this is required in order to specify the phenomena that the underlying mechanisms purport to explain. Moreover, it must describe the species-typical mechanisms in virtue of which such regularities hold. Further, on the overwhelmingly plausible assumption that human beings are unique in some psychological respects, it must also describe those unique regularities and the mechanisms in virtue of which such regularities obtain.

Third, the causal essentialist picture accommodates the fixity-specifying function of human nature. As with the nomological conception, it will yield counterfactual robustness, and for exactly the same reason: nomological natures are comprised of nomological regularities. In addition to this, however, there are good empirical reasons to suppose that many of the mechanisms that are responsible for the manifestation of such species-typical regularities are environmentally canalized. For so far as we know, mechanisms for perceptual processing, learning, memory and so on are highly conserved across environmental variation.

Finally, the causal essentialist view accommodates the traditional causal explanatory function of human nature. This is, in my view, what makes it preferable to the nomological conception of human nature. Proponents of the latter view must seek ersatz causal-explanatory work for human nature. In contrast, the advocate of casual essentialism can attribute the exact same causal explanatory function that human nature has traditionally been intended to play: viz. an underlying entity that explains more readily observable, reliably occurring generalizations that hold of human beings. Thus where the nomological conception accommodates only three central roles for human nature, the causal essentialist picture accommodates at least four; and to that extent it provides a better replacement notion than the nomological conception.

4.4 What Causal Essences Will Not Do

What of human nature's presumed taxonomic function? I maintain that given the biological facts *nothing* could play the traditional proximal causal role of human nature *and* perform this taxonomic function. There are two natural arguments for this claim. The first is probably not a good one; but the second probably is.

The (Probably) Bad Argument

Those psychological and neural mechanisms that causally explain the regularities that hold of modern humans are extant structures – they exist in the here and now. In contrast, if evolutionary biologists are to be believed, then species are genealogically individuated. In which case, it seems possible that an organism could possess the mechanisms that comprise human nature, and yet fail to be human because it lacks the relevant relationship to the past. (Think of Davidson's Swampman or Putnam's Twin.) In which case, proximal mechanisms of the sort that cognitive scientists care about cannot be kind individuating.

As it stands, this is a bad argument; and it's bad because it ignores the well-known possibility that extant states and mechanisms can be individuated *historically*. Suppose, for example, that the mechanisms for human visual perception are partially individuated by historical facts about human evolution. Then it would not be possible to possess a *human* visual system without being human. Of course, there might be – and indeed are – perceptual systems that are very much like our own. Still, no matter how similar in structure or function, on the present view, such mechanisms would not be *our* visual mechanisms unless they shared the same evolutionary history. But if this is so, then the present objection to the claim that causal essences individuate kinds requires that the relevant mechanisms not be (even partially) individuated by human evolutionary history. The problem (for me at least) is that this seems highly implausible. Perhaps psychological states and mechanisms *per se* are not individuated historically.[33] But the claim that being a *human* psychological state or mechanism is determined in part by genealogical relations seems no less plausible than the claim that the species, *Homo sapiens*, is historically individuated. In which case, if we are to cleave to a genealogical conception of species individuation, then we should also probably reject the present argument.

The (Probably) Good Argument
Let's leave aside questions about the individuation of mechanisms. The real problem with treating proximal causal essences as kind individuating is that it is possible to be a member of the kind and yet *lack* the relevant causal essence. By way of illustration, consider once more the case of visual perception. Psychophysics and vision scientists have identified a huge array of species-typical regularities regarding human vision; and on the present proposal the mechanisms that explain these regularities are aspects of human nature. But we know that these mechanisms – cognitive, neural, and developmental systems of various sorts – are *not* possessed by all humans. In particular, there is a host of disorders – both genetic and environmentally produced – that result in the absence of such mechanisms. For all that, the people who lack these mechanisms are still human beings; and this, I take it, suffices to show that human nature, construed as a proximal causal essence, cannot play its traditional kind individuating role.

5. Conclusion: Returning to Hume

In this paper I have articulated a conception of human nature on which it should be identified with a suite of mechanisms and

---

[33]   This is, of course, a longstanding issue in the philosophy of psychology. See Gabriel Segal, *A Slim Book about Narrow Content* (Cambridge, MA: MIT Press, 2000).

structures – a causal essence – that is implicated in the explanation of species-typical psychological regularities. The account is presented as a replacement for the more traditional (taxonomic) essentialist conception of human nature. More specifically, it has been fashioned to a) captures how cognitive and behavioral scientists tend to deploy the notion of human nature whilst, b) evading standard evolutionary objections, and c) allowing human nature – and theories thereof – to fulfill many of their traditional theoretical roles. In developing this account I have argued that the proposal is preferable to one competitor – the nomological conception of human nature – because it more fully accommodates these traditional theoretical roles. Further, I have argued that its failure to fulfill all the traditional roles of human nature is a consequence of the fact that – given very general considerations – *nothing* can jointly satisfy all these conditions. Finally, I have sought to integrate the proposal within a more general account of natural kinds – the HPC view – in a manner that reflects the way in which traditional human nature essentialism is an instance of a more general essentialist conception of natural kinds.

Though there are no doubt many issues and objections that a comprehensive treatment of the notion of human nature ought to address, I propose to conclude with a discussion of just one, which should help clarify how I think about causal essentialism's relation to historical usage of the notion of human nature.

The objection I envisage runs as follows: Though you purport to have articulated a replacement notion of human nature, what you have really done is show that there is no such thing as human nature. The notion of human nature has *always* been expected to fulfill both a proximal causal function *and* a taxonomic function. This is (so the objection continues) as close to a conceptual truth about human nature as anything is. But if what you say is true, then nothing could play both these roles. In which case, there is no such thing as human nature.

Of course, I accept that nothing conforms to the traditional (taxonomic) essentialist conception of human nature. That's my starting point. But I deny that there is a single univocal notion of human nature. Indeed, I deny that traditional taxonomic essentialism is even the only historically *prominent* conception of human nature. Another prominent conception – one that clearly manifests itself in Hume's work – appears exceedingly close in spirit to the causal essentialist picture developed here. For Hume, the term 'human nature' functions in the first instance to pick out – in rough and ready fashion – a suite of psychological phenomena; and a theory of

Richard Samuels

human nature is an empirical, causal explanatory psychological theory: a 'mental geography' or 'anatomy of the mind' that provides a 'delineation of the distinct parts and powers of the mind'.[34] As such, for Hume, a theory of human nature is a specification of the underlying proximal psychological processes, structures and mechanisms responsible for human behavior and mental activity. Yet there is not the slightest suggestion that Hume *also* expected his theory to perform the taxonomic function of specifying what it is to be human, still less that he thought of human nature in traditional essentialist terms. For Hume this just does not seem to be part of human nature's remit.

In Hume, then, we have a prominent historical figure that viewed human nature as something of immense importance, and yet did not see it as involving any commitment to kind individuating essences. If what I have said in the forgoing sections is correct, then much the same is true of contemporary cognitive and behavioral scientists. Much of their research is oriented towards characterizing the mechanisms and structures responsible for species-typical psychological phenomena —whether it be a specification of components of the visual system, a theory of working memory, a model of causal inference, and so on. Indeed, specifying such mechanisms – such causal essences – is arguably *the* central goal of contemporary cognitive science. In this regard at least, we are the intellectual descendants of Hume.[35]

The Ohio State University

[34] David Hume *Enquiry concerning Human Understanding, in Enquiries concerning Human Understanding and concerning the Principles of Morals*, edited by L. A. Selby-Bigge, 3rd edition revised by P. H. Nidditch. (Oxford: Clarendon Press, 1975)
[35] Earlier versions of this paper were presented at the Royal Institute of Philosophy Annual Conference at Oxford Brookes, Washington University, the University of Pittsburgh and the ISHPSSB conference held at the University of Utah. I am grateful for the many helpful suggestions that were offered on these occasions. Special thanks are due to Mark Cain, John Doris, John Dupre, Steve Downes, Frederick Eberhardt, Hans-Johann Glock, Paul Griffiths, Maria Kronfeldner, Sandy Mitchell, P.D. Magnus, Gillian Russell, Constantine Sandis, Roy Sorensen, Kim Sterelny and Karola Stotz. I would also like to thank Tim Schroeder, Eduoard Machery, P.D. Magnus, and Carl Craver for stimulating discussions of the issues covered in this paper.

Essentialism, Externalism, and Human Nature

M.J. CAIN

1. Introduction

Psychological essentialism is a prominent view within contemporary developmental psychology and cognitive science according to which children have an innate commitment to essentialism. If this view is correct then a commitment to essentialism is an important aspect of human nature rather than a culturally specific commitment peculiar to those who have received a specific philosophical or scientific education.[1] In this article my concern is to explore the philosophical significance of psychological essentialism with respect to the relationship between the content of our concepts and thoughts and the nature of the extra-cranial world. I will argue that, despite first appearances, psychological essentialism undermines a form of externalism that has become commonplace in the philosophy of mind and language.

2. Psychological Essentialism

As its name suggests, psychological essentialism is related to the traditional philosophical doctrine of essentialism.[2] One can draw a rough distinction between two versions of essentialism. According to the first, many of the individual things that populate the world have essences, where an essence is a property (or collection of properties) that is central to the identity of that thing so that it couldn't lose

---

[1] This latter view of essentialism is endorsed by Jerry Fodor in *Concepts: Where Cognitive Science Went Wrong* (Oxford: Oxford University Press, 1998).

[2] Historical advocates of essentialism include Aristotle and Locke. Perhaps the most prominent recent champions of essentialism are S. Kripke, *Naming and Necessity* (Oxford: Blackwell, 1980) and H. Putnam, 'The meaning of "meaning"', in his *Mind, Language and Reality: Philosophical Papers Volume 2* (Cambridge: Cambridge University Press, 1975).

doi:10.1017/S1358246112000033   © The Royal Institute of Philosophy and the contributors 2012
Royal Institute of Philosophy Supplement **70** 2012   29

the property without ceasing to exist. For example, it might be claimed that it is part of my essence that I am human but not part of my essence that I am an academic philosopher. Call this essentialism with respect to individuals. According to the second version of essentialism, it is categories of things that have essences. For example, in order to belong to the category HUMAN it is essential to be a mammal. This leaves it open as to whether any individual human is essentially human or as to whether any particular thing has an essence as such (as opposed to an essence relative to a particular category to which they belong). Call this doctrine essentialism with respect to categories.[3]

Psychological essentialism is a view within developmental psychology – and cognitive science more widely – that has come to prominence over the last two decades. In its boldest form it is the view that children are innately essentialist with respect to many of the categories for which they have concepts. For example, in virtue of an innate commitment to essentialism, a child who has acquired the concept DOG thinks of dogs as being bound together by a hidden essence so that any dog is a dog in virtue of possessing the relevant essence. Put this way, the implication would appear to be that children are, first and foremost, essentialists about categories as opposed to individuals.[4] Essences are conceived of as being hidden and causally responsible for the observable properties of things. Due to this causal connection categorising things on the basis of their observable properties will generally result in their being assigned to categories to which they belong. However, such a procedure falls short of being foolproof as, for example, something could appear to be a dog without being a dog and something could appear not to be a dog whilst being a dog. Typically, psychological essentialists regard children as holding a placeholder conception of essence; that is, children do not usually have any substantial views as to the precise nature of the essences of the categories that they adopt an essentialist attitude towards.[5] With respect to the breadth of childhood essentialism there

---

[3] See Ellis, *The Philosophy of Nature: A Guide to the New Essentialism*, (Cheshum: Acumen, 2002) and J.L. Mackie, *How Things Might Have Been*, (Oxford: Oxford University Press, 2006) for a more detailed account of this distinction.

[4] S. Gelman, *The Essential Child*. (New York: Oxford University Press, 2003) is clear on this point.

[5] D. Medin and A. Ortony, 'Psychological essentialism'. In S. Vosniadou (ed.) *Similarity and Analogical Reasoning*, (New York: Cambridge University Press, 1989).

Essentialism, Externalism, and Human Nature

is considerable disagreement. Keil[6] argues that childhood essentialism is restricted to the biological domain. Gelman[7] thinks that children are essentialist about a wider domain of reality that includes the psychological and substances such as water but does not include artefacts. And Bloom[8] holds that children are even essentialist with respect to artefacts such as coffee pots and works of art. What is important to appreciate is that as the psychological essentialist is making a claim about the metaphysical commitments of children she is not thereby committing herself to the truth of essentialism qua metaphysical doctrine.

As advocates of psychological essentialism portray a commitment to essentialism as a deeply entrenched, universal and innate characteristic of children it is natural to regard them as making a substantial claim about human nature: specifically, that it is part of our distinctive human nature to hold an essentialist outlook on the world (at least when we are children).

At this point a comment about the relationship between psychological essentialism and the kind of essentialism discussed by contemporary metaphysicians is in order. Contemporary essentialism about categories is often characterised as a view about natural kinds, where natural kinds are conceived as objective categories the existence and membership of which is independent of human interest and judgment.[9] This immediately implies that essentialism is not a doctrine that applies to types of artefacts. Moreover, it is often said that Darwin's theory of evolution by natural selection implies that essentialism doesn't apply to biological categories. For example, dogs don't have an essence as any property that dogs currently have need not be present in their descendents.

All this might appear to suggest that psychological essentialism, with its frequent references to the biological and the artefactual, is a misnamed doctrine. However, such a view would be a mistake for two reasons. First, what contemporary philosophers who take

[6] F. Keil, *Concepts, Kinds, and Cognitive Development.* (Cambridge, MA: MIT Press, 1989).
[7] S. Gelman, *The Essential Child,* op. cit.
[8] P. Bloom, *How Children Learn the Meaning of Words* (Cambridge, MA: MIT Press, 2000); P. Bloom, *Descartes' Baby: How the Science of Child Development Explains What Makes us Human* (New York: Basic Books, 2004); and P. Bloom, *How Pleasure Works: The New Science of Why we Like what we Like* (London: Bodley Head, 2010).
[9] A. Bird, 'Essences and Natural Kinds'. In R. Le Poidevin, P. Simons, A. McGonigal and R.P. Cameron (eds.), *The Routledge Companion to Metaphysics*, (Abingdon: Routledge, 2009).

essentialism seriously are saying is that essentialism isn't plausible with respect to biological and artefactual categories. But it doesn't follow from this that to think of the biological or the artefactual in essentialist terms is incoherent. Thus it becomes an empirical question as to whether children (or anyone else who is philosophically or scientifically unsophisticated) are essentialist about dogs, coffee pots, and the like. Second, the notion of essentialism that the contemporary metaphysician operates with seems to be unduly restrictive in only allowing properties such as intrinsic physical properties and their kin to belong to essences. But why can't having a particular history or bearing a specific relationship to the human mind be part of a category's essence given that histories and mental states are as much a part of the natural world as intrinsic physical properties?

Considerable empirical evidence has been presented in favour of psychological essentialism.[10] To get a flavour of this consider Frank Keil's[11] classic experiment. Keil showed children and adults a picture of a racoon. When asked these subjects answered that the picture was of a racoon. They were then told that the pictured animal underwent a series of changes including changes to its appearance (through fur-dying and plastic surgery), the insertion of a smell sac, and modifications to its behaviour. They were then presented with a picture of an animal resembling a skunk and told that it was of the original animal post-modification. When asked about the identity of the animal at this stage children over the age of seven and adults systematically answered that it was a racoon despite its appearance, indicating that for them something's being a racoon is a matter of its origins and/or hidden nature rather than its observable properties.

In this paper my concern is to not to evaluate the evidence for psychological essentialism but, rather, to determine the philosophical significance of the doctrine. The particular philosophical issue that I will focus on is that concerning the relationship between the contents of an individual's mind and the world external to her skull.[12]

---

[10]   See S. Gelman, 'Psychological Essentialism in Children', *Trends in Cognitive Sciences*, **8** (2004) 404–409, and S. Carey, The Origin of Concepts. (New York: Oxford University Press, 2009) ch 13, for helpful overviews.

[11]   F. Keil, *Concepts, Kinds, and Cognitive Development*, op. cit.

[12]   A number of philosophers and cognitive scientists have utilized a commitment of psychological essentialism in addressing philosophical issues. For example, S. Laurence and E. Margolis, ('Radical Concept Nativism' *Cognition* 86 (2002), 25–55) and S. Carey, (*The Origin of Concepts*, op. cit.) employ psychological essentialism in seeking to undermine Jerry Fodor's argument for radical concept nativism. (J. Fodor, *The*

3. Externalism

According to externalism the relationship between the contents of an individual's mind and the world beyond her outer surfaces goes beyond the mere causal. Rather, the very identity of the concepts and thoughts she has will depend on the nature of the external world that she is embedded in. Consequently, it is in principle possible for two individuals to be molecule for molecule replicas (or identical in terms of their intrinsic physical properties) yet have divergent concepts and thoughts due to the fact that they inhabit quite different environments. Externalism contrasts with internalism. Internalists reject the view that there exists this non-casual relationship between the mind and the external world. For them, the contents of an individual's concepts and thoughts supervene upon their intrinsic physical properties so that molecule for molecule duplicates would share their concepts and thoughts no matter how much the environments in which they resided diverged.[13]

Over the last thirty years externalism has become near orthodoxy in the philosophy of mind.[14] This is in no small part due to the influence of Hilary Putnam's paper 'The Meaning of "Meaning". At the heart of Putnam's argument is a thought experiment that is usually

---

Language of Thought. (Cambridge, Mass: Harvard University Press, 1975); J. Fodor, 'The Present State of the Innateness Debate' in his *Representations* (Cambridge, MA: MIT Press, 1981); and J. Fodor, *Concepts*, op. cit.). And J. Prinz, (*Furnishing the Mind* (Cambridge, MA: MIT Press, 2002)) appeals to psychological essentialism in motivating his proxytype theory of concepts.

[13] This way of characterizing the debate between externalists and internalists might seem to be problematic as it assumes a materialist or physicalist view of the mind when Descartes, that paradigmatic advocate of internalism, was a dualist. My reply is that this characterization will work for present purposes as most contemporary externalists reject dualism. See K. Farkas, *The Subject's Point of View*, (Oxford: Oxford University Press, 2008) and T. Williamson, *Knowledge and its Limits* (Oxford: Oxford University Press, 2000) for an attempt to characterise the debate in a manner that doesn't presuppose materialism or physicalism.

[14] However there are critics. For example: T. Crane, 'All The Difference in the World', *Philosophical Quarterly* **41** (1991), 1–25; N. Chomsky, *New Horizons in the Study of Language and Mind*, (Cambridge: Cambridge University Press, 2000); G. Segal, *A Slim Book About Narrow Content*, (Cambridge, MA: MIT Press, 2000); A.S. Wikforss 'Social Externalism and Coneptual Errors', *Philosophical Quarterly* **51** (2001) 217–3; and K. Farkas, *The Subject's Point of View*, op. cit.

M.J. Cain

described along the following lines. In a distant part of our galaxy there is a planet called Twin Earth that is very much like our own planet. On Twin Earth there is a community of individuals who speak a language very much like English, a community that has a member – call him Oscar2 – who is a physical duplicate of Oscar, a fellow who lives here on Earth. Members of both these linguistic communities apply the word 'water' to the local colourless, odourless liquid that falls as rain, fills their rivers and streams, quenches their thirst, and so on, and intend to apply that word only to stuff that is the same liquid as the local 'water'. One significant difference between Earth and Twin Earth is that the stuff they call 'water' on Twin Earth – the colourless, odourless liquid that fills their rivers and lakes, falls as rain, quenches their thirst, and so on – has a physical microstructure that differs from that of the stuff that we call 'water'. For, it is XYZ rather than H_2O. In virtue of this difference the English word 'water' has a different extension than that of the Twin English word 'water'; H_2O, and only H_2O, falls within the extension of the former whereas XYZ, and only XYZ, falls within the extension of the latter. Similarly, English sentences containing the word 'water' have different truth conditions than their Twin English counterparts. For example, the English sentence 'water is wet' is true if and only if H_2O is wet whereas the corresponding Twin English sentence is true if and only if XYZ is wet. Due to this difference of extension and truth conditions, the word 'water' has one meaning on Earth and quite another on Twin Earth. And an upshot of this it that the twins, being fully fledged members of their respective linguistic communities, mean different things by the word 'water' (or understand that word differently) despite their physical similarity. This leads Putnam to conclude that the meaning of a natural kind word on an individual's lips is partly determined by the nature of the external world that she inhabits.

Putnam was primarily concerned with linguistic meaning and with undermining description theories of meaning according to which the reference of a term is determined by its sense or intension (where sense or intension is conceived as a matter of a description associated with the term by the individual).[15] However, his argument can easily be extended to generate a parallel conclusion about concepts and thoughts. Here is how such an extension might run. We use language

---

[15]   For a helpful overview see D. Braun, 'Names and Natural Kind Terms'. In E. LePore and B.C. Smith (eds.) *The Oxford Handbook of Philosophy of Language*, (Oxford: Oxford University Press, 2006).

to express our concepts and thoughts. For example, Oscar uses the word 'water' to express one of his concepts and the sentence 'water is wet' to express a belief of his that contains that concept as a constituent. Reflecting the linguistic case, due to the nature of his home environment this concept applies to, and only to, H_2O and the belief containing it is true if and only if H_2O is wet. Similarly, the concept that Oscar2 expresses with the word 'water' applies to and only to XYZ and the belief that contains it is true if and only if XYZ is wet. Due to this difference in extension and truth conditions, Oscar's WATER concept and thoughts differ in content from those of his twin. And as concepts and thoughts are classified partly in terms of their content, the twins diverge in their concepts and thoughts.

This is a tale that has been told many times but there are important features of Putnam's reasoning that, following many recent commentators,[16] I have downplayed. As will become clear, it is important to rectify this situation as I will now do. Putnam assumes that the word 'water' (along with 'gold', 'tiger' and 'lemon') is a natural kind term. What makes it a natural kind term is not merely the fact that most of the samples of liquid that members of the English speaking community characterize as 'water' belong to a common natural kind. All those samples also share certain superficial properties and there is in principle nothing to stop there being a word with a meaning such it that applies to something if and only if that thing has certain superficial properties. What is crucial to a word's being a natural kind term is the state of mind of its users; they must have relevant intentions and make relevant assumptions. This is brought out at several points in the 'Meaning of "meaning"'. For example, imagining himself ostensively defining 'water', Putnam[17] writes:

> Suppose I point to a glass of water and say 'this liquid is called water' . . . My 'ostensive definition' of water has the following empirical presupposition: that the body of liquid I am pointing to bears a certain sameness relation (say, *x is the same liquid as y*, or *x is the same$_L$ as y*) to most of the stuff I and other speakers in my linguistic community have on other occasions called 'water'.

---

[16] For example, M. Rowlands, *Externalism* (Cheshum: Acumen, 2003) and R. Wilson, *Boundaries of the Mind: The Individual in the Fragile Sciences* (Cambridge: Cambridge University Press, 2004).

[17] 'The Meaning of "Meaning"', op. cit, 225.

M.J. Cain

When discussing the case of 'gold' Putnam[18] writes:

> when Archimedes asserted that something was gold . . . he was not just saying that it had the superficial characteristics of gold . . .; he was saying that it had the same general *hidden structure* (the same 'essence', so to speak) as any normal piece of local gold.

In fact, Putnam thinks that related intentions and assumptions are in place with respect to words that are normally contrasted with natural kind terms, for example, those, such as 'pencil', that name types of artefacts:

> When we use the word 'pencil' we intend to refer to whatever has the same *nature* as the normal examples of the local pencils in the actual world.[19]

Returning to the case of 'water' one might ask what it is for two samples of a liquid to bear the same$_L$ relation to one another. Putnam's answer is that it is for them to have 'the same important physical properties'[20] that is, the same physical microstructure. Consequently, given that the samples of liquid that we routinely call 'water' in our world are invariably collections of H_2O molecules the word 'water' in the English speaking linguistic community has a meaning such that H_2O, and only H_2O, falls in its extension. It is important to note that this doesn't require anyone to know that the crucial property of the liquid they interact with is being H_2O. Although this fact is common knowledge nowadays it wasn't known by anyone prior to the chemical revolution of the 18th century.

In sum then, for Putnam, mental states of members of the linguistic community – in the form of intentions and assumptions – play a key role in making it the case that the nature of the external world enters into the meaning of words such as 'water'.

A second important feature of Putnam's account is his claim that meaning has a social dimension in that what a word means on the lips of an individual is inherited from what it means on the lips of other members of her linguistic community. This is reflected in Putnam's invocation of the division of linguistic labour. An individual might not be able to distinguish between beeches and elms but this does not imply that the words 'beech' and 'elm' (along with her underlying concepts) mean the same thing on her lips. For, she is willing to defer to experts with respect to whether a given tree is an elm or a

[18] Ibid., 235.
[19] Ibid., 243.
[20] Ibid, 232.

beech. What connects this with Putnam's point about the role of mental states in determining meaning is that he holds that the social dimension of meaning depends upon individual speakers having appropriate intentions and thoughts in general. For, meaning wouldn't have a social dimension if individual speakers didn't intent to mean by a given word what their fellows mean by that word or if they didn't recognize the existence of experts and intend to defer to their judgement with respect to the application of words.

4. Externalism and Cognitive Science

Arguments echoing that of Putnam have been developed by Kripke and Burge.[21] What is perhaps a little surprising is how much they have influenced naturalistically orientated philosophers of mind, that is philosophers of mind who see their enterprise as being closely linked to the empirical study of the mind. For, these standard externalist arguments rely upon intuitions and bizarre thought experiments and make little reference to empirical work in psychology and cognitive science. Moreover, much mainstream work on concepts in cognitive science over the last few decades threatens to deliver a different result by implying that Putnam's twins express the same concept by means of 'water'.

The most prominent theory of concepts within cognitive science developed over the last thirty years is the prototype theory.[22] This began life as a reaction to the so-called classical theory of concepts according to which possessing a concept involves knowing or representing necessary and sufficient conditions for falling under the concept. A prototype is a complex mental representation that, rather than specifying necessary and sufficient conditions, specifies the characteristics that any item falling within its extension is likely to have. For example, on this view the concept DOG is a complex

[21]   S. Kripke, *Naming and Necessity, op. cit.* T Burge, 'Individualism and the Mental', In P.A. French, T.E. Ueling Jr. And H.K. Wettstein (eds), *Midwest Studies in Philosophy IV*, (Minneapolis, MN: University of Minnesota Press, 1979, 73–121).

[22]   E. Rosch, 'Principles of Categorization.' In E. Rosch and B. B. Lloyd (eds.) *Cognition and Categorization* (Hillsdale, NJ: Erlbaum, 1978). L. J. Rips, E.J. Shoben and E.E. Smith, 'Semantic Distance and the Verification of Semantic Relations', *Journal of Verbal Learning and Verbal Behavior* **12** (1973), 1–20. J.A. Hampton, 'Polymorphous Concepts in Semantic Memory', *Journal of Verbal Learning and Verbal Behavior* **18** (1979), 441–461.

representation that specifies properties that dogs generally have, properties that something is likely to have if it is a dog. Examples of such properties might be those of having four legs, having fur, having a tendency to bark, and so on. Thus, the DOG prototype constitutes a description of a prototypical or stereotypical dog and grasping the concept DOG is a matter of having this description encoded in one's head. A prototype also includes a similarity metric so that, for example, determining whether an item x falls within the extension of DOG involves employing a similarity metric in order to determine whether x resembles the prototypical dog to a sufficient extent. A Labrador or a Golden Retriever would be a serious candidate for a prototypical dog but, presumably, a Great Dane or a Pekinese would not be. That an individual would categorise a Pekinese, but not a Siamese cat, as a DOG reflects the fact that employment of the similarity metric generates the result that the former, but not the latter, is sufficiently similar to the prototypical dog to fall within the extension of the concept DOG.

Generally speaking, advocates of the prototype theory regard prototypes as being learned on the basis of experience and as referring to properties that are readily perceivable rather than abstract.[23] A closely related view is the examplar theory of concepts.[24] According to this, at the heart of an individual's concept C is a representation of a particular instance (or number of instances) of C encountered by the individual. Accordingly, deciding whether something falls under the concept in question involves comparing it with the exemplars. For example, central to my concept DOG might be a representation of the dog I had as a child so when I seek to determine whether something that I have encountered is a DOG I do so by working out whether it is sufficiently similar to the dog I had as a child.

With respect to externalism, a key point about prototype and examplar theories of concepts is that they don't sit too happily with that doctrine. For, it would appear that the prototypes or exemplars in the head of Oscar and Oscar2 will be indistinguishable implying that the twins express the same concepts by means of the word 'water' (for, recall, prototypes and exemplars tend to represent observable properties). Thus, if one wants one's view of concepts and thoughts to be empirically motivated then it seems that one shouldn't be too impressed by externalist thought experiments.

[23] This point is emphasized by both J. Prinz, *Furnishing the Mind*, op. cit. and S. Gelman, *The Essential Child*, op. cit.
[24] D.L. Medin and M.M. Shaffer, 'Context Theory of Classification Learning', *Psychological Review* **85** (1978), 207–238.

Essentialism, Externalism, and Human Nature

One obvious reply to this is to say that psychologists who work on concepts are primarily interested in the mechanisms by means of which we categorise things and the internal processes by means of which we manipulate the representations associated with our concepts. On this front there is no difference between Oscar and Oscar2. Nevertheless, if concepts are involved in delivering us knowledge about the external world then the identity of the external items that they refer to will be of crucial importance and with respect to this Putnam did establish something important. For, he established that no matter how similar Oscar and Oscar2's prototypes are, as they were constructed in response to samples of different types of stuff they support the possession of concepts that diverge in their reference or extension.[25]

I'm not convinced that prototype and exemplar theories of concepts can be squared with externalism quite so easily. The danger is that the externalist is begging the question when she asserts that Oscar and Oscar2's prototypes where constructed in response to different types of stuff. Of course, Oscar interacted with H_2O and Oscar2 with XYZ. But H_2O and XYZ agree with respect to the properties that figure in the prototypes in their respective heads so one might equally say that those prototypes were constructed in response to the same type of stuff as belonging to the relevant type is a matter of observable rather than hidden properties. In other words, the externalist has no right to regard the twins' concepts as being natural kind concepts. After all, if the prototype theory is correct then determining whether something falls under a given concept will typically be done on the basis of a consideration of its observable properties.

It might be objected that the above point ignores that very aspect of Putnam's line of thought that I have sought to emphasise. This is the idea that when ostensively defining 'water' an individual points at a sample of water and resolves to apply the term 'water' only to stuff bearing the $same_L$ relation to the ostended sample. My response to this objection is that from the point of view of someone who advocates the prototype theory of concepts this represents a mistaken view of how concepts are acquired. Either, a child acquiring concepts doesn't think of what she interacts with in the manner of the

---

[25] Something like this line of thought is presented by Susan Carey, *The Origin of Concepts*, op. cit. who, following Ned Block ('Advertisement for a Semantics for Psychology'. In P.A. French (ed.) *Midwest Studies in Philosophy* (Minneapolis, MN: University of Minnesota Press, 1986)) endorses a two-factor theory of concepts.

individual in Putnam's scenario or if she does her doing so doesn't enter into the nature and identity of those concepts.

5. Psychological Essentialism Again

It is at this point that psychological essentialism becomes relevant for it offers an empirically motivated theory that challenges key aspects of prototype and exemplar theories of concepts and would appear to sit more happily with externalism. Indeed, as both Gelman[26] and Carey[27] point out, psychological essentialism was partly motivated by Putnam and Kripke's reflections.

Psychological essentialism implies that with respect to many of their concepts children think that the items that those concepts group together share a hidden essence in virtue of which they fall under the concept in question. Thus, for example, falling under the concept DOG is a matter of having the relevant hidden properties rather than having any superficial properties that dogs typically have. Hence, from the child's perspective, something can appear to be a dog without being a dog and something can be a dog without appearing to be being a dog. This is inconsistent with the prototype theory as that theory implies that the concept DOG is such that being a dog is wholly a matter of satisfying a prototype made up of features that are both readily observable and statistically salient in the child's environment.

According to psychological essentialism the relevant hidden properties are often not known by the child who thinks of them as being a matter of how things in the external world really are in and of themselves. This perspective of the child clearly sits happily with that of Putnam as it implies that a child's concepts work just as he supposes concepts like WATER and ELM work. Moreover, it suggests that it is likely that children will defer to experts. For, if a child recognises that she doesn't know what the essence of being a dog is then she will be disposed to defer to someone who she takes not to be hampered by such a lack of knowledge. Note also that the psychological essentialist's emphasis on the perspective of the child echoes Putnam's emphasis on the psychological state of the individual ostensively defining 'water'.[28]

---

[26] S. Gelman, *The Essential Child*, op. cit.
[27] S. Carey, *The Origin of Concepts*, op. cit.
[28] None of this is to say that the psychological essentialist is compelled to deny the existence of prototypes. For, she can accept that such structures

6. Psychological Essentialism and Externalism

In the remainder of this paper I will argue that the relationship between psychological essentialism and externalism isn't as clear-cut as I have thus far implied. Rather, psychological essentialism serves to undermine the kind of externalism that is commonplace in contemporary philosophy of mind. This is not to say that psychological essentialism implies that externalism is false; rather, that the way in which the external world determines the contents of our concepts and thoughts is severely constrained and directed by our underlying mental states. Consequently, an individual's mental states play a more substantial role in determining the content of her concepts and thoughts than is recognized by orthodox externalists. In arguing for this conclusion I will tend to focus on natural language words but my reasoning applies just as much to the concepts expressed by such words. I will do this for ease of exposition and to maintain consistency with Putnam's description of his externalism.

To explore the issue I will begin by considering a problem that Devitt and Sterelny[29] raise for a purely causal theory of reference. Recall that one of Putnam's targets was the description theory of reference and (along with Kripke) he is often characterized as wishing to replace such a position with a causal theory. Now, consider an individual pointing at a sample of water and saying 'I'll call that type of stuff "water"' (or, alternatively, pointing at a dog and saying 'I'll call that kind of thing "dog"'). The problem is that the sample or token in question doesn't just belong to the type *water* (or *dog*) but to many others. For example, *thirst quenching liquid, my favorite drink, stuff that expands when frozen* (or *pet, mammal, vertebrate*). This raises the qua-problem: when the individual points at the sample of water what is it that determines that she succeeds in referring to the sample qua-water as opposed to qua-thirst quenching liquid or qua-my favourite drink, or qua-stuff that expands when frozen. Similarly, what determines that she points at the dog qua-dog rather than qua-mammal, qua-pet or qua-vertebrate? Without a convincing answer to this question it would seem that the advocate of the causal theory of reference is saddled

---

exist and are routinely employed in making categorization decisions on the hoof so long as she resists identifying them with the concepts that they so help deploy.

[29] M. Devitt and K. Sterelny, *Language and Reality*, (Oxford: Blackwell, 1987).

with the unfortunate conclusion that terms like 'water' and 'dog' have indeterminate references. Devitt and Sterelny suggest that the correct response to the qua-problem is to retreat from a purely causal theory of reference and adopt a causal-descriptive theory instead. Accordingly, although 'water' and 'dog' got their reference partly as a result of interactions with samples of water and dogs this fact alone wasn't enough to secure their reference. In addition, the individual ostensively defining these words had an appropriate description in mind: she thought of what she was attempting to name as being a natural kind whose tokens tend to have particular observable properties.

One comment on this line of thought is that it seems to cohere well with Putnam's own. That is, he is not arguing for a pure-causal theory as he portrays the individual ostensively defining 'water' as intending to use that word to refer only to samples of stuff that bear the 'same$_L$ relationship' to the sample she points at. Moreover, he represents the individual as having a 'stereotype' in mind that she associates with the word in question. So his point is not so much to establish a pure casual theory of reference but to undermine the idea that an individual's internal mental states are the sole determinants of the reference and meaning of the words on her lips.

Nevertheless, the qua-problem does gesture towards something that I think is very important with respect to the viability of externalism and its relationship to psychological essentialism. Focusing on the example 'water' what is it to bear the same$_L$ relationship to the ostened sample of colourless, odourless, thirst quenching liquid? As we have seen, Putnam thinks that it has to do with having the same microstructure and in the case in question that would involve being composed of H_2O molecules. That being composed of H_2O molecules is what is needed to bear the same$_L$ relationship to the ostended sample is not knowable a priori according to Putnam, a line of thought which sits happily with place-holder conceptions of psychological essentialism. Rather, it is a matter for science to discover. But this raises a further question: does the individual need to think that to bear the same$_L$ relationship to the sample of liquid before her a sample of liquid has to have the same microstructure? Putnam is committed to a negative answer to this question. This is because he thinks that the meaning of words like 'water' and 'gold' have remained constant over centuries so that they meant just what they mean now at a point in time when no-one had the scientific sophistication to think of the same$_L$ relation in microphysical terms. What I want to suggest is that however this question is answered there are serious repercussions for externalism in the light of psychological essentialism. Thus, the question poses a dilemma for the externalist neither horn of which she should find attractive.

Suppose that, following Putnam, we answer the question negatively in saying that the individual need not think of the same$_L$ relation in terms of microstructure. Let's accept that what makes water water is a matter of microstructure. In other words, that water is essentially H_2O. However, a parallel point could not be made of all types of liquid for which we have concepts. Consider, for example, milk. Any sample of milk will have a particular microstructure and a physical makeup in general. It will largely consist of molecules of H_2O along with various vitimins, minerals and fat molecules. Such physical properties will provide the causal basis for the observable properties of the sample, such as its colour, its taste and smell, how it responds to being heated along with its powers to nourish. But having such physical properties is not what makes the sample milk. In other words, milk doesn't have the same sort of essence as water, that is a microphysical or physico-chemical essence. To see this consider the following thought experiment. On an arid planet a team of super-intelligent robots who have never previously encountered water, synthesise a collection of H_2O molecules that they store in a beaker in their laboratory. These molecules form a colourless liquid that any visiting human would be unable to distinguish from water. Would this stuff be water? I contend that it would even though it has different origins from the water here on Earth and even though it doesn't play anything like the same role in the life of its home planet that water does here. For example, it doesn't fall as rain, fill any lakes or rivers or help sustain the life of any living creature. This is a simple consequence of water's having a microsphysical essence.

Now suppose that the robots take the water they have manufactured and mix it with a range of vitamins, minerals and fats that they have also synthesized so as to make something that is identical at the physico-chemical level to the glass of milk that I have just poured from a plastic bottle in my fridge. They don't drink this liquid and if they did it would certainly not provide them with any nourishment. Neither did they make it with the intention to provide nourishment for any other things. In fact, they are not in contact with any living things that would be nourished by the liquid. Qeustion: is the liquid they have made milk? My answer is that it is not as what makes milk milk is not its physico-chemical properties per se. Rather, the essence of milk has to do with its origins and function; that it is manufactured in the body of a living creature with the function of sustaining and nourishing its young offspring. In short, the milk-like liquid the robots manufacture doesn't have the relevant origins and function to be milk.

Now consider Twin Earth where the liquid that they call milk – a liquid that is produced in the bodies of the creatures they call 'mammals' and is made and used to provide nourishment for the young offspring of those creatures – is largely made up of XYZ. Question: is this liquid milk? I would deliver an affirmative answer on the basis that it has a relevant origin and function.

In sum then, a sample of liquid can fail to be milk whilst being identical at the physico-chemical level to the milk in my glass and something can be milk whilst being very different at the physico-chemical level to that milk. What this implies is not that milk doesn't have an essence but that its essence isn't microsphysical or chemico-physical; rather it is functional or bio-functional. Neither does it imply that 'milk' isn't a kind term or MILK a kind concept, just that the relevant kind is functional or bio-functional rather than physical. Some philosophers might baulk at this suggestion that 'milk'/MILK is a kind term/concept on the grounds that it groups together items whose behvaour is governed by different physical and chemical laws and distinguishes between items whose behaviour is governed by the same physical and chemical laws. I would respond that they are operating with an unduly restrictive notion of 'kind' but I don't have to insist on this point for the purposes of my argument. As will become clear, all I need is for my claim about what makes milk milk to be true.

Both the terms and concepts 'water'/WATER and 'milk'/MILK are prominent in our linguistic and mental lives and it is important that a child acquires them early in her development, something that a typical child can be expected to do. Now imagine an individual pointing at a sample of milk whilst saying 'milk' alongside the intention to use that word in future only to refer to stuff that bears the same$_L$ relation to the stuff before her. What meaning will she have bestowed upon 'milk'? What concept will she have acquired? Will it be *milk*/MILK or some orthogonal physico-chemical concept? Echoing the kind of scenario highlighted by Devitt and Sterelny[30] the sample of liquid before her falls both under the concept MILK and under some distinct chemico-physical concept. Earlier I posed a dilemma and we are now investigating the first horn of that dilemma. This involves following Putnam in committing oneself to the view that the individual doesn't think of the same$_L$ relation as being a matter of

---

[30]   M. Devitt and K. Sterelny, *Language and Reality*, op. cit.

sharing a common-microstructure with the ostended sample. Rather, she has a neutral or unarticulated idea of the relation. But this gives rise to an indeterminacy problem: why would the naming ceremony privilege the attribution of the meaning *milk* to 'milk' (and the acquisition of the concept MILK) rather than an alternative meaning relating to physico-chemical properties? Here, unlike the kind of cases that Devitt and Sterelny discuss, appeal to a stereotype or in-head description relating to observable properties won't help to disambiguate the pointing act. Let me explain why. When the individual points at a dog she is also pointing at a mammal. So what meaning is attributed to the word 'dog' at the naming ceremony? Is it *dog* or is it *mammal*? It seems that the stereotype or description in the head of the individual settles this question at least to the extent that it rules out *mammal*. For the description will refer to properties that dogs tend to have but that mammals in general don't have so that the description or stereotype will 'fit' dogs in general in a manner in which it won't fit mammals in general. Another way of putting this is to say that the description would serve in the identification or detection of dogs but not of mammals in general. As we have seen, to say this fits well with Putnam's picture. But in the case of the sample of milk such a move won't help. Any stereotype or in-head description will fit the physico-chemical kind just as much as it fits milk as anything that is like the ostended sample at that level will share the kind of observable properties that will figure in the stereotype or in-head description.

The upshot of this is that if the individual operates with an unarticulated notion of the nature of the same$_L$ relation then she is not going to be successful in attributing a determinate meaning or reference to 'milk' or in acquiring a determinate concept when she attempts to bestow meaning on that word.

But the same holds with respect to 'water'. The sample of water ostended will fall under a concept that binds together samples of liquid that have a common origin, 'lifestyle' and role in human life and life in general. One might describe this as the concept of a liquid that fills rivers and streams, falls as rain, comes out of taps, and is fundamental to the survival of most living things. Earlier I argued that MILK is a bio-functional concept. With respect to the concept I am now describing, it might be described as a functional concept. Call this concept FWATER. In the environment of the individual ostensively defining 'water' everything that falls under FWATER also falls under the concept WATER and vice versa. However, the concepts are not co-extensive as the XYZ on Twin Earth falls under FWATER though it is not water. And the H_2O

M.J. Cain

synthesized by the super-intelligent robots described above falls under WATER but not FWATER.

So the question is this: why does 'water' get attributed the meaning *water* rather than *fwater*? I don't see how any plausible answer can be given to this question if one holds onto the idea that the individual in the naming ceremony operates with an unarticulated notion of the same-L relation.

So far I have focused on the use of ostensive definition to bestow meaning on a word. But ostension can also be used to teach the meaning of word that already has its meaning fixed to another individual. Consider an individual who means *water* by 'water' attempting to teach the meaning of 'water' to someone else by means of an ostensive definition. If what I have said so far is true then for this attempt at teaching to be successful the would-be learner must have an appropriately articulated understanding of the $same_L$ relation in her mind. Without this there will be no fact of the matter as to whether she comes to attribute 'water' the meaning *water* or *fwater*.

Is the second horn of the dilemma any more promising? Taking this horn involves attributing the individual ostensively defining a word such as 'water' (or attempting to learn the meaning of such a word on the basis of an ostensive definition) a more fully articulated notion of the $same_L$ relation, where she thinks that bearing that relation to the ostended liquid involves having the same microstructure. There are a couple of worries with this suggestion. The first relates to the plausibility of the idea that when the word 'water' first entered the language it did so as the result of a naming ceremony involving an individual who thought of the liquid she was pointing at as having a microphysical essence. As such an event would have had to have taken place considerably before the scientific revolution of the eighteenth century one might reasonably doubt that anyone operated with such a thought.

The second worry is this. Perhaps the individual will succeed in bestowing the meaning *water* on 'water' and on acquiring the concept WATER but she runs the risk of bestowing a meaning other than *milk* on 'milk' and so not acquiring the concept MILK. Given that milk and water have quite different essences the individual will need to desist in thinking of the $same_L$ relation as being a matter of microstructure in the case of 'milk'. Instead, she would need to operate with an alternative (yet still articulated) idea of what the $same_L$ relation amounted to in the case of milk, one that characterised that relation in terms of bio-functional role. One might wonder why the individual would be motivated to regard the sample of milk so differently from the sample of liquid in operating with different

46

notions of the same$_L$ relation with regard to them. After all, it is not as if the milk doesn't have a microstructure or that the water doesn't have distinctive origins and a particular important role in our lives. Nevertheless, the second horn of the dilemma does seem to be preferable to the first for it does explain how 'water' and 'milk' could have come to mean what they mean and how an individual could learn the meanings of these words on the basis of being given an ostensive definition.

What are the implications of this for the viability of externalism? The mere fact that the individual ostensively defining 'water' is interacting with a sample of water does not ensure that she will bestow the meaning *water* on the word 'water' or succeed in teaching that meaning to anyone else. She could just as well bestow or teach the meaning *fwater* (along with her doppelganger on Twin Earth). For the microstructure of the ostended sample of water to have a semantic significance it must be thought of in a relevant way by both the definer and the learner. They must think of the ostended sample as having a physical microstructure and intend to apply the word 'water' only to samples of liquid that have that very microstructure. In other words, they must have an articulated notion of what the same$_L$ relation amounts to in this case. But they must also have at their disposal alternative notions of the same$_L$ relation that they utilize when dealing with words such as 'milk'.

None of this implies that externalism is false for one can construct a twin scenario where an individual on Earth attempts to bestow meaning on the word 'water' operating with the relevant articulated notion of the nature of the same$_L$ relation. Here the word water will acquire the meaning *water* and she will acquire the concept WATER. Her twin on Twin Earth, operating with just the same notion of the same$_L$ relation, will bestow a different meaning on 'water' and acquire a different concept. However, the resultant externalism will be somewhat chastened as the implication of my reasoning is the that extent to which the external world shapes the meaning of one's words and the content of one's concepts is very much constrained and directed by one's internal mental states. For inhabitants of Earth and Twin Earth respectively to mean different things by 'water' (or express different concepts by means of that word) they must have quite specific mental states lying behind their interactions with the external world, mental states that the external world itself doesn't guarantee that they have. This serves to undermine the kind of externalism that dominates contemporary philosophy of mind and language according to which the mere fact that the samples of liquid that we interact with and label 'water' implies that that word refers to, and only to, H_2O and that H_2O, and only H_2O, fall under the concept expressed by that word. It also serves to undermine Putnam's position even though he emphasises the importance of mental states in contributing to the determination of meaning.

So far I have focused on the case of language but my reasoning applies just as much to concepts. Thus, for an individual to acquire the concept WATER from her interactions with water (be those interactions direct or mediated by her experiences of her fellows' use of the word 'water') she needs to think of the target concept as grouping together items in virtue of their having a common microstructure. If she thinks of the target concept in some alternative but equally articulated way then she will acquire not WATER but some other concept (FWATER, perhaps). And if she is neutral on the question of what binds together the items that fall under the target concept then she runs the risk of failing to acquire a determinate concept.

I now want to consider a potential objection to my line of argument. This draws upon essentialism as a doctrine about particulars as opposed to categories. The idea is that although the sample of liquid that figures in the ostensive definition of 'water' is both water and fwater it is essentially the former and only contingently the later. It is this difference that explains why 'water' has the meaning *water* rather than *fwater* bestowed upon it. Thus there is no need to demand of the individual that she has a richly articulated notion of the same$_L$ relation.

I have three points to make in response to this objection. First, it runs the risk of making it a mystery as to how 'milk' means what it does and how we acquire the concept MILK. For, if the essence of a sample of water relates to its microstructure then why doesn't the essence of a sample of milk? One might respond by saying that the essential function of milk relates to biology (that it is produced within the bodies of biological systems for the use of their offspring) so making milk a biological kind and so something in the scientific domain. Whereas, fwater isn't a biological kind but more of an artefactual kind so falling outside of the scientific domain. However, I'm not convinced by this as the essential function of fwater partly relates to its usage by biological systems whose survival depends upon it and which have evolved to utilize it. So why isn't fwater a biological kind? Moreover, if it is conceded that FWATER is an artefactual concept it might be pointed out that some prominent psychological essentialists[31] argue that our innate essentialist commitments cover the

---

[31]   For example, Paul Bloom, *Descartes' Baby*, op. cit.

artefactual so that there is an empirical basis for thinking that a particular can have an artefactual essence.

My second point is that such an essentialism about particulars is hardly mandatory. Thus the advocate of this objection needs to produce some justification for it. Such a justification isn't going to come from developmental psychology as psychological essentialists are quite clear that our innate essentialist commitments relate to categories and kinds and not particulars. Thus, there is little empirical support for the claim that it is part of our innate metaphysical perspective on the world that particulars have essences. And even if it were that wouldn't be much help given that, as indicated in the previous paragraph, psychological essentialists often argue that our essentialist commitments spread beyond the domain of physics and biology. This implies that if empirical work in developmental psychology is invoked to settle the issue there is the real prospect that it will support the claim that from the perspective of the typical human the essence of a particular thing that is an artefact relates to its being an artefact as much as its falling under any kind recognized by science.

A third point is that we have to make sense of how all of the words that we use mean what they mean, of why all of our concepts have the content that they have. As we have plenty of words that refer to artefacts and as the acquisition of many artefactual concepts is fundamental to a child's development the advocate of the objection under discussion runs the risk of making a mystery of how we could have such words and concepts.

I can envisage another objection to my line of thought that runs as follows. Perhaps it is correct to say that a range of articulated notions of essence are needed to ground the meanings of the words of our language and the concepts that we use them to express. But it doesn't follow from this that every individual need have and employ such a range of articulated notions of essence. For we mustn't forget that one of Putnam's key points relates to the social dimension of meaning. It is only the individual members of the linguistic community who first coin a word – or the experts with respect to the application of that word – who need to have and employ the relevant articulated notion of essence (be it microstructuaral, bio-functional, or whatever).

I have two replies to this objection. The first is that it makes it too easy to know the meaning of a word or grasp a concept and rules out as impossible perfectly normal phenomena such as failing to understand a word and misunderstanding a word. Being a competent member of a linguistic community doesn't imply that one knows the meanings of all the words of the community's language or grasps all the concepts expressed by those words. Suppose an individual has encountered the word 'vitamin' but knows little about what vitamins are. Then they could can hardly be said to grasp the concept VITAMIN or mean *vitamin* by that word. In such a case the individual could be expected to be aware of their ignorance so as not to make any claims about understanding the word or concept in question. But there are other cases where an individual mistakenly believes that she knows what a particular word means in the wider community. A common example relates to the word 'disinterested'. Many people think this word means *uninterested* rather than *unbiased*. If such a person were to describe someone as 'disinterested' they would be saying that they were uninterested rather that unbiased. This would be so regardless of the meaning of the word in the wider community and even if the individual intended to mean by 'disinterested' just what everyone else meant. In sum then, the familiar phenomena of failing to understand the meaning of a word and misunderstanding a word that one uses suggest that for an individual's linguistic knowledge and concepts to line up with those of her fellows considerable demands are placed on her underlying mental states.

None of this is to deny the existence of a division of linguistic labour. Suppose I can't tell elms from beeches. I can till mean different things by the words 'elm' and 'beech' and mean what the experts mean by them. But that this is the case requires me to meet various conditions. I know that 'elm' and 'beech' name distinct species of trees and so employ the concepts TREE and SPECIES in connection with those words. I think that the respective species picked out by 'elm' and 'beech' are different in ways broadly similar to those in which oaks and sycamores (which I can tell apart) differ. Hence, I think they differ with respect to leaf shape, size, DNA, evolutionary history, and such like. I also accept that there are experts and would defer to them but I have some idea about what makes an expert an expert, how to find one, and the kinds of techniques they would use. So it would seem that the divide between me and the experts isn't so extreme and that to avail myself of the division of linguistic labour I have to have quite a rich body of specific mental states.

My second reply is that the objection doesn't sit very well with practice in developmental psychology where it is taken as a real possibility that individuals undergo conceptual development as they mature. Thus, for example, a developmental psychologist might argue that the concept that a typical five year old child expresses by means of the word 'cause' differs from that expressed by a typical ten year old when she uses 'cause', which in turn differs from that expressed by a typical adult when she uses 'cause'. But if the power of the wider linguistic community to enter into the mind of the individual is as great as the objection implies, then such conceptual development is an impossibility. But rejecting the coherence of orthodox developmental psychology seems to me to be too high a cost of endorsing the objection under consideration.

7. Conclusion

In this article I have argued that, despite first appearances, psychological essentialism undermines the kind of externalist view of the content of our concepts and thoughts that has become commonplace in the philosophy of mind and language. This a consequence of the psychological essentialist's emphasis on a range of concepts that includes those of biological phenomena and artefacts as well as those of types of physical stuff. If a child is to acquire such a wide range of concepts then she will need to have at her disposal a range of articulated notions of essence and bring the relevant notion of essence to bear in each particular case. For example, the articulated notion of essence that she will need to deploy in acquiring the concept WATER will be different from that that she needs to deploy in acquiring the concept MILK. Without the appropriate articulated notions of essence a child will not acquire these concepts no matter how much water and milk she interacts with. This is not to say that the extra-cranial world plays no role in determining the contents of our thoughts and concepts but the extent to which it does is severely constrained and directed by our internal mental states.

Oxford Brookes University
mcain@brookes.ac.uk

Human Nature and Grammar

WOLFRAM HINZEN

1. Introduction

Seeing human nature through the prism of grammar may seem rather unusual.[1] I will argue that this is a symptom for a *problem* – in both discussions of human nature and grammar: Neither the theory of grammar has properly placed its subject matter within the context of an inquiry into human nature and speciation, nor have discussions of human nature properly assessed the significance of grammar.[2]

In philosophy, the standard setting for such discussions in the last decades has been the philosophy of biology, where the search for a human nature is placed in the context of a discussion of 'sex and death'[3]: the vagaries of genetic reproduction under the ruthless regime of changing environments and natural selection. Discussions characteristically begin from a doubt as to whether human nature can be real – given an even more basic doubt, in a Neo-Darwinian context, of whether species are. If these reduce to mere variants, it is of their essence to change and for genetic and phenotypic variation among their members to exist, which is in turn a reflection of historical contingencies and the selection processes they trigger. Hull[4] concludes that if human nature denotes something real, it cannot be grounded in biology. Even if there *were* universally distributed traits in *Homo sapiens*, which he argues there aren't, it must be 'largely a matter of evolutionary happenstance'[5] which as

---

[1]   Though see T. Roeper, *The Prism of Grammar* (Cambridge, MA: MIT Press, 2009).

[2]   For exceptions to this generalization, apart from Roeper ibid., see W. Hinzen, *Mind Design and Minimal Syntax*, (Oxford: Oxford University Press, 2006) and N. Mukherji, *The Primacy of Grammar* (Cambridge, MA: MIT Press, 2010).

[3]   K. Sterelny and P. E. Griffiths, 1999. *Sex and Death* (Chicago: University of Chicago Press, 1999).

[4]   D. Hull, 'On Human Nature'. In Hull and Ruse (eds.) *The Philosophy of Biology* (Oxford: Oxford University Press, 1998).

[5]   Ibid. 385.

doi:10.1017/S1358246112000045   © The Royal Institute of Philosophy and the contributors 2012
Royal Institute of Philosophy Supplement **70** 2012   53

such can't have the metaphysical, ethical and epistemological significance that philosophers have taken human nature to have.

Another denial of human nature comes from the 'blank slate' conception of the human mind in the sense of Pinker,[6] which amounts to a rejection of 'innateness', a notion to which human nature has been closely linked in recent discussions. According to this conception and the radical empiricist tradition more generally, classically represented by Skinner,[7] biology has left the structure and contents of our minds largely unshaped. Internalist determinants are neglected in favour of external ones. In the limit, there is no relevant biological basis to the human mind at all. According to Rorty,[8] our minds are being left to the shaping influences of culture and historical-cultural contingency. Innateness is also often argued to be an inherently confused notion and not to fit with what has been called the 'interactionist consensus'[9] – the view that all traits arise from an interplay of genetic inheritance, ecological and epigenetic resources in a developing system.[10]

One can thus arrive at a rejection of human nature on various paths – Neo-Darwinian, empiricist, pragmatist or relativist. Whatever route we take, human nature comes out as historical, contingent, and variable. An innate 'Universal Grammar' (UG) is frequently denied on similar grounds, like the ubiquity of linguistic variation and the character of language as a socio-cultural construction, for which there is no linguistically specific biological basis.[11]

Where the notion of human nature has prominently survived in recent years, it is in the specific context of the evolutionary psychologist's take on the Neo-Darwinian synthesis. Here the claim is that our minds largely consist of dedicated functional 'modules' that are hardwired into the human brain as task-specific evolutionary

[6]   S. Pinker, *The Blank Slate: The Modern Denial of Human Nature* (Harmondsworth: Penguin, 2003).
[7]   B. F. Skinner, *Verbal Behavior* (New York: Appletonn-Century-Crofts, 1957).
[8]   R. Rorty, 'The Priority of Democracy Over Philosophy. In A. R. Malachowski, (ed.) *Reading Rorty* (Oxford: Blackwell, 1990).
[9]   K. Sterelny and P. E. Griffiths, 1999. *Sex and Death*, op. cit.
[10]   P. E. Griffiths and E. Machery, 'Innateness, Canalisation and "Biologizing the Mind', *Philosophical Psychology* **21** (2008), 395–412.
[11]   N. Evans, and J. Levinson, 'The Myth of Language Universals: Language Diversity and its Importance for Cognitive Science', *Behavioral and Brain Sciences* **32** (2009), 429–492; M. Christiansen, and N. Chater 'Language as Shaped by the Brain', *Behavioral and Brain Sciences* **31** (2008), 489–558; M. Tomasello, *Constructing a Language*. (Cambridge, MA: Harvard University Press, 2005).

adaptations.[12] According to Pinker's[13] classical conception of the generative program in linguistics, grammar is one of these modules. But because it consists of arbitrary formal rules on this conception, its significance for human nature, general cognition, and human reason is unclear. In fact, the consistency of such a module with Darwinian evolutionary principles is often denied.[14]

As things stand, neither textbooks such as Sterelny and Griffiths[15] nor anthologies such as Hull and Ruse[16] or Rosenberg and Arp[17] thematize either human language or grammar in any essential way, despite a long tradition of biolinguistic inquiry in which a notion of human nature has been a central topic.[18] The philosophy of mind, similarly, remains focused on issues such as phenomenal experience, consciousness, and the Self, giving grammar no systematic status. Against this state of art I will here make a case that (Universal) grammar (UG) is (at least a crucial part) of the answer to the problem of human nature, and vice versa. In short, grammar is the essential science that needs to illuminate human nature, and human nature in turn is the central issue that needs to illuminate the theory of grammar. Neither the notions of innateness nor of essence or of modularity will centrally enter into this conception.

Section 2 makes two claims: firstly, the rejection of human nature in the paradigms mentioned above is ultimately based on what Chomsky[19] has called 'methodological dualism': it treats the study of human nature as different from the study of other aspects of nature. Given that such dualism is unjustifiable under naturalistic premises, the rejection in question is so as well. Secondly, such methodological dualism is notably absent in the early modern project of a

[12]   S. Pinker, *How the Mind Works*. (New York: Norton, 1997).
[13]   S. Pinker, *The Language Instinct* (Harmondsworth: Penguin, 1994).
[14]   For example, Christiansen and Chater, op. cit.
[15]   Op. cit.
[16]   D. Hull and M. Ruse, (eds.) *The Philosophy of Biology* (Oxford: Oxford University Press,1998).
[17]   A. Rosenberg, and R. Arp, *Philosophy of Biology* (Oxford: Wiley-Blackwell, 2010).
[18]   N. Chomsky, *Aspects of the Theory of Syntax* (Cambridge, MA: MIT Press, 1965); N. Chomsky, *Cartesian Linguistics*, Third edition, ed. J. McGilvray (Cambridge: Cambridge University Press, 1966/2009); E. Lenneberg, *Biological Foundations of Language*, (New York: John Wiley & Sons, 1967); M. Piattelli-Palmarini, J. Uriagereka, and P. Salaburu 2009. *Of minds and language*. Oxford: Oxford University Press.
[19]   N. Chomsky, *New Horizons in the Study of Language and Mind*. (Cambridge: Cambridge University Press, 2000).

'natural philosophy', in which the notion of human nature was a central concept: the early modern naturalists used a uniform notion of naturalistic inquiry and engaged in no essentialist speculations. In Section 3 I argue that human nature needs to be illuminated through the theory of grammar, which arguably has identified a real singularity in nature. Nonetheless, as Section 4 argues, the uniform methodological naturalism propagated by Chomsky nonetheless falls short of an important dimension of the study of grammar, which precisely illuminates its epistemological and philosophical significance. Section 5 identifies this dimension as grammatical mediated forms of deictic reference, which I argue are a defining feature of the human mind, and around which grammar is organized. Section 6 summarizes the argument.

2. Methodological Dualism and the Rejection of Human Nature

The argument I want to consider in this section is that human nature is obsolete because, if it exists, it must be grounded in biology, and biology does not vindicate any such thing. Hence a human nature does not exist. This argument is carried out in the spirit of naturalism: we cannot ground human nature metaphysically, the idea is, so we have to do it on the basis of the results of science. But the traditional notion of human nature comes with pretensions to universality and essentiality, and biology, at least, bears no such thing out. This stance coheres with a vision of biology on which, as Mayr puts it, 'laws and experiments have no significant place in biology'[20], its methodology being that of 'historical reconstruction' and the testing of 'competing historical narratives'. In that case, biology has a special status among the sciences, and species including *Homo sapiens* cannot be studied in the same way as other objects of nature. They are essentially historical objects. The naturalistic stance then naturally entails that we need to apply a methodology to *Homo sapiens* that we would not apply to other aspects of physical nature. The methodology will be that of studying the contingent adaptive history of the hominid lineage.

But as Hinzen[21] points out, there is an alternative to this conception within biology itself, as is clear from an anti-Darwinian

---

[20]   E. Mayr, 'Darwin's Influence on Modern Thought', *Scientific American* (July 2000), 80.

[21]   W. Hinzen, *Mind Design and Minimalist Syntax*, op. cit.

developmentalist undercurrent ever since the Darwinian revolution began. It assumed a more uniform notion of causal explanation even in the living realm and retained a focus on laws, as in the generic developmental laws of von Baer and Haeckel in the early and middle 19th century, or the earlier 19th century tradition of 'rational morphology'.[22] This tradition was centered on the question of the origin of order and form more than the vagaries of natural selection, which it does not see as a genuine source of evolutionary novelty, anticipating similar claims today.[23] In fact, all we need to counter the attack from historicity in the study of human nature is to follow Darwin himself in stressing that there are *two* (partially independent) laws of evolution: 'Unity of Type, and the Conditions of Existence.'[24] While the latter law is natural selection (and would eventually dominate the other in Darwin's own overall functionalist rather than structuralist vision[25], the former refers to *generative principles* that underlie the striking commonalities of structure and form found across wide ranges of animal phyla, quite independently of the habits of life involved.[26] As Darwin marveled, addressing the subject of 'Morphology':

> What can be more curious than that the hand of a man, formed for grasping, that of a mole for digging, the leg of the horse, the paddle of the porpoise, and the wing of the bat, should all constructed on the same pattern, and should include the same bones in the same relative proportions.[27]

The pre-Darwinian vision of organic forms as immutable natural forms or types that are not necessarily different in kind from inorganic ones and built into the general order of nature does not conflict

---

[22]   S. J. Gould, *The Structure of Evolutionary Theory* (Cambridge, MA: Harvard University Press, 2002), ch. 4.

[23]   S. A. Newman, and G. B. Müller, G. B. 1999. 'Morphological Evolution: Epigenetic Mechanisms'. In *Embryonic Encyclopedia of Life Sciences*. (London: Nature Publishing Group, 1999). Available at: http://www.els.net; G. Webster and B. Goodwin, *Form and Transformation: Generative and Relational Principles in Biology* (Cambridge: Cambridge University Press, 1996).

[24]   C. Darwin, *On the Origin of Species by Means of Natural Selection* (Harmondsworth: Penguin, 1859/1968), 206.

[25]   Gould, op. cit, ch. 4.

[26]   R. Amundson, 'Two Concepts of Constraint', *Philosophy of Science* **61** (1994), 556–78; R. Amundson, 'Typology reconsidered', *Biology and Philosophy* **13** (1998) 153–77.

[27]   Op. cit., 434.

with an adaptationist outlook: clearly, the afunctional givens of physical law will necessarily *interact* with the conditions of historical circumstance. But we don't expect the latter to greatly distort the canalizing influence of physical law. Nor is this perspective in any way foreign to contemporary biology. As revitalized today within the Evo-Devo paradigm, the developmentalist tradition puts stress on 'physicochemical, topological, and biomechanical factors, as well as generic, stochastic and self-organizational properties of developing tissues' in development, viewed as factors independent of, though cooperating with, natural selection.[28] As Denton *et al.*, put it:

> when deploying matter into complex structures in the subcellular realm the cell must necessarily make extensive use of natural forms (…) which like atoms or crystals self-organize under the direction of natural law into what are essentially 'pre-Darwinian' afunctional abstract molecular architectures in which adaptations are trivial secondary modifications of what are evidently primary givens of physics.[29]

In this way, some have seen Theodosius Dobzhansky's famous dictum that 'in biology, nothing makes sense except in the light of evolution' to stand on its ear: 'Evolution, it turns out, makes no sense except in the light of biology – developmental biology, to be precise'.[30]

Surveying this anti-Darwinian undercurrent in Hinzen[31] and its continuation today,[32] I argued that the tradition of Universal

[28] S. A. Newman, and G. B. Müller, G. B. 1999. 'Morphological Evolution: Epigenetic Mechanisms', op. cit., note 23; W. Arthur, 'The Emerging Conceptual Framework of Evolutionary Development Biology', *Nature* **415** (14 Feb. 2002), 757–64.

[29] M. J. Denton, P. K. Dearden, and S. J. Sowerby, 'Physical Law *Not Natural Selection* as the Major Determinant of Biological Complexity in the Subcellular Realm: New Support for the pre-Darwinian Conception of Evolution by Natural Law, *BioSystems* **71** (2003), 297–303. See also M. J. Denton, 'Laws of Form Revisited', *Nature* **410** (22 March 2001), 417.

[30] E. Pennisi, 'Evo-Devo Enthusiasts Get Down to Details', *Science* **298** (2002), 953–5.

[31] W. Hinzen, *Mind Design and Minimal Syntax*, op.cit., ch. 3. Also see: W. Hinzen, 'Spencerism and the Causal Theory of Reference' *Biology and Philosophy* **21** (2006), 71–94; and W. Hinzen, 'The Philosophical Significance of Universal Grammar', (*University of Durham*, Ms., 2011).

[32] See, for example: M. Pigliucci, and G.B. Müller (eds.) 2010. *Evolution: The Extended Synthesis* (Cambridge, MA: MIT Press, 2010); A. Wagner, *The Origins of Evolutionary Innovations* (Oxford: Oxford

Grammar (UG) in the sense of Chomsky[33] could be construed in very similar terms, as an instance of the 'Unity of Type' applied to human linguistic diversity. It reflects an attempt to make language accessible as an object of scientific inquiry, regarding it as governed by universal natural laws, hence as rational in some way rather than arbitrary. Language becomes, as Chomsky[34] puts it, 'a real object of the natural world'. With language being so isolated in the biological world, exhibited in the human species alone, we would expect it to pose a formidable new challenge to biology – which it is the hope of the field of the field of biolinguistics to address – rather than to be merely answerable to particular established conceptions of what biology is supposed to be.

I will not return to this case here, but rather point out in what way it answers the challenge to human nature based on biology above. We will now say that this challenge consists in the imposition of a particular methodological constraint on the study of *Homo sapiens*: historical narrative is to be the appropriate method, which obviously is not applied to physical phenomena of other sorts. Whatever 'nature' humans come out to have, in that case, it is bound to come out as historically contingent and variable. But the imposition of this constraint is unwarranted. It applies a double standard in the study of nature, an instance of 'methodological dualism' in Chomsky's sense.

Such dualism is objectionable. While there can be no objection to applying different methodologies to the study of different objects, we cannot *start* from a certain metaphysical conception of what an object is like or how it is to be explained. We cannot, for example, as Descartes did, *start* from a conception of what a 'body' is and how its motions are to be explained, and on this basis rule out a priori scientific theories on which the world doesn't work that way. There cannot be, within naturalistic inquiry, an injunction against using

---

University Press 2011); E. H. Davidson, and D. H. Erwin 2006. 'Gene Regulatory Networks and the Evolution of Animal Body Plans', *Science* **311** (10 February 2006), 796–800; M. Y. Sherman, 'Universal Genome in the Origin of Metazoa: Thoughts About Evolution', *Cell Cycle* **6** (2007), 1873–1877; and A. Bejan and J. H. Marden. 'Unifying Constructal Theory for Scale Effects in Running, Swimming and Flying', *The Journal of Experimental Biology* **209** (2006), 238–248.

[33] N. Chomsky, *Aspects of the Theory of Syntax* (Cambridge, MA: MIT Press, 1965).

[34] N. Chomsky, *The Minimalist Program* (Cambridge, MA: MIT Press, 1995), 11.

any particular methodology: for such inquiry is to be judged by its fruits, and furthermore, only the inquiry itself will determine the ontology of the domain. To say that the human is historical and cultural and no methods from non-historical sciences can be applied to its study is to place a roadblock in the path of naturalistic inquiry. If an essentialist definition of 'biology' as a historical science is used to constrain such inquiry, the opponent of human nature thus falls prey to his own essentialist critique. It can of course turn out not to be fruitful to study language or the human mind 'as a natural object', in the sense above. But this is another matter and needs to be shown on other grounds.

Such double standards have been notably *absent* in how the study of human nature was conceived in the early days of modern science. The Enlightenment project of a 'Science of Man' was, as Tomaselli[35] summarizes, 'very broadly speaking, expected to provide a description of the nature and extent of human cognitive capacities, of the way the mind works, as well as afford an understanding of the processes by which human beings come to be the way they are, the manner by which they acquire their character and individuality, their tastes, desires and ends'. Hume's wording is often telling: '[M]an is a being, whom we know by experience, (...) and whose projects and inclinations have a certain connexion and coherence, according to the laws which nature has established for the government of such a creature.'[36] What these laws are is a subject matter of naturalistic inquiry.

It is particularly anachronistic to shoulder Hume's *Treatise of Human Nature* (1739–40) with a notion of human nature that is essentialist in character. The Science of Man was part of Galilean science, in which essences had long disappeared. The message of the *Saggiatore* (1623) had been that the task of science is to bring nature into a mathematical form, not to dig deeper into the 'true natures' of things and their ultimate rationales. This amounts to denouncing certain 'why'-questions. Post-Newtonian science would further abandon certain 'how'-questions as well, including the ideal of mechanical explanation. While Descartes had still upheld that ideal – final causes and occult forces were expelled from physical nature – by the end of the very century in which the 'mechanical

---

[35]   S. Tomaselli, S. 1995. 'Human Nature'. In J. Yolton *et al.* (eds.), *The Blackwell Companion to the Enlightenment*. (Oxford: Blackwell, 1995), 229.

[36]   D. Hume, *An Enquiry Concerning Human Understanding*, ed. L. A. Selby-Bigge, 3rd edn. rev. by P. H. Nidditch (Oxford: Clarendon Press, 1975), section XI:144).

philosophy' was born, those non-mechanical forces of 'attraction and repulsion' were back on the scene.

The natural philosophers of the day seem to have largely acquiesced to this unexpected situation, and I will illustrate this briefly with Locke and Hume. Locke contended that although the mechanical philosophy had been shown wrong, it was nonetheless also clear, insofar as our understanding goes, that 'bodies can act on one another only through contact, since it is impossible for us to comprehend that a body can act on what it does not touch; for this would mean that it could cause an effect where it is not'.[37] Therefore, Newton's 'gravitation from matter to matter', though working in a way 'incomprehensible' to us, proves that God could do something that could neither be derived from our conception of body nor explained through our knowledge of matter. But if 'our comprehension is no measure for the power of God' and gravitation had proved mysterious yet natural, why couldn't God have superadded a faculty of thinking to matter as well?[38] After all, matter had ceased to be wholly 'material', as Leibniz notes.[39] Thus, if one were to continue to defend the Cartesian dualism of two substances, it had become pointless to insist on the 'immateriality' of the mental substance. The mind-body problem, therefore, becomes unformulable in its original form, as was widely concluded in the sciences of the day, particularly by Priestley.[40]

Hume articulates a skepticism not unlike Locke's: 'the powers and forces, by which [the course of nature] is governed, be wholly unknown to us'. We 'are ignorant (...) of the manner in which bodies operate on each other: Their force or energy is entirely incomprehensible.'[41] We are equally 'ignorant of the manner or force by which a mind, even the supreme mind, operates either on itself or on the body.'[42] It is a small surprise, then, to find that the 'Science of Man' was to be strictly *non*-metaphysical in character. Its only foundation could be careful 'experience and observation', and its

---

[37]　Quoted in G. Leibniz, *Neue Abhandlungen über den menschlichen Verstand*. (Hamburg: Meiner, 1704/1996), 18, 23.

[38]　J. W. Yolton, *Thinking Matter: Materialism in 18th-Century Britain* (Minneapolis: University of Minnesota Press, 1983).

[39]　Op.cit, 20.

[40]　N. Chomsky, *New Horizons in the Study of Language and Mind*, op. cit., 112–3.

[41]　D. Hume, *An Enquiry Concerning Human Understanding*, ed. L. A. Selby-Bigge, 3rd edn. rev. by P. H. Nidditch (Oxford: Clarendon Press, 1975), section V, part II, §44, 54.

[42]　Ibid., section VII, part I, §57, 72.

objective to further knowledge was no more ambitious than that of 'natural philosophy': philosophy as an integral part of the sciences of the day.[43] The Science of Man thus did not aim at essences, its inability to 'explain ultimate principles' being a defect it shared with 'all the sciences'. The *anti*-foundationalism of the enterprise seems important and striking.[44]

There is, then, in early modern philosophy, a philosophical framework in place for the naturalistic study of human nature, which we find unaffected by the essentialism that mars the enterprise according to its contemporary critics. Naturalistic inquiry into human nature as conceived in this way will simply yield whatever results it may. Hume is now widely considered to be wrong in his conclusion that the laws governing our mind are the 'laws of association' applying to contiguous 'ideas',[45] showing that his science of human nature makes falsifiable empirical claims, but not that significant generalizations are not possible. In this light we might compare the widely entertained claim today that 'there is no human nature' to the claim, ahead of inquiry, that there are no general laws of animal locomotion, or that all we can do is catalogue diversity and construct adaptive histories in regards to the various ways in which animals have come to walk, fly, or swim. As it turns out, in this particular and striking case, there *are* laws and substantive generalizations to be had, across very different 'habits of life' and 'conditions of existence.'[46]

One could be *skeptical* about the science of human nature, in short, but this does not vitiate the enterprise. Many Enlightenment thinkers shared such skepticism, fearing that man might in the end turn out to be 'the plaything of time and historical circumstances.'[47] Thus, M. le Roi, in his *Encyclopédie* entry for 'Homme (morale)' (1765), despaired that man defied definition, and that human motivations were too diverse to fall into a pattern that would allow theoretical study. But such overwhelming human diversity was regarded as an essentially frustrating fact that appeared to render a certain theoretical project fruitless or unfeasible. It wouldn't render it illegitimate. It

[43]   D. Hume, *A Treatise of Human Nature*, ed. L. A. Selby-Bigge, 2nd edn. (Oxford: Clarendon, 1978), xvii.
[44]   See W. Hinzen, Mind Design and *Minimalist Syntqx*, op. cit., part 1.
[45]   See, for example, S. Carey, *The Origins of Concepts* (Oxford: Oxford University Press, 2009).
[46]   A. Bejan and J. H. Marden. 'Unifying Constructal Theory for Scale Effects in Running, Swimming and Flying', *The Journal of Experimental Biology* 209 (2006), 238–248.
[47]   S. Tomaselli, 'Human Nature', op. cit, 232.

did not point to another theory, based on some kind of new and historical conception of human nature, but to a theoretical defeat.[48]

As things stand, we are in the same situation today as was M. de Roi: we still do not know whether his particular skepticism is justified, which is the question that the current paradigm of 'Universal Moral Grammar' targets.[49] To conclude, ahead of such inquiry into our nature, that human nature is arbitrary rather than rational in some way and subject to substantive generalizations is to remain wedded to a metaphysical and essentialist conception of human nature that naturalistic inquiry of its nature does not support.

3. Grammar As Science and As Carving Nature At Its Joints

What then *are* relevant generalizations in the case of human nature, and from which specific science will they come? Relevant generalizations will not come from aspects of human beings that are not sapiens-specific and hence will not inform us about human nature specifically. It so happens, however, that while a UG in the distinctive sense of Pinker[50] is widely denied today, particularly in linguistic typology, it is *not* controversial that grammar is universal in human populations, pathologies aside. No human population without a grammatically structured linguistic medium of communication operative at a population level has ever been found. Cultural and technological innovations moreover, including writing, appear to leave our basic grammatical ability largely unaffected, allowing us to characterize all language families on the globe in essentially the same terms.[51] Assuming the current consensus in regards to the singularity of our species as originating in the same Sub-Saharan African population, and the dispersion of that species up to Australia until around 40,000 years ago, we may further assume that the language faculty

---

[48]   W. Hinzen, *Minimalist Syntax*, op.cit., 10.

[49]   J. Mikhail, *Elements of Moral Cognition: Rawls' Linguistic Analogy and the Cognitive Science of Moral and Legal Judgment* (Cambridge: Cambridge University Press, 2010).

[50]   S. Pinker, *The Language Instinct*, op. cit.

[51]   This generalization is crucially consistent with claims such as D.L. Everett's ('Cultural Constraints on Grammar and Cognition in Pirahã: Another Look at the Design Features of Human Language', *Current Anthropology* 46 (2005) 621–46), to the effect that some languages have some grammatical constructions that do not exhibit formal properties that the same constructions exhibit in other languages.

had essentially genetically fixated at a species level by that time, and that it has not been subject to relevant change since.[52,53]

At the same time, there is strong evidence for the essential *absence* of meaningful grammar in non-human communication systems, crucially including the communications of the so-called 'language-trained' apes, which Tomasello[54] argues 'contain basically no relational or grammatical structuring of any kind'. It is a striking feature also of animal communication in the wild that the primitive elements of relevant call systems (present e.g. in monkeys but notably absent in the other great apes) make up a rigid and finite list, failing to combine in a meaningful way. Moreover, they appear to be largely indexical in character and to depend on the 'online' processing of a perceptual stimulus, the repeated occurrence of which they track for adaptive reasons.[55] The use of words is generally not indexical in this sense.[56] We systematically use words symbolically, as a reflection of 'offline' thinking in which the referent of the word is not present, words always have a grammatical category, and they tend to appear in the context of other words.

[52] T. J. Crow (ed.), *The Speciation of Modern Homo Sapiens* (Oxford: Oxford University Press, 2004).

[53] D. Dediu and D.L. Ladd ('Linguistic Tone is Related to the Population Frequency of the Adaptive Haplogroups of Two Brain Size Genes, ASPM and Microcephalin', *PNAS* 104 (2007), 10944–10949) present interesting evidence for a causal connection between genetic and linguistic diversity in regards to the acquisition of tonal contrasts in a language, suggesting some on-going gene-language co-evolution. Insofar as this co-evolution affects the phonological externalization of language rather than its syntax or semantics, it is perhaps quite expected, and it certainly does not disturb what has been called the 'psychic unity of mankind'.

[54] M. Tomasello, *The Origins of Human Communication* (Cambridge, MA: MIT Press, 2008), 249.

[55] See K. Zuberbühler ('Linguistic Prerequisites in the Primate Lineage. In M. Tallerman (ed.), *Language Origins* (Oxford: Oxford University Press, 2005)) for a discussion and careful qualifications of the claim that Campbell monkeys can process a combinatorial rule. Given relevant doubts even about the analogy between the relevant call and human words (D. Bickerton, *Adam's Tongue* (New York: Hill and Wang, 2009)), talk of a rule of 'modification' is tenuous. Semantic compositionality seems a long a way off.

[56] Interestingly, not even in the case of so-called 'indexicals' such as 'here', 'I', or 'now'. 'I', in particular, need not refer to the speaker, and 'here' need not refer to the place of utterance (P. Schlenker, 'A Plea for Monsters', *Linguistics and Philosophy* 26 (2003), 29–120).

If grammar is universal in the species at a population level and at the same time marks a fundamental discontinuity with other species, it may well be a key to our problem. Moreover, it tells us that the relevant science telling us about human nature is not going to be biology but the science of grammar, which is not integrated with biology yet. Experiments on linguistic processing at the level of the brain, in particular, depend on a sound linguistic framework within which results are meaningfully interpretable.[57] This broad conclusion conflicts with the pre-theoretical view that grammar simply isn't a science but rather a social-normative convention which is arbitrary in character. A science of grammar, on the other hand, *has* been one of the first and longest-standing human speculative endeavours, even though the relevant history is somewhat scattered and the endeavour got re-started and re-invented several times. Grammar was conceived as a science in Classical India beginning around 2,500 years ago;[58] in the High Middle Ages in 13th century Europe;[59] in the Port Royal tradition in the 17th century;[60] and in Chomsky's uptake of this last tradition in the wake of the 'second' cognitive revolution in the 1950s.[61] Larson's *Grammar as Science*[62] is a notable contemporary introduction to grammatical theory written as an exercise in scientific theory construction.

If one doubts the science of grammar's successes and achievements or indeed its status as a science, we should, given the principles of naturalistic inquiry suggested above, resist making this verdict on the basis of some conceptual, metaphysical or a priori conception of what grammar *is*. Again, the character and ontology of a field of inquiry is only determined in the course of that inquiry. Rejecting grammar as a science and as the essential path to empirical generalizations and insights into human nature and specificity is no less an

---

[57] A. Moro, *The Boundaries of Babel* (Cambridge, MA: MIT Press, 2010); W. Hinzen and D. Poeppel, 'Semantics Between Cognitive Neuroscience and Linguistic Theory', *Journal of Cognitive Processes* (in press).

[58] B. K. Matilal, The Word and the World: India's Contribution to the Study of Language (Oxford: Oxford University Press, 1991).

[59] M. Covington, *Syntactic Theory in the High Middle Ages: Modistic Models of Sentence Structure* (Cambridge: Cambridge University Press, 2009).

[60] A. Arnauld and E. Lancelot, *Grammaire Générale et Raisonnée de Port-Royal.* (Paris, 1660/1966).

[61] N. Chomsky, *Aspects of the Theory of Syntax*, op. cit.

[62] R. K. Larson, *Grammar as Science.* (Cambridge, MA: MIT Press, 2010).

instance of methodological dualism. Arguably, biology is no more fundamental as a science in regards to grammatical generalizations than physics was in relation to chemical ones in 19th century chemistry.[63] It is grammar, not biology, which, as of now, needs to yield the relevant generalizations, whatever we take the ultimate metaphysical nature of grammar to be. Whatever we choose as the subject matter of naturalistic inquiry, it has to be studied in its own terms and with whatever methodologies it requires.

In the rest of this section I would like to explore a different road, however, on which to see grammar not only as a science but indeed as 'carving nature at its joints': i.e., as isolating a real joint of nature, giving the human mind a proper place in the physical world. A recognizably modern human culture is essentially present in the Aurignacian revolution in Europe around 43–35,000 years ago, where, in a relatively sudden way, the archaeological record begins to show us evidence of symbolic representation, delicate engravings on bone and stone plaques, painted images, implements made of soft materials (bone, antler), needles, song and dance, music on bone flutes, fish hooks and net sinkers, serious hunting with darts, spears, bows, and arrows, and long-distance trade.[64] Perhaps the most crucial element of this sequence of innovative and essentially modern behaviours is symbolic representation as required for language. That element can arguably be backdated to around 70–80,000 years, given evidence especially from South-African findings.[65] This brings us closer to the origins of the speciation of modern *Homo sapiens* itself.[66] The apparent absence of symbolic representation before this time entails the absence of language in either the Neanderthal and the African precursors of *sapiens*, and would explain the sharply contrasting cultures (or lack of cultures) that we find in these species.[67]

[63] W.H. Brock, *The Fontana History of Chemistry* (London: Fontana, 1992).

[64] P. Mellars, 'The Impossible Coincidence: A Single-Species Model for the Origins of Modern Human Behavior in Europe', *Evol. Anthropo* **14** (2005), 12–276; R. Klein and B. Edgar, *The Dawn of Human Culture*, (New York: John Wiley and Sons, 2002).

[65] C. S. Henshilwood, 'Modern Humans and Symbolic Behaviour: Evidence from Blombos Cave, South Africa'. In G. Blundell (ed.) *Origins* (Cape Town: Double Storey, 2006).

[66] T. J. Crow (ed.), *The Speciation of Modern Homo Sapiens*, op. cit.

[67] This is not to say that Neanderthal did not *vocalize*, which is a different issue (for some evidence and discussion in regards to the FOXP2 gene see R. E. Green, *et al*. ('A Draft Sequence of the Neandertal Genome',

With still some tens of thousands of years to go between the specia-tion of modern *Homo sapiens* between 200,000 and 150,000 years ago and the early African findings, moreover, it is a natural conclusion that this curious time lag, before we see novel cognitive abilities emer-ging as reflected in a very different culture, is explained by the need (and the initial lack) of a relevant external trigger: most plausibly, language.[68] Even apart from that, the terms describing the novel cog-nitive abilities often appear as linguistic categories in disguise. Thus the creativity in combining symbolic expressions itself is what grammar centrally represents. Grammatical structuring in a symbolic medium based on words correlates with a mode of thought that has unique features and entails the capacity to construct symbolic worlds and share them in a culture. In contradistinction to this per-spective, Tomasello[69] argues that the key to the evolution of human linguistic communication is shared intentionality crucially viewed as non-linguistic and as based on the essential 'skill' of 'recursive mindreading'. A genetic change thus made us recursive mind-readers, and a more complex grammar was then needed to express it. Yet, where other minds are represented as thinking some particular thought, this would seem to require these representations to have certain inherent structural properties – like the occurrence of an (un-endorsed or unasserted) proposition within another proposition, as in *[He believes [I am here]]* – which seem uniquely mapped from gram-matical configurations instantiating the relevant recursions, however these are then pronounced. Moreover, evidence for higher-order in-tentionality in non-grammatical creatures is hard to come by, and there is considerable evidence of its absence.[70] If so, the radical re-structuring of thought that we need to posit would not pre-date grammar. It is grammar.

I want to argue, then, that becoming human is reflected in a novel creativity and variability that hominid culture now comes to exhibit, with grammar-based symbolic articulation as a basis and as an exter-nal sign linked to some internal underlying system of thought that is

---

Science **328** (2010), 710–722); S. Mithen, *The Singing Neanderthals* (London:Phoenix, 2006).

[68]   I. Tattersall, 'A Putative Role for Language in the Origin of Human Consciousness'. In R. Larson *et al*. (eds.), *The Evolution of Human Language* (Cambridge: Cambridge University Press, 2010).

[69]   M. Tomasello, *The Origins of Human Communication*, op. cit., 321.

[70]   W. T. Fitch, *Language Evolution* (Cambridge: Cambridge University Press, 2010), section 4.11.

Wolfram Hinzen

expressed in it. Not only are there symbolic rather than merely indexical units now, but they can be string together with other symbols
grammatically, yielding an endless array of new meanings in systematic ways, which the external environment only weakly controls. No
such ability for generating new meanings productively is attested in
bird song, despite its formal complexity, as it is not a system of symbolic reference in the same sense as language is.[71] It is also missing in
musical cognition, which the Neanderthals may have had.[72] The
emergence of a system of grammatical meaning in the hominid
mind is thus a crucial dividing line, and reference is its crucial aspect.

Let us now go a step further and say, with Mukherji,[73] that a cognitive system is 'computational-representational' if it satisfies three
essential criteria: it is symbolically articulated; it is unbounded, exhi-
biting discrete infinity or recursion; and it is only weakly controlled
externally, making its operations largely stimulus-free. Mukherji
argues that only a narrow set of systems satisfies these criteria apart
from language, namely logic, arithmetic, and music. From these,
both logic and arithmetic likely depend on language. As for music,
it arguably not only exhibits recursion but also an internal organization into tones and melodies allowing for a notion of 'musical
meaning' relevantly analogous to the notion of 'grammatical
meaning' above, even if music is clearly not *referential* in the way
that language is. As Bickerton[74] points out, systems sharing such
crucial and unique properties could not plausibly each have had separate evolutionary histories. Let us therefore assume that they had a
common origin in the human speciation event itself: Mukherji[75]
calls them the 'hominid set'. Further evidence supporting this conclusion comes from the 'Musilanguage'-Hypothesis: the view, on
one version of it, that the exact same computational system that is
posited to underlie human language in recent Minimalist syntax[76]
also underlies musical processing,[77] with the only difference
between the two systems arising from the primitive elements that
are combined.

[71] P. Marler, 2000. 'Origins of Music and Speech'. In N. Wallin, B.
Merker, and S. Brown, (eds.), *The Origins of Music*, (Cambridge, MA:
MIT Press, 2000).
[72] S. Mithen, *The Singing Neanderthals*, op. cit.
[73] N. Mukherji, *The Primacy of Grammar*,op.cit.
[74] D. Bickerton, *Adam's Tongue*, op. cit.
[75] N. Mukherji, *The Primacy of Grammar*, op. cit., 189.
[76] N. Chomsky, *The Minimalist Program*,op.cit.
[77] J. Katz, and D. Pesetsky 'The Recursive Syntax and Prosody of
Tonal Music' (Ms., MIT, 2009).

In the wake of the cognitive revolution we are accustomed to characterize such systems *computationally*, where we crucially not only mean by this that a computational model can be applied in studying them, but that the organism in question genuinely *performs* such computations. The distinction is needed since virtually any device, from stomachs to particle systems in physics to crystals to eco-systems can be *modeled* computationally, i.e. as a function from particular inputs to outputs. Theories characterizing the genesis of grammatical meanings computationally are therefore meant to apply to what the human brain actually does, in a way that theories modeling behaviour computationally *need* not do: indeed, using techniques such as electroencephalography (EEG) or magnetoencephalography (MEG) we can *see* the human brain performing such computations on a millisecond per millisecond basis. By contrast, we don't want to say that physical particles and eco-systems compute the differential equations that describe their behaviour.

We could, of course, decide that generative grammar as a theory of such computations in the brain should not be interpreted realistically either. This would be in a similar sense as when many prominent 19th century chemists maintained that their theories and generalizations should not be interpreted realistically, providing mere computing devices instead.[78] But it would be equally questionable, and it would be out of tune with actual linguistic practice, where a robust realist interpretation of theoretical generalizations is generally assumed today.

I will therefore assume that the scope of 'computational-representational' theories of mind is narrower than it might have been. Birdsong, as noted above, is not a reasonable instance, and similar doubts arise in many other cases of cognitive performance in non-human animals that have been described computationally, from insect navigation to the caching behaviour of scrub jays. Gallistel[79] makes a strong case on the basis of such abilities that the computational system characterized in linguistic theory is *not* a novelty arising with language. But with 'computational-representational' construed as above, the issue is open again, and doubts in fact arise from the very beginning. For example, are the primitive units of such non-human systems, which often causally co-vary with environmental

[78]   W.H. Brock, *The Fontana History of Chemistry*, op. cit.
[79]   C. R. Gallistel, 'The Foundational Abstractions'. In M. Piattelli-Palmarini, J. Uriagereka, and P. Salaburu (eds.), *Of Minds and Language*. (Oxford: Oxford University Press, 2009).

variables, really like human concepts in the sense of the meanings that are expressed in symbols that are words? There also appears to be no analogue of grammatical meaning here in the sense above, an analogue of which arguably does exist in music, as noted.

What matters for present purposes is that if these doubts are justified, the range of computational systems in nature, as characterized by computational-representational theories of mind, is narrower than a general caution about the term 'computation' itself suggests. In essence it will be *confined* to the 'hominid set', as Mukherji[80] conjectures, which will thereby be established as a real joint of nature that is distinct and isolated from everything else. Here, and only here, will we have the relevant *independent* evidence – lacking in ants, bees, and jays (let alone particles and crystals) – that the relevant computations do indeed take place in the devices that are modeled by means of them. For there is, in this instance, a symbolic *culture* in which the creative use of the relevant computational abilities is externally attested. As Descartes[81] argued, symbolic expression in words is the best possible evidence for the presence of thought in an organism, for 'all men, the most stupid and the most foolish, those even deprived of the organs of speech, make use of signs' to express their thoughts, while non-human animals don't.

In summary, I have argued in this section that grammar is to be the science within which we need to place inquiries into the human, and that, as of now, no other science will do, taking the notion of human nature out of what I do not think is (as of now) its natural home: biology. Moreover, it appears that the theory of grammar, in isolating a specific computational system claimed to be instantiated in human brains, has isolated a system that is literally found nowhere else in nature except there, where it causes the sweep of cultural innovation that has marked out a modern human culture against all others ever since.

4. Language as a Natural and As a Rational Object

In Section 2 I suggested that methodological naturalism is an appropriate attitude from which to explore the notion of human nature today, that it has been practiced, with good results, in early modern 'natural philosophy', and that the rejection of human nature in the 20th century reflects a methodological dualism in regards to the

[80] N. Mukherji, *The Primacy of Grammar*, op. cit., ch. 7.
[81] R. Descartes, *Discours de la Méthode* (Paris: Vrin, 1637/1984).

study of human nature, which naturalistic inquiry by its nature does not support. In Section 3 I have further argued that grammar is the essential key to the mystery of the 'human revolution' around 40,000 years ago, and that it should be regarded as a science interpreted realistically and in fact as isolating and targeting a joint of nature, defining our species and perhaps explaining its origins.[82] Notably, adaptationist considerations have not entered into how we arrived at these conclusions. Indeed the conclusion challenges such considerations, for the hominid set is a clear *discontinuity* in nature requiring a substantive account of speciation, for which traditional assumptions of gradualism and reproductive isolation provide no keys in this instance.[83]

In the remainder of this paper I will argue the following point. Although the attitude of methodological naturalism championed by Chomsky[84] is an essential step towards re-instigating the notion of human nature as a subject matter of scientific inquiry and as a central concept of philosophy, Chomsky's specific *take* on the study of 'language as a natural object'[85] has left its role in the genesis of our mind too underspecified in order for it to play the role in evolution that I am claiming it did. I will contend that more can be said in how exactly grammar is the motor behind the human revolution, and what it is about it that got things moving in human terms. It is in this regard that I think the theory of grammar should become more constrained by considerations of human speciation, rather than merely the other way round.

Generative grammar in the 20th century is born, of course, in a 'rationalist' spirit, as an instance of 'Cartesian linguistics' in the sense of Chomsky[86] and Arnauld and Lancelot.[87] Yet, it is actually quite unclear, in the way that grammar has factually come to be studied, what it is about it that is 'rational'. Chomsky, of course, has convinced many that grammar is a system of 'knowledge' (rather than, say, a mere skill or convention) that has a systematic and deductive structure to it that can only partially be acquired

---

[82] T. J. Crow, 'The "Big Bang" Theory of the Origin of Psychosis and the Faculty of Language', *Schizophrenia Research* **102** (2008), 31–52.

[83] T. J. Crow (ed.), *The Speciation of Modern Homo Sapiens*, op.cit.

[84] N. Chomsky, *New Horizons in the Study of Language and Mind*, op. cit.

[85] Cf. Ibid., ch. 5.

[86] N. Chomsky, *Cartesian Lingusitics*, op. cit.

[87] A. Arnauld and E. Lancelot, *Grammaire Générale et Raisonnée de Port-Royal*, op.cit.

from perceptual data. From this we obtain a case for an 'innate language organ'. Yet, at least until the advent of linguistic Minimalism in syntactic theory in the 1990s,[88] if not beyond, this module was by and large described as a purely 'formal' system in the spirit of the 'autonomy of grammar', leaving a separate discipline of 'semantics' in charge of matters of 'content'. In one sense, the previous section supports such autonomy in strong and novel terms: the grammaticalization of the hominid brain goes along with the evolution of a new cognitive mode that is *sui generis*. Yet there is another and more traditional sense of autonomy, invoking the formal 'arbitrariness' of grammar: the lack of a functional or semantic motivation for its basic formal rules and elements.[89]

It is precisely that arbitrariness and formality that is plausibly to be blamed for the relative lack of interest in the theory of syntax in the philosophy of language, and the fact that grammar is not taught in philosophy departments. If meaning is the essential philosophical issue and syntax (or 'form') does not speak to it by the lights of the generative grammarians themselves, why bother? In fairness, it must be said that the cross-linguistic generalizations that the Government and Binding framework in generative linguistics unearthed[90] really *did* seem arbitrary rather than reflecting any principles of rationality, semantics, or logic. In contrast to phonological rules, which are grounded in phonetics, and semantic rules, which were meant to be grounded in the nature of some non-linguistic system of thought and else our relation to the world, constraints on syntactic well-formedness just didn't seem to make any deeper sense. In short, although linguists should not blamed for pursuing syntax independently. But, the fact remains that as grammar became autonomous, semantics and philosophical logic became autonomous as well, developing their own primitives (e.g., semantic types, possible worlds, etc.) and combinatorial operations (e.g., function application, abstraction, etc.), conceived as being independent from those of grammar.

---

[88] N. Chomsky, *The Minimalist Program*, op.cit.

[89] As re-stated in a recent editorial of the journal *Lingua*, the autonomy of grammar consists in the following claim: 'phonological and semantic rules can refer to syntactic information, but syntactic rules cannot refer to phonological or semantic information' (J. Rooryck, N. Smith, A. Liptak, and D. Blakemore (eds.). 'Editorial Introduction to Special Issue on Evans and Levinson's "The Myth of Language Universals"', *Lingua* **120**, 2655).

[90] L. Haegeman, *Introduction to Government and Binding Theory* (Oxford: Blackwell, 1994).

This mutual autonomy prevails today and is reflected in textbooks in the philosophy of language, where meaning is primarily discussed in relation to *words* rather than grammar, and even more specifically in relation to words that are *names*, which seem to exhibit no inherent grammatical structure at all. This then raises a question about the meaning of *sentences*, which do not seem to be names. The principle of compositionality has been the traditional answer: quite simply, sentence meanings arise by 'composing' the meanings of words (or, in practice, by assigning some words a 'function' that maps the meanings of some words to that of the sentences whose meaning one wanted to explain). The relevant operations of composition, crucially, are *semantic* operations. In this sense, grammatical relations and operations essentially never enter into the genesis of linguistic meaning.

In syntax, in turn, semantics is not only not regarded as conditioning the grammar, but Chomsky[91] argues that the basic semantic notion of reference does not apply to natural language, making semantic theory, insofar as it is based on this notion, empirically empty. But no alternative theory of meaning is suggested, nor is there a principled account of what 'grammatical meaning' *is*, i.e. of how grammar, once it intrudes into the human brain in evolution or development, *affects* the organization of meaning. Indeed, one could view the Minimalist Program[92] as effectively pursuing the *opposite* research program: to keep syntax maximally minimal, generic, and free of meaning, reducing it in essence to the maximally simple combinatorial operation Merge, which can be applied to *any* discretely infinite system.[93]

Syntax so described is clearly not linguistically specific, however. Linguistic specificity is rather said to come from how this core generative system is embedded in two 'interface systems', namely sensory-motor systems (S-M) on the one side and 'conceptual-intentional' (C-I) systems on the other, with the latter regarded as primary over the former.[94] The C-I systems are taken to pre-date language in evolution and to condition the outputs of the narrow syntactic

[91] N. Chomsky, *New Horizons in the Study of Language and Mind*, op. cit.

[92] N. Chomsky, *The Minimalist Program*, op. cit.

[93] C. Boeckx, *Bare Syntax* (Oxford: Oxford University Press, 2008).

[94] N. Chomsky, 'Approaching UG from Below'. In U. Sauerland and H.-M. Gärtner, (eds.) *Interfaces + Recursion = Language? Chomsky's Minimalism and the view from syntax-semantics*, (Berlin, New York: Mouton de Gruyter, 2008).

component through usability constraints. C-I is thus already there when recursion and grammar arrive. So they are not explained. And as recursion is described, it is unclear – and there is no account, except for commonly appealing to compositionality – of how grammatical meaning arises from whatever meanings or concepts are available pre-grammatically. In fact, there still *is* no real theory of grammatical meaning to be had: a principled idea of how the organization of meaning changes, when grammar intrudes. Perhaps the hope even is that it *doesn't* change.

Yet, linguistic specificity can hardly come from systems that are non-linguistically specific by definition.[95] Moreover, it seems implausible, in light of the substantive cognitive impoverishment we find in Neanderthals or chimpanzees, to suppose that the emergence of grammar will not systematically *affect* what meanings exist or what thoughts a creature can think, and hence substantially *re-organize* the C-I systems. It may even bring them into *place*, as Davidson[96] and Bickerton[97] argue. Indeed, the absence even of *concepts* in the non-human animal mind – given the need to keep these terminologically distinct from *classifications* and *categorizations* based on perceptual feature grouping – is a possibility that we cannot neglect. For any semantic entities that are inherently complex and structured, such as propositionally structured thoughts, this conclusion grows stronger, and it will be supported by evidence that non-human primates do not think propositionally.[98] While this evidence is controversial we can hardly claim that the chimpanzee thinks *all* the complex thoughts we think – refers to abstractions, ponders the truth, the causes of his being, etc. – while only a tragic sensory-motor deficit keeps him from speaking out loud. The deficit, no doubt – and no less than in the Neanderthal or *Homo Heidelbergensis* – is a cognitive (at least) *as much as* a sensory-motor one. So there must be a cut-off point where pre-linguistic meaning – whatever it may be, possibly only instinctually driven and perceptually based *categorization* – ceases and grammatical meaning begins. But the problem is that we simply do

---

[95] W. Hinzen, 'Minimalism'. In T. Fernando and R. Kempson, (eds.) *Handbook of Philosophy of Linguistics* (Elsevier, in press).

[96] D. Davidson, 'Rational Animals', *Dialectica* **36** (1982) 317–327.

[97] D. Bickerton, *Adam's Tongue*, op.cit.

[98] H. Terrace, 'Metacognition and the Evolution of Language', in H. Terrace and P. Metcalfe (eds.), *The Missing Link in Cognition* (Oxford: Oxford University Press, 2005); D. C. Penn, K. J. Holyoak, and D. J. Povinelli, 'Darwin's Mistake: Explaining the Discontinuity Between Human and Nonhuman Minds', *Behavioral and Brain Sciences* **31** (2008), 109–130.

not have a conception of grammar that would speak to this question: of how we became rational, capable of generating meanings of a radically different kind.

As Leiss[99] argues, this predicament is rooted in the rationalism of generative grammar itself. For the grammarians of Port Royal, rational thought was essentially a given. It is structured by logic, and grammar is 'rational grammar' insofar as it *reflects* the logical structure of thought. Hence grammar is not *generative* of thought, but only *expressive* of it. Ipso facto, we lack a genuine (empirical, naturalistic) *theory* of thought, a theory of how it arises and why it takes the specific human format that it does. If language is merely a suitable device for *expressing* it, it won't provide the needed explanation. On the contrary, thought is today widely used to explain language. In order for language to serve its function of expressing thought, the idea is, it has to be of a certain kind. Therefore it exhibits the format it does.[100] Tomasello's approach is particularly telling in this regard (as we saw above), as is Christiansen and Chater's,[101] who point out:

> A standard assumption is that thought is largely prior to, and independent of, linguistic communication. Accordingly, fundamental properties of language, such as compositionality, function-argument structure, quantification, aspect, and modality, may arise from the structure of the thoughts language is required to express.

This stance however merely shifts the burden of explanation. The thought system that Christiansen and Chater appeal to is too linguistic in character to play the explanatory role that is here required of it. Essentially the entire semantic structure that is specifically expressed in human language sentences is presupposed, and regarded as something that is available prior to – and hence may explain – the evolution of the system that happens to come with the relevant meanings. There is no reason to deny that non-human animals have mental representations that can track environmental features and enter computations, in the 'broad' sense above. But these mental representations are not autonomously manipulable, they are surely not Nouns and Verbs, or subjects and predicates, and hence they are also not the kind of constituents that we need in order to obtain a propositional meaning. No

---

[99]   E. Leiss, *Sprachphilosophie*. (Berlin:De Gruyter, 2009).

[100]   R. Jackendoff, *Foundations of Language*, op. cit.; M. Tomasello, *The Origins of Human Communication*, op. cit.

[101]   M. Christiansen, and N. Chater 2008 'Language as Shaped by the Brain', op. cit., 501.

Wolfram Hinzen

such meanings, to my knowledge, have been found in species communicating non-linguistically, and Davidson[102] gives a conceptual argument that they will not be: thinking propositionally requires a concept of intersubjective truth – an inkling that what we are thinking, if it has the right format, is true or false in some objective sense. But where this concept of truth would come from if not from sharing a language, is unclear. Indeed we see that where language is used but not shared, as in schizophrenia, the sense of truth is disturbed as well.

There is a motivation, therefore, for pursing the research program of systematically looking at grammar as a device for obtaining the very propositional forms of reference in question, as exhibited in any act of human (rational) language use. But this, as noted, is exactly not, it at first appears, what generative linguistic theory, which has expelled the notion of reference from the scope of its theorizing, can help us with: it has been characterized by an 'internalist' move that regards meaning, to the extent that it is addressed in this approach, as generated internal to the organism and as separate from the realm of reference and truth.[103] Coherent with this, Chomsky's line of thought in regards to language evolution in recent years has been that language first evolved internally, as a 'language of thought'. Only then the organism gradually adapted its articulatory system to the task of expressing this internal language and the meanings it generates. The way in which the syntactic system interfaces with thought is thus primary, while sensory-motor externalization is secondary, given externalization no constitutive role in the genesis of thought. Reference, however, including propositional forms of reference, is intuitively a 'public'-language phenomenon: we use *public* language symbols to reference an object for an interlocutor, and there is no reference in this sense in the privacy of our own minds. There is a question, therefore, how syntax as conceived in the internalist tradition will illuminate notions such as reference and truth.

A coherent reaction to this problem has been to precisely *eliminate* these notions from semantic theory, leaving them to the interaction of grammar post-grammatical cognitive systems.[104] In the concrete

---

[102] D. Davidson, 'Rational Animals',op. cit.

[103] W.Hinzen, *Mind Design and Minimal Syntax*, op. cit.; W. Hinzen, *An Essay on Naming and Truth* (Oxford: Oxford University Press, 2007).

[104] P. Pietroski, 'Meaning Before Truth'. In G. Peter and G. Preyer (eds.), *Contextualism in Philosophy*, (Oxford: Oxford University Press, 2005).

formalization of Pietroski,[105] semantic theory specifically consists in a recursive and compositional specification of how predicates conjoin, where the meanings of such predicates are pre-linguistic 'concepts'. By conjoining predicates we get ever more restricted meanings, i.e. a situation that is described in ever more detail: a killing, say, that is done with pleasure, in the morning, by Tom, with a knife, etc. As Pietroski shows, we also get an account of quantification, and inference. But we will not get the kind of expression that we use in an act of singular reference, or in asserting something. We may have reasons to believe, however, that what *gives* us a sense of objectivity and truth *is* grammar, and that nothing else is known to give us that. In that case, the revolution that the intrusion of grammar into the hominid brain induced is undersold by an internalist stance in semantics. I will outline an argument that the grammar *is* an arbiter of reference in the final section.

For now we may summarize the situation as follows. Modern linguistic theory has followed a rationalist intuition: thought is universal and somehow just there ('innate', perhaps), with its rationality characterized by logic. Grammar, therefore, can only be 'rational' by aligning with logic. To the extent that it does not, it is an expressive tool that is simply deficient and arbitrary. This basic intuition gave rise to the 'rational grammars' of the 17th and 18th centuries. It came into disrepute in the early 19th century, however, when linguists aligned their discipline with psychology instead. The terms 'sentence' and 'judgement' could in this period be used virtually interchangeably.[106] By the end of the 19th century, on the other hand, *anti-psychologism* in logic as propagated by Bolzano, Frege, and Husserl had become increasingly established, giving rise to the logical analysis of the forms of judgement, irrespective of how human grammar happened to pattern cross-linguistically, which had become the main subject matter of linguistic theory. Half a century later, Chomsky would revive rationalist linguistics. Unlike early 19th century linguists, he did propagate a Universal Grammar. However, he not only strongly resisted the equation of the science of language and the science of thought – first articulated with remarkable clarity by Friedrich Max Mueller (1887/1909) – but he turned grammar into an autonomous 'module' consisting of functionally arbitrary and formally characterized algebraic rules.

[105] P. Pietroski, P. 2011.'Minimal Semantic Instructions'. In C. Boeckx (ed.). *The Oxford Handbook of Linguistic Minimalism* (Oxford:Oxford University Press, 2011).
[106] G. Graffi, *200 years of syntax*. (Amsterdam: John Benjamins, 2001).

This is the very conception that, as embedded in the evolutionary context of adaptationist biology by Pinker,[107] draws the scorn of those theorists today who want to link grammar meaningfully to human thought and psychology,[108] leading to the crisis of UG today.

In this way, the task of theory of thought has remained – no account of the fundamental shift in our mode of thought is available, which I argue here is linked to the intrusion of grammar and via this linked to the cause of human speciation itself. As things stand, no such theory is forthcoming from within the theory of grammar either. Quite the contrary, if we follow Chomsky's deepest speculations within what has been called the 'Strong Minimalist Thesis',[109] language may be like a crystal: built from structurally simple, few, and elegant principles, rooted in natural law. There is no intrinsic connection between the internal structure of this crystal and its rational use. As Chomsky has once put it, the computational system of language could be just what it is now, yet used for purposes of locomotion.[110] In this way, the spirit of autonomy has lived on, and the Minimalist Program has driven the rationalist research program to an unsuspected peak.

5. How Grammar Might be Rational

I have argued that while it is coherent to study language as a 'real object of the natural world', the *kind* of natural object it has come out to be will not allow us to perceive grammar and human rationality as inherently linked – leaving the origins of a humanly unique format of thought opaque. In this final section I briefly indicate, based on longer elaborations made elsewher,[111] how I think this link can be re-instituted, leading to a theory of grammar as identical with a humanly specific mode of thought. Let us begin by not taking issue with – i.e., simply accept – the idea that humans and many

[107] S. Pinker, *The Language Instinct*, op. cit.

[108] R. Jackendoff, *Foundations of language.* op. cit.; N. Evans, and J. Levinson, 'The Myth of Language Universals: Language Diversity and its Importance for Cognitive Science', op. cit.; M. Christiansen, and N. Chater 'Language as Shaped by the Brain', op. cit.; M. Tomasello, *The Origins of Human Communication*, op. cit.

[109] W. Hinzen, *Mind Design and Minimal Syntax*, op. cit.

[110] N. Chomsky, *New Horizons in the Study of Language and Mind*, op. cit., 27.

[111] W. Hinzen, 'The Philosophical Significance of Universal Grammar', (*Ms.*, University of Durham, 2011).

Human Nature and Grammar

non-human creatures share concepts. Crucially, then, these concepts cannot be the meanings of words. This is because every word has a formal syntactic category – it is a grammatical entity – and no concept has that. Since the grammatical category of a word systematically enters into its meaning, as we shall see shortly, it follows that whatever meanings concepts have will not exhaust the meanings of words. At this very junction, the question of which principled difference grammar makes to meaning can be usefully re-raised. For the difference between a word and a concept is the very difference between grammar and no grammar.

A crucial phenomenon to look at in this regard is category conversions in the many languages where these are possible, of which English is one. What is the difference in meaning between (1) and (2)?

(1)   Mary's smile
(2)   Mary smiles

In this example the two words *smile* and *smiles* access the same root concept in the human lexicon. Let us denote it, following philosophical convention, as the concept SMILE. Whatever it exactly means, we may assume it means something, and indeed the same thing in both expressions. In what way, then, do the two meanings of the two words also *differ* in meaning, given that they *do* so differ? The answer is that they differ in terms of the formal ontology they invoke, in the sense that in (1) it is a smile under an 'objectual' perspective that we refer to, while in (2) we do so under an 'eventive' perspective. One consequence of this is that, in the second case, what we are referring to is placed in time in relation to the point of speech (it is tensed), and that it is specified for Aspect (it is ongoing as the speech event takes place). Nothing like that happens in (1). Crucially, these differences in how we refer have nothing to do with 'semantic' reference. The external world doesn't determine whether we refer to it objectually or eventively. The situation of language use could be exactly the same, and yet we may use the nominal, or the verb. Nor does the *conceptual* system determine this, which as such cannot even make the relevant ontological distinction: for the distinction to become available, a decision on which word is chosen to express the concept has first to be made.

It wouldn't make sense, therefore, to explain the difference in the meaning of the two words in (1) and (2) by stipulating that they semantically refer to different objects: a certain object in the first, a certain event in the second. If we said that we would have to repeat the same stipulation for just about every conceptual root that can enter such conversions. The difference in question is not a difference in semantic reference, any more than it is one in conceptual content. It is a *grammatical* difference. Yet this doesn't mean it is meaningless. And therefore we need to find a different term to characterize it.

The term I have chosen is *deictic reference*. Deictic reference originates in pointing, which is not uniquely linguistic but sharply restricted when it is not: one cannot point to an event that happened yesterday with one's index finger, nor can one draw an interlocutor's attention to *the fact that p* or *p's being true*. Grammar is needed for all of these things, and in this sense, grammar is a *device of extended deixis*. It does not organize our *concepts* and the forms of 'semantic' reference they have (substantive lexical content), but it organizes the forms of deictic reference that are based on them.

This makes a common assumption stand on its head: grammar, on this common assumption, is there for *combining concepts*. If I am right, it essentially never does that. Combining the root concept SMILE with a verbalizing morpheme *v* to give us the verb *smiles* is not naturally described as combining two *concepts*. Quite the contrary, when we take a root out of the conceptual system, verbalize it, and then tense it, this does not reflect a process of combining concepts or predicates, but a process of progressively making a given concept *referentially more specific*, embedding it in time (and space): first it is specified to be ontologically an event, say, which as such is specified as extended in time and can then related to the speech event. Grammar, thus, describes a progression from concepts to acts of reference, not a mapping from concepts to concepts. No more descriptive or substantive conceptual content is added to a given concept when it becomes grammaticalized. What changes is not description but reference.

Once we look at grammar in this fashion – as a device for extensionalizing intensional (conceptual, predicative) information – we find the same phenomenon everywhere. Starting from a given concept, we can nominalise it and obtain, say, the word *wine*. By adding grammatical structure we can then expand to *bottles of wine*, then to *three bottles of wine*, then to *these three bottles of wine*. Then the expansion stops. With each step, nothing in the conceptual content or semantic reference of WINE changes. What changes is deictic reference, or the relating of a given predicative concept to a referent that falls under this concept, where the referent is always located at some distance to the deictic centre of the speaker: the Now, Here, and Self of speech. In the nominal case, only embedding or identifying a referent in *space* is an option, where the referent is deictically classified as being either first, second, or third person; in the verbal case, aspectual specification govern embedding in *time*; for embedding in *discourse*, a full clause is needed. With each addition of a functional element to a given conceptual root, (deictic) reference not only changes systematically, but reference becomes more specific and extensional. *These three bottles of wine* refers to three individual objects; *Three bottles of wine* refers to a set whose members are sets of bottles of wine with three members each; *Bottles of wine* refers to a larger set of which the previous is a (small) subset, yet all of whose members are bottles; *Wine* refers to a yet larger set which contains bottles and non-bottles alike.

Beyond characterizing grammatically mediated forms of reference broadly as deictic, we can more specifically distinguish three referential strategies: indefinite quantificational reference, as in *a man*; definite specific reference, as in definite descriptions such as *the man*; and 'rigid' or 'object' reference as in *Tom*. Sheehan and Hinzen[112] show, updating an account by Longobardi,[113] that the grammar is systematically sensitive to these three forms of reference and organizes them, and that the exact *same* three forms can be found in the case of the reference of clauses, yielding familiar distinctions among the ontology of the clause, as in referring to a mere *proposition*, to a *fact* (a proposition evaluated as true), or to a *truth*.

If so, and if the relevant grammatical generalizations hold cross-linguistically, grammar is the very mechanism behind the humanly specific forms of reference that there are, that are commonly assumed to be universal, and that describe the core elements of human rationality as philosophers have viewed them since antiquity. It does not give us concepts, but it allows us to put them to a referential use, in a communicative context in which both the concepts and the grammar are shared and the grammatical meanings encoded in the grammar can have some objectivity. In that case, there is nothing left for external and independent systems of 'thought' to explain, *beyond* supplying the concepts on which the grammatical engine feeds. Grammar is not now an arbitrary system or module, which is only contingently related to its use or to thought. It is the very basis of human rationality, and the cornerstone of our minds and nature.[114]

---

[112] W. Hinzen and M. Sheehan, 'Moving Towards the Edge', *Linguistic Analysis*, 2011(in press).

[113] G. Longobardi, G. 1994. 'Reference and Proper Names', *Linguistic Inquiry* **25** (1994), 609–665; G. Longobardi, 'Towards a Unified Grammar of Reference', *Zeitschrift für Sprachwissenschaft* **24** (2005), 5–44.

[114] The connection between the fragmentation of grammar and the breakdown of the deictic frame (and hence human reason) in Schizophrenia argued for by Crow (T. J. Crow, 'The "Big Bang" Theory

Wolfram Hinzen

6. Summary

Human nature has been standardly discarded on grounds of its inconsistency with biology, its epistemological dubiousness, and its putative metaphysical nature. Yet a methodological naturalism free of metaphysical prejudice should be allowed to be applied to the study of *Homo sapiens* as an object of nature as much as to any other object. Such a project has affinities with the efforts of early modern natural philosophers to pursue a Science of Man free of a metaphysical and scholastic heritage.

Unique and universal in humans is a grammatical way of structuralizing communicative signals. As this phenomenon has been subjected to naturalistic scrutiny, its features make it appear isolated in the biological world, yet as falling under one relatively well-defined natural type, a joint of nature. While this is in itself an interesting result, the generative program in linguistics has characterized its object of inquiry in a paradigmatically rationalist fashion that does not allow us to see its role in the genesis of human reason and our species itself. In that situation, a theory of the novel format of thought that supports the human revolution has escaped us, and a mechanism behind it is missing.

If am right, grammar is that mechanism, as grammar, accessing pre-human and pre-linguistic concepts, turns them into devices of reference in situations of communicative language use. Cross-linguistic research will need to reveal whether the basic forms of deictic reference in the sense above are indeed universal, and whether they are uniformly supported by the grammatical mechanisms in question.[115]

Durham University
wolfram.hinzen@durham.ac.uk

---

of the Origin of Psychosis and the Faculty of Language', op. cit.) is a powerful further support for this conclusion, which came up during the Human Nature conference and which unfortunately I cannot go into here for reasons of space.

[115] This research was made possible by the grant 'Un-Cartesian Linguistics' (AHRC/DFG, AH/H50009X/1). I thank my co-workers Uli Reichard and Michelle Sheehan for numerous conversations on the issues of this paper, and the organizers of the Human Nature conference for stimulating such useful discussions.

Can Evolutionary Biology do Without Aristotelian Essentialism?

STEPHEN J. BOULTER

1. Introduction

It is usually maintained by biologists and philosophers alike that essentialism is incompatible with evolutionary biology, and that abandoning essentialism was a precondition of progress being made in the biological sciences. These claims pose a problem for anyone familiar with both evolutionary biology and current metaphysics. Very few current scientific theories enjoy the prestige of evolutionary biology.[1] But essentialism – long in the bad books amongst both biologists and philosophers – has been enjoying a strong resurgence of late amongst analytical philosophers with a taste for metaphysics.[2] Indeed, to impartial observers it is likely to appear that both evolutionary biology and essentialism are as well supported in their respective domains as could reasonably be expected. There is thus at least a *prima facie* tension here between evolutionary biology,

---

[1] Stearns and Hoekstra rightly insist that "The ideas of evolution have survived many controversies and tests and are now considered as reliable as any ideas in science." *Evolution: An Introduction* (Oxford: Oxford University, 2005, 23).

[2] It all began with Kripke's classic *Naming and Necessity* (Oxford: Blackwell, 1972), although perhaps the laurel ought to go to Ruth Barcan Marcus – see her "Essentialism in Modal Logic" and "Essential Attribution" in *Modalities: Philosophical Essays* (Oxford: Oxford University Press, 1993). See also Alvin Plantinga, *The Nature of Necessity* (Oxford: Clarendon Press, 1974); Hilary Putnam, *Mind, Language and Reality* (Cambridge: Cambridge University, 1975); Kit Fine, "Postscript", in *Worlds, Times and Selves*. Fine and Prior (eds) London: Duckworth, 1977); David Wiggins, *Sameness and Substance* (Oxford: Blackwell, 1980); and David Charles, *Aristotle on Meaning and Essence* (Oxford: Clarendon Press, 2000). For a general overview of contemporary formulations of essentialist theses see Graeme Forbes, "Essentialism", in *A Companion to the Philosophy of Language*. Hale and Wright (eds). (Oxford: Blackwell, 1999, 515–533).

doi:10.1017/S1358246112000057   © The Royal Institute of Philosophy and the contributors 2012
Royal Institute of Philosophy Supplement **70** 2012   83

Stephen J. Boulter

metaphysics (of a reputable sort) and, as we shall see, pre-theoretical common sense.[3]

The question regarding the compatibility or otherwise of essentialism and evolutionary biology also touches upon the highly contentious, because often politicised, issue of human nature. Most assume in their pre-theoretical moments that there is something, a "nature", in virtue of which we as members of *Homo sapiens* are distinguished from the rest of the animate and inanimate world. And while we used to have recourse to theology, and latterly the great works of art and literature, for an understanding of this nature, it is now more commonly held that evolutionary biology and psychology are the more likely sources of reliable information on this score. But beneath the surface of this phrase "human nature" are essentialist assumptions, in particular, that there is such a nature that all human beings have that distinguishes us from everything else. So what is one to make of these apparent inconsistencies? Can biology, and evolutionary biology in particular, tell us anything about human nature? Or rather, does evolutionary biology tell us that there is no such thing as human nature at all?

To put my cards on the table immediately, I maintain that there is a human nature; that evolutionary biology has much to tell us about this nature; and that all this is compatible with Aristotelian essentialism. It is this final point which is the focus of attention in this paper. I will argue that far from being incompatible with essentialism, evolutionary biology in fact *presupposes* Aristotelian essentialism inasmuch as the truth of the former requires the truth of the latter. This claim puts me sharply at odds with orthodox philosophy of biology. But I believe this conflict can be resolved amicably once essentialism is properly understood. To make good this claim it is necessary to begin with an account of both theories. A further preparatory step is to lay out explicitly the standard incompatibilist arguments and some possible responses already mooted in the literature. I can then proceed to the core of the paper, the presentation of two arguments in support of the thesis that evolutionary biology *cannot*

---

[3]   The resolution of such tensions is the bread and butter of philosophy. For an extended discussion of this understanding of the nature of philosophy see Stephen Boulter, *The Rediscovery of Common Sense Philosophy* (Houndsmill: Palgrave Macmillan, 2007, ch. 1); Nicholas Rescher, *Aporetics: Rational Deliberation in the Face of Inconsistency* (Pittsburgh: Pittsburgh University Press, 2009); and Nicolai Hartmann, *Grundzüge einer Metaphysik der Erkenntnis.* 5th ed. (Berlin: W. de Gruyter, 1965).

do without essentialism. After floating a suggestion as to what bio-logical essences might be I revisit the original set of incompatibilist arguments to show that they are easily brushed aside once one is fam-iliar with the outlines of Aristotelian essentialism and the metaphys-ical commitments of evolutionary biology.

I turn then to the characterisation of both theories.

2. Aristotelian Essentialism

An adequate understanding of any theory requires familiarity with the problems it is meant to address. This is certainly true of Aristotelian essentialism (from here on in just "essentialism" unless otherwise specified). It is also important for a proper appreciation of essentialism to compare it to the alternative solutions suggested by other metaphysicians (something rarely done in the philosophy of biology literature).

Aristotle's essentialism is the result of the attempt to provide a metaphysical account of what is implicit in our everyday dealings with the world. In particular the essentialist wants to maintain that:

(i)   The world contains, amongst other things, mind-indepen-dent middle-sized items like minerals, plants, animals, and stars;
(ii) These items are irreducible;
(iii) These items can persist through some changes, but not all; and
(iv) These items are intelligible.

Traditionally the problem posed by this set of propositions has been understanding how real items can persist through change. Perhaps the easiest way to see the difficulty is as follows: If an item a persists through a change, then a prior to the change is the same item as a at then end of the process (a at time$_{t1}$ is identical to a at time$_{t2}$). But by Leibnitz's Law if a is identical to b then any property of a must also be a property of b. But if a has undergone a change then it must have some property after the change that it previously did not have, or have lost a property it previously had. In either case not everything true of a at time$_{t1}$ is true of a at time$_{t2}$; so by Leibnitz's Law a at time$_{t1}$ is not identical to a at time$_{t2}$, and so a has not persisted through the change but has been replaced by something else. Generalise this result and one ends up denying that change is possible.

Stephen J. Boulter

Aristotle's solution, designed to respect i–iv, is to accept the following claims:[4]

1. The world is primarily constituted by individual substances belonging to discrete natural kinds, each kind having its own essential properties.
2. F is an essential feature of kind K if and only if F is a feature used to define kind K.
3. The definition of a kind plays two important roles. First, the definition provides the existence and identity conditions of instances of the kind. These allow one to track an instance of a kind through its career and any changes it might undergo by allowing principled answers to questions of the form "is *a* the same as *b*?" Second, a definition stating the essence of a kind has an explanatory role in that it is adverted to when explaining why an instance of the kind has the properties and behaviour patterns that it does.
4. There are biological kinds.
5. (1) – (4) are grounded in the nature of things independently of our thought or representations of them.

Such a theory allows the essentialist to maintain the target theses at the expense of some qualification of Leibnitz's Law (it does not apply unqualifiedly across times). (1) and (5) do justice to the reality of middle-sized items mentioned in (i) and (ii); (2) and the first part of (3) accommodate the claim that these items can persist through some changes but not all by distinguishing between essential and non-essential properties, the loss of the latter being consistent with the continued existence of the items through the change, while the loss of the former marks the passing out of existence of the item in question; (2) and the second part of (3) marks a commitment to the intelligibility of these items mentioned in (iv). (4) simply points out that natural kinds are not restricted to items falling exclusively within the domains of physics and chemistry. Crucial to the position is the distinction between essential and non-essential properties. Only if such a distinction is recognised can an entity undergo a change without passing out of existence altogether:

---

[4]   The literature on Aristotle's metaphysics is very extensive and extraordinarily sophisticated, and there is, unsurprisingly, room for rational debate regarding the details of his position. What I provide here, however, is relatively uncontroversial among Aristotle scholars. I follow the account given in Charles, op. cit. note 2.

accommodating this common sense view is the primary motivation behind essentialism.

Providing a metaphysics which allows one to uphold i–iv is difficult without recourse to essentialism; indeed every competing metaphysical system abandons one or more of these desiderata. For example, in asserting the mind-independent nature of middle-sized items the essentialist is at odds with Kant and all forms of constructivism. The essentialist's commitment to (ii) distinguishes him from Plato (who maintained, at one stage at least, that extra temporal and spatial Forms alone are ultimately real); from Democritus and other atomists (who reduce middle-sized items to aggregates of atoms, the latter alone being fully real); and from Spinoza (who maintained that there is only *one* ontologically basic item). (iii) distinguishes the essentialist from Heraclitus, modern day phenomenalists, and trope theorists (who deny the existence of *persisting* objects of any kind). The essentialist's commitment to (ii) and (iii) together distinguishes him from Parmenides, Plato, Heraclitus, Democritus and modern day perdurance theorists who deny that any change is possible in real entities, and from Spinoza who maintains that all changes are merely phase changes of one underlying substance. Finally the essentialist's commitment to (iv) distinguishes him from Parmenides, Heraclitus, Plato and the skeptics who all denied that the world of ordinary sense experience is fully intelligible. We shall enter into some of the details of these points below; but it is worth noting at the outset that the rejection of essentialism comes at a high price to ordinary common sense intuitions. If one is inclined to believe that individual horses and cabbages, say, are as real as anything can be; that an individual horse and individual cabbage can undergo some changes while remaining a horse or a cabbage respectively, while other changes bring about their respective ends; and if one believes that we can understand something of horses and cabbages (for example, that we can explain why horses have the standard vertebrate limb and cabbage plants can photosynthesise); then Aristotle's essentialism proves indispensable, for the other major metaphysical systems threaten precisely these sorts of claims.[5] Let this suffice as an account of Aristotle's essentialism, and let us now turn to a similarly brief account of evolutionary theory.

---

[5] It is not for nothing that Lawson-Tancred deemed Aristotle's "the received metaphysics of the Western world." (In Aristotle, *Metaphysics*. Translation by Lawson-Tancred (London: Penguin, 2004, xxiii).

Stephen J. Boulter

3. Evolutionary Biology

Again let us start with the questions evolutionary theory is meant to address. Evolutionary biologists are particularly concerned to provide an understanding of biological diversity and organismal design. A word on each of these features of the living world is in order.

The Diversity and Disparity of the Living World

Biologists are impressed by the fact that there are so many different kinds of organisms built on such different body plans. The evolutionary biologist seeks to provide some way of making sense of this bewildering variety by finding order in the diversity. But the biologist is also impressed by the fact that this variety is limited. There are many logically possible organisms the biologist can conceive of in "design space" which she does *not* find in the real world. In fact it would appear that most logically possible organisms never become actual. Thus the biologist also wants to explain why the living world has the pattern it actually has, and why it is not more varied than it actually is. Why, for instance, are there no flying pigs or frogs, or grass eating snakes (there are vegetarian lizards, so why no vegetarians snakes?) If there are eusocial insects, why are there no eusocial birds? Why are there no species with 3 or more sexes? Why do organisms come in discreet packages – species – rather than all organisms looking the same, or each individual appearing radically different? Why, indeed, has the living world not produced any radically new body plans since the Cambrian 500mya?

Adaptation

A feature of the living world noted by all is the fact that organisms are usually, and often conspicuously, well-equipped to deal with their environment. How does this come about? An interesting wrinkle here, however, is that it is as often as not the fact that organisms display less than optimal adjustment to their environment that biologists want to explain. The human eye, for example, though historically used as an instance of intelligent design by a creator, is in fact rather poorly designed from an engineering point of view (retina is at the back rather than the front). Why should this be?

 These are the big questions facing evolutionary biologists, and the theory of evolution is designed to address precisely these issues. With these questions in mind we can turn to the distinctive claims of evolutionary theory. These are as follows:

1. Evolutionary change has occurred. The living world is not stable, with species coming into and passing out of existence.
2. All life on this planet descends from a single remote ancestor (i.e., there was no separate or special creation of each individual species) and Life has a branching pattern.
3. New species form when a population splits into two or more groups and these begin to adapt to different circumstances. (Usually a sub-population on the periphery becomes geographically, and so reproductively, isolated from the main population, and begins to adapt to their new and different circumstances.)
4. Evolutionary change is gradual, not rapid. Off-spring that differ radically from their parents due to significant mutation rarely if ever survive to reproduce. All change must be relatively conservative, and so significant changes to a lineage require many small steps taking many generations.
5. The mechanism of adaptive change is natural selection.

This set of claims has been called the "received" view, but there is debate about a number of these.[6] Most biologists accept (1) the fact of evolution, and (2) the branching pattern of evolution stemming from a single source (although the shape of life might more closely resemble a mosaic than a tree in single celled organisms). This is virtually universal. (3), the theory of speciation (Mayr's contribution), is highly regarded, but not as solid as (1) and (2). It is probably one way new species emerge, but it might not be the only way, or the most prevalent way. (4), the commitment to gradualism, is perhaps more firmly established than it once was now that the excitement that first surrounded Gould's theory of punctuated equilibrium has died down, but developments in evolutionary developmental biology have put this issue back on the table. (5) is the ingredient in the received view that has attracted most attention. It is subject to much debate, but most biologists agree that natural selection has at least some role to play in dealing with the explananda outlined earlier. At issue is whether it is the only significant force driving adaptive change, or whether it needs to be supplemented by other

---

[6] For further discussion see chapter 2 of Sterelny and Griffiths, *Sex and Death: An Introduction to Philosophy of Biology* (Chicago: University of Chicago Press, 1999).

forces which might well be more powerful, and whether it can account for the general shape of Life. But for the time being we can say this:

The *fact* of evolution is established easily. It follows from three readily made direct observations of the living world:

a. *Phenotypic variety* (organisms are not identical, but differ within a specific range on a variety of features).
b. *Differential reproduction* (organisms do not reproduce in equal numbers. Some produce many more off-spring than their con-specifics, many much less, some not at all).
c. *Principle of heredity* (off-spring resemble their parents more than they resemble other con-specifics).

These facts guarantee that the traits found within a population will change from generation to generation. But if this change is to be adaptive, and if adaptive change is to play a role in speciation, then additional conditions must be met. The change needs to be cumulative, i.e., the same reproductive pattern must take place over many generations. Cumulative selection requires:

d. stability in the direction of selection (the same sorts of features need to be favoured over a long period of time)
e. each step on the adaptive path must be better than the last (there can be no retreat the better to advance in evolutionary processes)
f. The right ratio of mutation rate or available variation to selective pressure. If the selective pressure is too hard it will drive the variation rate down to nothing very quickly, eliminating the chance of further evolution (the experience of animal breeders); but if the selective pressure is too low, then it will not eliminate enough of the variations to make any significant difference to the gene pool as all will survive in equal measure.

Let this suffice as an account of the main claims of the received view of evolution. We can now proceed to the grounds for the claim that the two theories are incompatible.

4. The Incompatibilist Case(s)

It might not be immediately obvious from the foregoing accounts precisely why the two theories are thought to be incompatible. Many different reasons have been suggested. It is worth spelling out these different lines of thought explicitly.

Evolutionary Biology do Without Aristotelian Essentialism?

It is said that essentialism about biological kinds is *not* consistent with evolutionary biology for the following reasons:

1. Essentialism about species implies species fixism. But species fixism is inconsistent with the view that species evolve. So essentialism about species is inconsistent with evolutionary theory.[7]

2. Essentialism about species implies clear, non-bridgeable boundaries between species. But this is inconsistent with Darwinian gradualism on two counts. First, no set of properties, at either the level of the phenotype or genotype, has been identified as jointly necessary and sufficient for membership of any biological species. That is, in the field (as opposed to the philosopher's armchair) what one actually finds is such a degree of variation within any species that no clear boundaries between species are found but rather a merging or blending at the edges of one species into another. Second, this degree of variation is a precondition of one species gradually evolving into another, as is demanded by orthodox Darwinism. Evolution between species with clear boundaries would only be possible if nature proceeded by jumps (saltations). But saltations are impossible according to orthodox Darwinian theory.[8]

3. Moreover, even if the naturalist were to identify necessary and sufficient conditions for membership in a species this would not be to the point. For if an organism were to differ markedly either phenotypically or genotypically from its parents, it would still be classed as a member of the species to which the parents belong. This is inconsistent with essentialism because the properties the essentialist is willing to countenance as part of an organism's essence must be intrinsic and not relational.[9]

---

[7] This argument is found in Ernst Mayr, "Darwin and the evolutionary theory in biology", *Evolution and Anthropology: A centennial appraisal*. Meggers ed. (Washington DC: Anthropology Society of Washington, 1959), and *The Growth of Biological Thought* (Cambridge Mass.: Belnap Press, 1982). It is also expounded in David Hull, "The effect of essentialism on taxonomy: two thousand years of stasis. Part 1", *Br. J. Philos. Sci.*, (1965), **XVI**: 1–18. See also M.T. Ghiselin, (1981) "Categories, life and thinking", *Behav. Brain Sci.*, (1981), **4**: 269–283, 303–310.

[8] This argument is also found in Mayr, op. cit. note 7.

[9] That this latter point is required for the argument to have any force is not always spelled out explicitly, but John Dupré is clear on this. He doubts that descent is "even a candidate for an essential property" because this

4. Essentialism is not simply the view that organisms have an essence. It also maintains that this essence has an explanatory role within biology inasmuch as one can explain at least some of the properties of an organism by adverting to the essence of the species of which it is a member. But no essence *with explanatory power* has been identified by evolutionary biology (or any other branch of biology for that matter). Therefore, essentialism is inconsistent with evolutionary biology inasmuch as one claims while the other denies that there are biologically explanatory essences.[10]

5. It has been argued that biological essences, were they to be discovered, would have no explanatory role in evolutionary biology.[11] In the population thinking characteristic of evolutionary biology, to determine the effects of evolutionary mechanisms one need only advert to statistical laws about the interactions of the individuals in a population. One needs no knowledge of the particular properties of particular individuals. It is only properties of populations that are truly explanatory. "Describing a single individual is as theoretically peripheral to a populationist as describing the motion of a single molecule is to the kinetic theory of gases. In this important sense, population thinking involves *ignoring individuals...*"[12] But in ignoring individuals, one ignores their essences. So essences are explanatorily irrelevant to evolutionary biology.

6. It is assumed by essentialism that each and every organism has one and only one essence, the essence of the species of which it is a member. But it has been argued that current evolutionary biology favours species pluralism, i.e., the view that organisms can be grouped into several equally real species depending on the species concept employed.[13] What is more, it is claimed

---

property is "purely relational". *The Disorder of Things: Metaphysical Foundations of the Disunity of Science* (Cambridge, Mass: Harvard University Press, 1993, 56).

[10] For an expression of this argument see Samir Okasha, "Darwinian Metaphysics: Species and the Question of Essentialism", *Synthese* (2002), **131**, 191–213.

[11] See Eliot Sober, "Evolution, Population Thinking, and Essentialism", *Phil. of Sci.*, (1980), **47**, 350–83.

[12] Op. cit., note 11, 370.

[13] See M. Ereshefsky, "Eliminative Pluralism", in *The Philosophy of Biology*. Hull and Ruse (eds). (Oxford University Press, 1998).

that the resulting species do not coincide. That is, it is not the case that reproductively isolated groups coincide with groups with common ancestors and groups subject to the same environmental selection pressures (groupings arrived at using the biological, phylogentic and ecological species concepts respectively). Since one and the same organism can fall into more than one group, and since no one of these groupings is privileged, it would seem that an individual organism can have more than one essence, contra essentialism.

But the incompatibility thesis has been contested on the following grounds:

1. Bernier argues that essentialism is not incompatible with evolutionary biology because species fixism, properly conceived, is not incompatible with one species giving rise to another distinct species via standard evolutionary processes.[14]

2. D. Walsh, relying on Pellegrin[15], D.M. Balme[16], and J. Lennox[17], argues that essentialism is not incompatible with evolutionary biology because essentialism properly conceived does not imply species fixism of any description. He writes: "On Aristotle's scheme essences or natures are not transcendent fixed "ideas"; they are goal-directed capacities immanent in the structure of the organism." These natures "…could change over time in just the way we have come to think that species do."[18]

3. Walsh argues, contra Sober, that evolutionary biology cannot rely simply on population thinking while ignoring individual organisms and their properties. While evolutionary change can be described as changes in gene frequency in a population (as Sober suggests) one cannot explain why such changes are

[14] See R. Bernier, "The Species as an Individual: Facing Essentialism", *Systematic Zoology* Vol. **33**, No. 4, (1984), 467.

[15] "Logical Difference and Biological Difference: the Unity of Aristotle's Thought", in *Philosophical Issues in Aristotle's Biology*, Gotthelf and Lennox (eds). (Cambridge: Cambridge University Press, 1987).

[16] *Aristotle's de Partibus Animalium and De Generatione Animalium I* (Oxford: Clarendon Press, 1972).

[17] "Material and Formal Natures in Aristotle's *de Partibus Animalium*" and "Kinds, Forms of Kinds, and the More and the Less in Aristotle's Biology", in *Aristotle's Philosophy of Biology* (Cambridge: Cambridge University Press, 2001).

[18] "Evolutionary Essentialism", *Brit. J. Phil. Sci.* **57** (2006), 431.

adaptive without adverting to features of individual organisms, in particular their developmental systems and phenotypic plasticity. Since these features are plausibly regarded as the essential nature of organisms, and since explaining adaptations is part of the raison d'être of evolutionary biology, evolutionary biology cannot fulfil its explanatory ambitions without presupposing essentialism. "Recent evolutionary developmental biology shows that one cannot understand how natural selection operating over a population of genes can lead to increased and diversified adaptation of organisms unless one understands the role of individual natures (essences) in the process of evolution."[19] Therefore essentialism is not inconsistent with evolutionary biology.

This collection of arguments is not exhaustive, but it includes the most pressing points advanced on both sides of the debate. It is worth noting immediately that the incompatibilist arguments are not consistent. Some deny there are biological essences (1–3); others are willing to countenance essences but deny them explanatory value (4 & 5); still others claim that organisms can have *more than one* biological essence, each possibly having explanatory value in some context or another (6). The same can be said of the arguments on the other side inasmuch as there is a difference of opinion as to whether species fixism is indeed a problem. Some claim that it is not (1), while others, at least by implication, assert that fixism would be a problem if it were entailed by essentialism (2). I take these inconsistencies on both sides of the house to indicate both the complexity of the issues and the need to return to first principles. Now the first principle shared by both theories is a commitment to the reality of change in the living world. It is on this shared principle that I build two presupposition arguments intended to show that evolutionary biology actually requires the truth of essentialism.

5. Two Presupposition Arguments

As stated at the outset, I maintain that both evolutionary biology and Aristotelian essentialism have independently established claims on our allegiance. Consequently, on the assumption that truth is one, it is methodologically appropriate to start with the assumption that the tensions between the two are not genuine but merely *prima facie*. Of course if this thesis cannot withstand scrutiny one will

[19]   Op. cit., note 18, 426.

have to accept that the tensions are genuine and a choice between the two will be forced. It is my view that this choice can be avoided.

It is important at the outset to be explicit about my limited aims. I am not concerned here to defend directly either the received view of evolution or essentialism. The question here is only as to their compatibility. I want to know whether the truth of either would imply the falsity of the other. As far as the argument of this paper is concerned *both* evolutionary theory *and* Aristotelian essentialism *might very well be false*. I happen to think both are true, and that this position will be supported in some measure if I can but show that they are at least compatible.

With this in mind I now present two arguments which invite the conclusion that evolutionary biology presupposes Aristotelian essentialism. Both are based on considerations drawn from reflection on the very problem of change that motivated essentialism in the first place. The gist of these considerations is as follows: If organisms are ontologically irreducible to entities of physics and chemistry; if biological species are natural groups of such organisms; if such species can undergo some changes without passing out of existence; and if one is willing to accept that speciation and extinction events do occur, then essentialism is forced – for an entity can persist through change only if it retains its essential properties while shedding or gaining an accidental property. Now it would appear that the only claim in these reflections at which some biologists might baulk is the claim that species are natural groups. For the autonomy of biology as a science requires organisms to be ontologically irreducible to physics and chemistry.[20] Moreover, all agree that a species can, say, increase or decline in numbers, or broaden or decrease its

[20] Of course there are good grounds for maintaining that organisms are ontologically irreducible. Mayr himself goes to considerable lengths to establish precisely this point, identifying eight characteristics of living organisms that have no parallel in the inanimate world (op. cit. note 7, 1982, 36–59). And even those who expect that such a reduction will be effected eventually acknowledge that such a reduction would require significant changes to our understanding of physics and chemistry, and most likely include a commitment to downward causation. For further discussion see E.F. Keller, "It is Possible to Reduce Biological Explanations to Explanations in Chemistry and/or Physics", in *Contemporary Debates in Philosophy of Biology*. Ayala and Arp (eds). (Oxford: Wiley-Blackwell, 2010, 19–31), and John Dupre, "It is not Possible to Reduce Biological Explanations to Explanations in Chemistry and/or Physics", in *Contemporary Debates in Philosophy of Biology*. Ayala and Arp (eds). (Oxford: Wiley-Blackwell, 2010, 32–47).

Stephen J. Boulter

range, i.e., change in some respect, without ceasing to exist. And of course no biologist is going to question the propriety of speciation and extinction events. The two arguments to follow are thus designed to show that evolutionary biology will have great difficulty in discharging its own self-imposed explanatory goals if it abandons the view that species are natural groups.[21]

An Argument From Diversity:

1. Evolutionary biology's fundamental claim with respect to biological diversity is that species have diverged to take advantage of the various ecological opportunities afforded to them. Ancestral species have given rise to distinct daughter species by a process of descent with modification, which results in the emergence of new biological forms and the expected degree of biological diversity. In short, biological diversity follows upon speciation events.
2. Setting aside questions regarding the various possible mechanisms of speciation, it is customary within evolutionary biology to take the following view of the origin of species. Once ancestral species A has cleaved into two new daughter species B and C, ancestral species A no longer exists, and daughter species B and C have come into existence (there has been two speciation events and one extinction). Moreover, B is not C, and neither is a continuation of A.[22]

[21] Of course these arguments are redundant for those who already accept that species are natural groups, the foregoing reflections on the problem of change being sufficient to force essentialism.
[22] That is, ancestral species A does not continue to exist in virtue of metamorphing into species B or C. Does this conflate sortal persistence conditions with diachronic identity conditions? Some metaphysicians want to distinguish the question "Under what conditions can x remain the kind of thing x currently is?" from "Under what conditions can x remain x?" Those who wish to preserve this distinction are motivated by the concern to allow for the possibility of metamorphosis of the sort associated with classical mythology, i.e., where Lucius, say, begins life as a human being, is transformed into an ass, and is ultimately returned to human form, all the while remaining Lucius. I think such scruples can be set aside here. For one, many will wonder whether the myths of metamorphosis are in fact fully intelligible (could Lucius really be an ass and remain Lucius?). For those whose intuitions prevent them from embracing metamorphosis as a genuine possibility sortal persistence conditions just are diachronic identity

3. This account of the origins of biological diversity presupposes that change is a real feature of the living world. In particular it presupposes that distinct species really do come into and pass out of existence. So speciation and extinction events are not illusory. Nor are they simply a function of our naming conventions – for mind-independent diversity cannot be explained by mind-dependent, i.e., non-natural, entities and processes. Furthermore, the biologist cannot maintain that speciation and extinction events are merely a function of a new arrangement of subatomic particles, or merely a phase change of an underlying substance, or temporal parts of an unchanging Tree of Life without abandoning the ontological irreducibility of organisms or the reality of change.

4. It is possible to maintain that A, B and C are distinct, natural species only if the existence and identity conditions of each are distinct.

5. This point is generalisable to cover all speciation and extinction events.

6. But the existence and identity conditions of x specify the Aristotelian essence of x. So,

7. Biological species, in virtue of having existence and identity conditions, have an essence.

The upshot of this argument is clear enough: The standard account of biological diversity provided by evolutionary theory presupposes essentialism. Note that this argument is built on the fact that species *do* come into and pass out of existence, a fact often thought to be inimical to essentialism. In fact quite the reverse is the case. Only if species have distinct essences can one say in a principled fashion that one species no longer exists and that two new distinct species have arrived on the scene, and one needs to be able to say this if one is to give the standard account of biological diversity.

An Argument From Organismal Design:

1. Evolutionary biology's fundamental claim with respect to organismal design is that many features of organisms are adaptations.

---

conditions because the identity of x is determined by x's sortal. But these considerations can be set aside in the current context because no evolutionary biologist believes that speciation events are cases of metamorphosis.

2.   An adaptation is a derived character or trait that evolved because it improved relative reproductive performance.

3.   Crucial to present purposes is the contrast between derived and ancestral characters. A trait or character is termed "ancestral" if it is possessed by an ancestral species shared by related daughter species. A trait or character is termed "derived" if it evolved after the ancestral trait in the lineage.[23]

4.   To determine whether a trait is derived one needs to know something of the transition from the ancestral to the derived condition of the character. That is, one needs to know the trait's phylogenetic history.

5.   To track the phylogenetic history of a trait the biologist employs phylogenetic trees.

6.   For a phylogenetic tree to be genuinely illuminating it must represent real relationships obtaining between natural species.[24]

---

[23]   The crucial point about adaptations is that they are features or characters that *at some point* in their phylogenetic history were derived. That is, for a trait to be an adaptation there must have been at one stage of its history a transition from the ancestral to the derived state. This does not mean that this trait ceases to be an adaptation if it is subsequently passed on without modification to another species after further cleavage in the lineage. Adaptations can be, and often are, ancestral traits with respect to a particular set of species, say species C, D and E, where C is a daughter species of ancestral species A, and D and E are daughter species of C.

[24]   That phylogenetic trees are genuinely illuminating is assumed whenever they are employed in biochemistry, immunology, ecology, genetics, ethology, biogeography and stratigraphy. This assumption also underwrites a major methodological procedure in biology. Comparative analyses are only illuminating if the classification of the items being compared and their relationships are assumed to be accurate reflections of mind-independent biological reality. Thus phylogentic trees taken to represent mind-independent biological reality are necessary to comparative anatomy, comparative physiology, and comparative psychology. It is worth noting in this regard that realism about species is advocated by Darwin himself in the famous thirteenth chapter of *On the Origin of Species*. "All the foregoing rules and aids and difficulties in classification are explained, if I do not greatly deceive myself, on the view that the natural system is founded on descent with modification; that the characters which naturalists consider as showing true affinity between any two or more species, are those which have been inherited from a common parent, and in so far, *all true classification is genealogical*; that community of descent is the hidden bond which naturalists have been unconsciously seeking, and not some unknown plan of creation, or the enunciation of general propositions, and the putting

7.   The standard relationship represented by a phylogenetic tree is that of an ancestral species A cleaving into two or more daughter species B and C.

8.   And as seen in the argument from diversity, the standard interpretation of this process assumes that after cleavage species A no longer exists, and species B and C have come into existence (there has been two speciation events and one extinction). Moreover, B is not C, and neither is a continuation of A.

9.   Thus in order to maintain that a trait genuinely is an adaptation the biologist must assume that distinct, natural species really do come into and pass out of existence. That is, speciation and extinction events are not illusory, nor simply a function of our naming conventions – for mind-independent adaptations cannot be explained by mind-dependent, i.e., non-natural, entities and processes. Furthermore, the biologist cannot maintain that speciation and extinction events are merely a function of a new arrangement of subatomic particles, or merely a phase change of an underlying substance, or temporal parts of an unchanging Tree of Life without abandoning the ontological irreducibility of organisms or the reality of change.

10.   It is possible to maintain that A, B and C are distinct, natural species only if the existence and identity conditions of each are distinct.

11.   But the existence and identity conditions of x specify the Aristotelian essence of x.

12.   In order to maintain that a trait is an adaptation the biologist must assume it is a feature of a species with an Aristotelian essence.

Again, the upshot of this argument is clear enough: The standard account of what it is to be an adaptation presupposes essentialism. Phylogentic trees can be genuinely illuminating only if they represent real relationships between natural groups which come into and pass out of existence. But it is only if species have distinct essences that

---

together and separating objects more or less alike". *On the Origin of Species*. In *From So Simple a Beginning. The Four Great Books of Charles Darwin*. E.O. Wilson (ed.). (New York: W.W. Norton, 2006, 717). If there is any question about how one is to read these lines, Darwin underlines his realism with the claim that "This classification is evidently not arbitrary like the grouping of the stars in constellations" (op. cit., 711).

Stephen J. Boulter

one can say in a principled fashion that one species no longer exists and that two new distinct species have arrived on the scene. Thus the standard accounts of biological diversity and organismal design both presuppose essentialism.

6. What Are These Essences, And Are They Explanatory?

It would certainly smooth the path of the arguments from diversity and organismal design if some account of these alleged biological essences were forthcoming. I have not made any suggestions as yet as to what these essences might be, or whether these essences are genuinely explanatory. Space considerations make it impossible to enter into these matters here as fully as one would like; but I can at least make a plausible suggestion on this score.

My main suggestion regarding biological essences is that they are found not in the genotype or the phenotype but in the species specific developmental programmes that map genotypes onto phenotypes. The key claims in this suggestion are that (i) only a portion of an organism's genome determines its species (not all of it); (ii) that *developmental control genes* (i.e., genes that control the expression of other genes) determine the developmental pattern of an organism; and (iii) that these developmental patterns are "lineage specific", i.e., shared by individuals of the same biological species understood as a smallest diagnosable cluster of organisms related by ancestry and descent.[25] On this suggestion two organisms belong to the same species and have the same essence if they share the same developmental programme regardless of how else they might differ. If a population of such organisms maintains the same developmental programme over several generations then no extinction or speciation event has occurred, regardless of any other changes that might have taken place.

Perhaps the most striking thing about this suggestion is that its plausibility is granted even by those who are not usually considered friends of essentialism. John Dupré, for example, has written:

It might reasonably be asked here whether these epigenetic mechanisms might not themselves serve as essential properties. And I think that if, as I speculated earlier, there are species for which these provide the best account of species coherence, we would have here perhaps the best candidates in biology for real essences.[26]

---

[25] See Stearns and Hoekstra for further discussion (op. cit. note 1, 137).
[26] Op. cit., note 9, 55.

One reason for taking species specific developmental programmes as serious candidates for biological essences is that they have great explanatory potential, an essential feature of Aristotelian essences. A developmental control gene can be seen as a selector switch that makes choices from a range of potential developmental fates. These switches are responsible for the "universal" properties of phenotypes. And these switch points allow for phenotypic alternatives that can become subject to selection pressures. Moreover, M.J. West-Eberhard has fixed upon these features of developmental programmes in the elaboration of her developmental plasticity theory of speciation. She writes:

> ... developmental plasticity in trait expression within a parent population can predispose descendent sister populations to speciation by facilitating the intraspecific evolution of contrasting specializations. The individuals expressing these specializations begin to show breeding separation...This creates two breeding populations, each one with one of the contrasting alternatives *fixed*. Phenotypic fixation ...promotes further divergence.[27]

The main lesson she draws from this line of thought is that "Phylogenetic gaps could have a developmental origin."[28] R. Raff, for one, would concur:

> Novel features arise in animal evolution as a result of modifications of developmental pattern.[29]
>
> Most of what goes on in the development of a new descendent species will utilise the same standard parts as the parent species. Novel forms will arise mostly from the modifications of existing modules in development.[30]

Now I cannot defend this thesis regarding biological essences here. It must suffice to make the suggestion, and draw attention to the attractions of the view. Of course there are outstanding questions that need to be addressed. Will this approach work for all organisms? Are developmental programmes as invariant as this proposal suggests? These are empirical questions best left to biologists. But we can say at least two things here. Even if this particular suggestion does not

[27] *Developmental Plasticity and Evolution* (USA: Oxford University Press, 2003, 528).
[28] Op. cit., note 27, 24.
[29] *The Shape of Life: Genes, Development and the Evolution of Animal Form* (Chicago: University of Chicago Press, 1996, 31).
[30] Op. cit., note 29, 360.

hold up under scrutiny, something else will have to be found to play the role of essences if evolutionary biology is to meet its self-imposed explanatory objectives. Second, while its confirmation lies ultimately in the hands of biologists, it is to be noted that the claim that species specific developmental programmes are biological essences does not fall to any of the original incompatibilist objections rehearsed at the outset of our discussion, and this serves as a kind of corroboration. I conclude, then, with a brief review of those original incompatibilist arguments with this thesis in mind.

7. Replies to Incompatibilist Arguments

Some of the replies to the incompatibilist arguments will be clear enough from the foregoing discussion. For example, it has already been pointed out that there is nothing in Aristotelian essentialism that implies species fixism, i.e., that species cannot evolve. In fact essentialism is required to allow for genuine change in the living world. Similarly, we can reject the second objection on the grounds that an organism's species specific developmental programme is that in virtue of which it belongs to a particular species, happy that this allows for the full range of phenotypic variability found in real populations. Until this suggestion is defeated on empirical grounds there is, contra this objection, an empirically plausible candidate for the role of biological essences.

The third objection is curious in that it appears to undercut evolutionary biology itself. For if offspring are always placed in the same species as the parent regardless of genotypic, phenotypic or developmental differences, as the argument alleges, then speciation events would be impossible. This is an argument against the receive view of evolutionary biology, not essentialism.

As to the fourth objection, which granted essences house room within biology but denied them explanatory power, perhaps enough has already been said. One of the main attractions of the thesis that species specific developmental programmes are biological essences is precisely their explanatory power, so the objection is simply false.

To the fifth objection – Sober's argument that the properties of individuals can be ignored in population thinking, so the essential properties of individuals (if they existed) are not explanatory – it can be countered that the statistical properties of populations are ontologically dependent upon the properties of the individuals that make up the population. So at some explanatory stage the properties of individuals must be factored in. Their essential properties will be among those adverted to in the course of this level of explanation. And there is no reason to think developmental programmes will not be involved, at least indirectly, in these explanations.

Finally, what are we to make of the claim that one and the same organism can belong to several, equally real biological species, so that one and the same organism can have several, equally real essences? This last objection falls foul of the principle of non-contradiction and so is charged with incoherence. If one and the same organism had more than one essence, then it would have more than one set of existence and identity conditions. But this would allow it to possess under one set of conditions a property which it does not have under another – a violation of the principle of non-contradiction. This result can be avoided in one of two ways: Either one can deny species realism, but at the cost of compromising the explanatory goals of evolutionary biology; or one might claim that two or more organisms can occupy exactly the same space at the same time, a claim few biologists would find intelligible.[31] It is much more plausible to avoid the contradiction altogether and maintain that each and every organism has one and only one developmental programme, and so each and every organism has one and only one essence.

So I conclude that the original incompatibilist objections leave unscathed the suggestion that biological essences are species specific developmental programmes. This in turn makes the acceptance of the two presupposition arguments easier to countenance. But the crucial point upon which all else depends is the commitment to the reality of change shared by evolutionary biology and essentialism. It is this shared metaphysical commitment that binds the evolutionary theorist to the essentialist.

Oxford Brookes University
sboulter@brookes.ac.uk

[31]   Some metaphysicians are willing to allow two objects to occupy the same space simultaneously. The standard example being a lump of clay and a vase composed of the clay. When the vase breaks the vase no longer exists but the clay remains, which means the vase was not the clay, and the clay was not the vase. One way to understand this is to maintain that the clay and the vase are two distinct objects which overlapped at one stage of their respective careers. But no one to my knowledge believes that this model can be extended to embrace the overlapping of two or more distinct organisms.

The Anthropological Difference: What Can Philosophers Do To Identify the Differences Between Human and Non-human Animals?

HANS-JOHANN GLOCK

This paper considers the question of whether there is a human-animal or 'anthropological difference'. It starts with a historical intro-duction to the project of philosophical anthropology (sct. 1). Section 2 explains the philosophical quest for an anthropological difference. Sections 3–4 are methodological and explain how philosophical anthropology should be pursued in my view, namely as impure conceptual analysis. The following two sections discuss two fundamental objections to the very idea of such a difference, biological continuity (sct. 5) and Darwinist anti-essentialism (sct. 6). Section 7 discusses various possible responses to this second objection – potentiality, normality and typicality. It ends by abandoning the idea of an essence possessed by all and only individual human beings. Instead, anthropological differences are to be sought in the realm of capacities underlying specifically human societies (forms of com-munication and action). The final section argues that if there is such a thing as the anthropological difference, it is connected to language. But it favours a more modest line according to which there are several anthropological differences which jointly underlie the gap separating us from our animal cousins.

1. Philosophical Anthropology

Hume's ambition was to establish a 'science of human nature'. His claims on behalf of that project were far from modest. 'There is no question of importance whose decision is not comprised in the science of man. ... In pretending to explain the principles of human nature we in effect propose a complete system of the sciences'.[1] Since the sixteenth century, the scientific investigation

[1]   D. Hume, *A Treatise of Human Nature*, ed. L.A. Selby-Bigge and P.H. Nidditch (Oxford: Oxford University Press, 1978), I.iv.16.

doi:10.1017/S1358246112000069

Hans-Johann Glock

of human nature had also been known under the label 'anthropology'. And Hume's great antipode Kant accorded a central role to that discipline, if not within the sciences in general then at least as regards philosophy. In his *Critique of Pure Reason* Kant famously distinguished three fundamental questions of philosophy: What can I know? What ought I to do? What may I hope for? In his *Logic* Kant less famously maintained that philosophy in a 'cosmopolitan spirit' (*Philosophie in weltbürgerlicher Absicht*), i.e. philosophy that pursues our ultimate concerns as rational creatures, can be 'summarized' (*lassen sich bringen auf*) by these three questions plus a fourth one: What is man? (*Was ist der Mensch?*). The first question is answered by metaphysics, the second by morality, the third by religion and the fourth by 'anthropology'. Nevertheless, Kant goes on to claim, even the first three questions can be regarded as belonging to anthropology, since they all 'refer to' (*sich beziehen auf*) the last question.[2]

Any such blanket statements about a particular discipline lying at the heart of philosophy, not to mention the sciences in general, are controversial, and for good reasons. Still, Kant's three initial questions do refer to the last one in at least one respect. They are phrased in the first-person singular, yet in a generic way such that 'I' can easily replaced by 'we'. Consequently they concern, respectively, the knowledge, moral obligations and spiritual prospects of *human beings*. Furthermore, assigning pride of place to anthropology is potentially illuminating in so far as many fundamental philosophical questions concern the nature of human beings and their place in the universe, either directly or indirectly. That is to say, they ultimately point to questions such as

Who are we?
What *kind* of creatures are human beings?
And what is our relation to the natural world?

In the nineteenth century, 'anthropology' won out over 'science of human nature' as a designation for the academic investigation of such questions. Following Kant, moreover, philosophy came to be clearly distinguished from the empirical sciences. It is in this context that Scheler distinguished 'philosophical' from 'theological'

---

[2] I. Kant, *Critique of Pure Reason*, trl. P. Guyer (Cambridge: Cambridge University Press, 1998), B 832–3. I. Kant, *Lectures on Logic*, trl. J.M. Young (Cambridge: Cambridge University Press, 2004), AA IX 24–5.

and 'scientific' anthropology.[3] In the sequel, the label 'philosophical anthropology' was popularized by a movement within German philosophy founded by Scheler and continued by Plessner and Gehlen. Their general aim was to interpret and synthesize scientific findings concerning human nature in a philosophical fashion. More specifically, the members of the movement were keen to explicate the concept of life in such a way that the differences between plants, animals and humans would become apparent. At the same time they attempted to resist Darwinism and its naturalistic tendencies in the name of a non-materialist biology. Finally, the movement was associated with the idea that we encountered in Hume and Kant. Human nature and its exploration is of particular importance to philosophy as a whole – the project is not just a philosophical anthropology but also an anthropological philosophy.

In the Germanophone world, the title 'philosophical anthropology' is still applied first and foremost to this particular school of thought, which continues to the present.[4] But in a wider sense philosophical anthropology is any philosophical – as opposed to religious, scientific or artistic – reflection on the nature of human beings. Over the past 10 years or so, philosophical anthropology in this wider sense has become increasingly prominent within the Anglophone world, prompting some to speak of an 'anthropological turn'. The reasons for anthropology's new place in the philosophical limelight are manifold. First, within the analytic tradition the philosophy of mind has replaced the philosophy of language as the most dynamic discipline, and the one most often accorded a foundational role.[5] And problems concerning the mind and its relation to the body have an obvious bearing on human self-understanding. Secondly, and relatedly, the actual or alleged advances of neuro-science have led many to question the idea that possession of a mind sets humans apart from the rest of creation. Thirdly, biology, especially evolutionary biology, is now widely regarded as the most exciting natural science. Indeed, Darwin's theory of evolution is sometimes even portrayed as *the*

---

[3]   M. Scheler, *Die Stellung des Menschen im Kosmos* (München: Nymphenburg, 1928).

[4]   For a historical survey see J. Fischer *Philosophische Anthropologie* (Freiburg: Alber, 2009). Ernst Cassirer's *An Essay on Man* (New Haven: Yale University Press, 1944) stands outside this tradition. It does not focus on the difference between humans and animals and does not draw on biology.

[5]   H.-J. Glock, *What is Analytic Philosophy?* (Cambridge: Cambridge University Press 2008), ch. 2.8.

discipline underlying all science, the far more credible claims of logic and physics notwithstanding. Fourthly, in biology and psychology the retreat from behaviourism and the rise of cognitive ethology has led to definite advances in the methods for observing and experimenting on animal behaviour, both in the laboratory and in the wild. These in turn ensued in astonishing discoveries concerning the intelligence and behavioural capacities not just of primates, cetaceans and other mammals (notably dogs and pigs), but also of species from other taxa, such as parrots, Caledonian crows and octopuses. Fifthly, the debate about animal minds stimulated by these discoveries has been linked to a debate about the moral status of animals that started in the 1970s and continues unabated. All these have been contributing factors to a more general crisis in our self-image as human beings. Many achievements that seemed to be the preserve of humans appear to be within the grasp of animals, computers or robots. Add to that, finally, the newly developed technologies for replacing many parts of human beings by prostheses or implants, and the question of what being human ultimately amounts to becomes more urgent than ever.

2. The Anthropological Difference as A Central Topic of Anthropology

For (philosophical) anthropology, non-human animals (henceforth simply animals) have always been a central topic, since they serve as *objects of comparison*. Traditionally the nature and place of human beings has been determined in relation to the divine looking up and to animals looking down. Most of our contemporaries still purport to know not just that there is a God, but also what HE is like (without their convictions regarding this second issue being even remotely compatible). Within academic circles, however, God has become too contested and obscure to serve as a point of orientation. Which leaves animals. 'It would be of little interest to know what animals are, if it weren't a means for knowing what we are', de Condillac opined.[6] In a similar vein Gehlen maintained: 'Any anthropology must define the essential difference between humans and animals'.[7]

---

[6]   E. de Condillac (1755), *Traité des Animaux*, (Paris: Vrin, 1987), 1 (my translation).
[7]   A. Gehlen, 'Die Resultate Schopenhauers', reprinted in V. Spierling (ed.), *Materialien zu Schopenhauer's 'Welt als Wille und Vorstellung'*, (Frankfurt a. M.: Suhrkamp, 1984), 323.

Indeed, this interest in animals constitutes one of the two central problems of anthropology down the ages. On the one hand, there is the question of *anthropological constants* or *universals*: Are there features shared by all ('normal') human beings, irrespective of their social and historical context. On the other hand, there is the question of the *human-animal* or *anthropological difference*:[8] Are there features that are *unique* to humans, i.e. set them apart from all animals?

However, there is nothing special about being special.[9] *Every* biological species differs from *all* the others, i.e. has unique features. There is an empirical reason for this: speciation proceeds by specialization, the exploration of a unique 'ecological niche'. Depending on one's understanding of species, there may also be a conceptual reason. Perhaps we should count two groups of animals as belonging to the same species if they share all features other than origin (more on this anon).

Thus only certain bacteria perform chemo-synthesis; only bats can navigate through ultra-sound. These examples of uniqueness concern higher taxa, yet instances of species uniqueness can be provided by going into finer detail or combining features. Thus beavers are the only species that can digest wood and (being mammals) suckle their young. Indeed, it is not beyond the wit of man to specify unique features of human beings. 'Man is the only creature that can partake of a hot meal in flight', as the German humorist Loriot observed. In their quest for the anthropological difference, however, philosophical anthropologists are looking for a difference with a difference. They are searching for features of homo sapiens that (a) set us apart 'categorially' or 'essentially' from all other animals; (b) are fundamental, in that (all) other relevant differences derive from them; (c) are important, notably to our self-image, for instance because they assure us of a higher spiritual or moral status than animals.

Because of (a), the search for the anthropological difference is *ab initio* linked to the search for anthropological constants. In conjunction, the two quests amount to a search for a *definition* of what it is to

[8]   The expression *anthropologische Differenz* hails from the German tradition of philosophical anthropology. There it continues to be used in a variety of ways, many of them obscure and idiosyncratic. My employment of it is in line with M. Wild, *Die Anthropologische Differenz* (Berlin: deGruyter, 2006), an exemplary historical investigation of the debate about animal mentality in early modern philosophy from the vantage point of contemporary ethology and philosophy of mind.

[9]   D. Radner and M. Radner, *Animal Consciousness* (Buffalo: Prometheus, 1989), 8; K. Sterelny, *Thought in a Hostile World* (Oxford: Blackwell, 2003); Wild, op.cit. note 9, 2–3.

be human, an answer to a Socratic 'What is X?' – or 'What are Xs?' - question. Such an analytic definition must specify conditions which are individually necessary and jointly sufficient for being human. Furthermore, since it is supposed to capture the nature or essence of human beings, the features specified by such a definition should not just *in fact* be possessed by all and only human beings; rather, it should be *necessary* that all and only human beings possess them. Only creatures possessing all of the features specified in the definition can be human, and any creature possessing them all is ipso facto human.

Accordingly, the anthropological difference is or would be something that could be used as a *differentia specifica* in such an analytic definition. (a) further ensures that this definition takes the form

> Human beings are the animals that Φ / are F rather than, for instance
> Human beings are the animals that Φ *more* or *most* / are F to a *higher* or *highest degree.*

Needless to say, not all definitions that take this form also satisfy the requirements for an analytic definition stating an anthropological difference. Plato, for instance, maintained that man is a featherless biped. Confronted by Diogenes of Sinope with the counterexample of a plucked chicken, he is supposed to have added 'with round nails' (as reported by Diogenes Laertius[10]). But not all human nails are round, and even if they were, having claw-like nails would certainly not disqualify an otherwise human-like creature from being human. Plato's definition also falls foul of conditions (b) and (c). Though far more serious, Loriot's characterization similarly fails at these two hurdles. Concerning (b), our capacity for heating up a meal in flight, striking though it may be, is obviously derivative of our technological capacities. The same holds for other advanced features that are obviously unique to humans. Only humans engage in organised sports, get married, construct airplanes, compose music or philosophize about the nature of their own species. But these characteristics presuppose other more basic capacities.

The history of ideas has also yielded several at least prima facie promising candidates for such more basic differences. Among the features that have, at various times, been held to constitute an anthropological difference are:

---

[10]   Diogenes Laertius, *Vitae philosophorum*, ed, H.S. Long, (Oxford: Oxford University Press, 1964), 6.40

thought (rationality, reason); concepts and abstraction; language; knowledge of necessary truths; consciousness or sentience; self-consciousness (knowledge of one's own mental states); knowledge of the mental states of others; an immortal soul; a moral sense; a sense of humour; a sense of history; anticipation of the future, including one's own death; a sense of beauty; tool use or tool manufacture; technology; free will; a capacity to act (for reasons); a capacity to follow rules (normativity); personhood or personality; a capacity for culture or cultural progression.

Trying to test the members of this list against conditions (a) – (c) would be a Gargantuan task. Fortunately, some headway can be made by noting the following point. Though decidedly diverse, these proposals share one highly general assumption. If there is such a thing as the anthropological difference, it must concern our *mental* properties and capacities. Thus Hacker states: 'The abilities distinctive of human beings are abilities of intellect and will'.[11] This is not to deny that some of our anatomical endowments may be important not just biologically but also philosophically—notably upright posture and the possession of a dexterous hand with opposable fingers[12]. But such physical peculiarities can only have contributed to our special status through being connected to our mental powers and/or their development.

Beyond this point of almost universal consensus, however, there is an ongoing controversy on every aspect of the idea of an anthropological difference. All of the proposals listed above have been contested, on both conceptual and empirical grounds. To take just one prominent case: traditionally, humans were regarded as *homo faber*, the only species capable of using or at any rate of manufacturing tools. Yet in 1961 Jane Goodall observed how a chimpanzee broke off the branch of bush, modified it and then used it to fish for termites in a mound. When she reported this to her colleague, the palaeontologist Louis Leakey, the latter famously remarked: 'Now we must redefine tool, redefine Man, or accept chimpanzees as humans'.[13] All three

---

[11] P.M.S. Hacker, *Human Nature: the Categorical Framework* (Oxford: Blackwell, 2007), 2.
[12] R. Tallis, *The Hand: a Philosophical Inquiry into Human Being* (Edinburgh: Edinburgh University Press 2003). Emil Zatopek's famous: 'Fish swim, birds fly, humans run' is a variation on the theme of upright posture.
[13] See D. Peterson, *Jane Goodall—the Woman who Redefined Man* (New York: Houghton Mifflin, 2006), 212.

options have been pursued, but only the second one is remotely palatable.[14]

Indeed, the very suggestion that there might be such a thing as the, or an, anthropological difference has attracted critical comments in recent years. More specifically, the question has been raised whether the idea of such a difference is compatible with the biological continuity between animals and humans, and whether it remains wedded to a scientifically outdated essentialism. Before considering these two fundamental worries in the final sections, however, I shall outline my methodological approach to anthropology in general and the anthropological difference in particular.

3. Philosophical Anthropology and Conceptual Analysis

My conception of philosophical anthropology is neither tied to the specific Germanophone tradition, nor as wide as the idea of a philosophical reflection on human nature. Instead, I pursue a third option. At a first approximation, that option is summarized by Peter Hacker, who characterizes philosophical anthropology as 'the investigation of the concepts and forms of explanation characteristic of the study of man'.[15] Nonetheless my own preferred characterization is slightly different. *Philosophical* anthropology investigates the specifically conceptual and methodological issues thrown up by our non-philosophical (*scientific* and *non*-scientific) discourse about the nature of human beings. I agree with Hacker that it should be part of philosophical anthropology to elucidate what types of *explanation* can afford what kind of insight into human beings and their behaviour. It is worth adding, however, that the concepts and explanations concerned are not just those of 'the study of man', or even of humans. They are not confined to the scientific or more loosely academic investigation of human beings. Instead, they pervade other forms of discourse, such as morality and law, and of course, first and foremost, our everyday parlance.

Henceforth I shall speak of 'anthropological concepts', keeping in mind that these include non-scientific concepts. Another point to keep in mind is that anthropological concepts in my sense are not confined to those which apply to all or only to human beings, their

---

[14]   Technology is a different matter, since it involves the production of tools for the purpose of repeated use, and in the context of collaborative social practices.
[15]   P.M.S. Hacker, op. cit. note 11, 4.

activities and productions. They do not need to signify an anthropological constant or difference (otherwise perspiration and soap, respectively, would qualify). They only need to be relevant to the philosophical discussion of the nature of human beings. Finally, such concepts may also fall under other philosophically relevant headings. Altruism, for instance, is relevant both to philosophical anthropology and to moral philosophy.

My major point of agreement with Hacker is this. The specifically philosophical as task concerning anthropology does *not* consist in collecting new data about human beings or in devising empirical theories. It does not even consist predominantly in synthesizing the empirical findings at a particularly abstract level. Instead it consists in clarifying *what it is* to satisfy various anthropologically relevant concepts and *under what conditions* such concepts can be ascribed.

In this respect, conceptual analysis follows the traditional philosophical search for analytic definitions. By contrast to that tradition, however, many variants of twentieth-century conceptual analysis do not seek *de re* definitions capturing the nature or essence of *F*s, something independent of the way we think and speak. Instead they are content with *de dicto* definitions, definitions which capture the meaning(s) of '*F*', something we have given to the expression by using it in a certain way. Finally, in its enlightened Wittgensteinian form, conceptual analysis leaves open what concepts, if any, actually *allow of* an analytic definition.

By this token, philosophical anthropology as conceptual analysis considers *what counts* as a human being, either in ordinary language, or in a specialized mode of discourse like ethology, or even in the context of a specific philosophical or scientific problem, theory or argument. More generally, like its traditional precursors philosophical anthropology as conceptual analysis pays attention not just to actual but also to possible instances of anthropological concepts. This is particularly important when it comes to considering what, if anything, the nature or essence of human beings consists in. For such an essence would have to be possessed not just by all and only those creatures that are human, but by all and only those creatures we would be prepared to *count* as human—a tall order, as we shall see.

Ignoring or distorting the distinctly conceptual dimension of anthropological investigations can have deleterious consequences. As we have seen, one of the central anthropological questions is whether humans are unique by dint of their special mental powers. The answer depends *not just* on empirical findings (whether observations in the field or experiments in the laboratory, whether behavioural or neurological), *but also* on how one explains and employs

Hans-Johann Glock

heavily contested *concepts* like that of a mind, of thought, of behaviour, etc. Now, because of our requirements as social primates, our mental concepts capture neither genetic nor neurophysiological differences, but differences in the kinds of *behavioural* and *perceptual* capacities we human beings are interested in. As a result, the criterion for the possession of mental powers by a species is not the DNA or even the brain of its members. These only come into play when one proceeds to explaining the ultimate or proximate causes of *why* these specimen possess the mental powers they do. They do not determine *whether* the animals possess such powers in the first place.

Nevertheless, the connection between the mind and behavioural capacities is denied by many contemporary philosophers. According to Searle, for instance, 'behaviour is simply irrelevant' to the attribution of thoughts, because 'my car radio exhibits much more intelligent verbal behaviour, not only than any animal but even than any human that I know'.[16] If one were to trust this passage, one would not envy Searle his company. The production of noise by a radio hardly even qualifies as behaviour. But if it does, it is exceedingly stupid. The radio fails the Turing test miserably. Even to its non-linguistic environment, moreover, it cannot react in an intelligent, i.e. responsive and flexible manner. This is why during a traffic jam, in the midst of a chorus of honking, it is capable of uttering things like 'Right now everything is serene and quiet here'. It is not the radio that behaves intelligently, but at best the person whose utterances it transmits; and even that very much depends on the station the radio is tuned to.

The operations of complex computers and robots appear far more intelligent. According to Searle, however, even they are incapable of consciousness or thought. In his opinion, the essential prerequisite for both is the presence of neurophysiological phenomena rather than the capacity for complex and flexible behaviour:

> Suppose we had a science of the brain which enabled us to establish conclusively the causal bases of consciousness in humans. Suppose we discovered that certain electrochemical sequences [XYZ] were causally necessary and sufficient for consciousness in humans…Now if we found XYZ present in snails but absent in termites, that would seem very strong empirical evidence that snails had consciousness and termites did not.[17]

[16] J. Searle, 'Animal Minds', *Midwest Studies in Philosophy* **XIX** (1994), 216.

[17] Op. cit., note 16, 215–216.

But one can establish that XYZ is the causal base of consciousness *only if* the phenomenon of consciousness has been *identified* on independent grounds. These grounds are the conditions for the applicability of the concept of consciousness. And these conditions are not merely a matter of epistemology – of how we come to know whether a creature is conscious. They are a matter of semantics – of what it is for a creature to be conscious. More generally, the conditions for the application of our established mental concepts determine at least the initial topics of any empirical investigation into the causal preconditions of mental phenomena. Searle dismisses as irrelevant the criteria for consciousness and thought employed not just by lay-people but also by cognitive ethologists. According to him it is part of the meaning of mental terms that they apply only to creatures with a certain neural outfit. This is at odds with the established understanding of these terms, on which Searle himself tacitly relies in identifying mental phenomena. It also has the unpalatable consequence that, contrary to Searle's avowed stance, extreme scepticism about animal minds is legitimate, since even the most knowledgeable among us are ignorant about the precise causal base of consciousness and about the extent to which it is common to humans and animals.

4. Impure Conceptual Analysis

As the last section shows, in anthropology conceptual and factual questions are intertwined. We must pay heed to the *conditions for the applicability* of mental terms. At the same time, however, the question to which creatures these terms *actually apply* obviously depends on facts about these creatures. This leads me to a first caveat concerning the idea that philosophical anthropology is the conceptual analysis of anthropological concepts. On the one hand, matters of meaning antecede matters of fact: it makes sense to investigate a phenomenon X only if it is clear what counts as X. On the other hand, we must avoid what I call 'Socratism', the mistake of thinking that one cannot establish empirical facts about X unless one already has an analytic definition of what 'X' is in Plato's *Meno* (80a – e), Socrates devises the following paradox. It is impossible to enquire into what X is since one cannot look for or recognize the correct answer, without already knowing it from the start. The underlying argument runs roughly as follows:

P_1 To recognize the correct definition of X we already have to know what X is

P_2 The definition of X tells us what X is

Hans-Johann Glock

C_1 We would already need the correct definition in order to recognize it

C_2 The search for a correct definition is pointless.

P_1 is mistaken, at least in conjunction with P_2, which identifies knowing what X is with knowing a definition of X. As Kant pointed out, definition marks at most the end-point of philosophical inquiry, not its beginning. And as Wittgenstein pointed out, to look for and recognize the correct definition of X, all one needs is a pre-theoretical understanding of 'X', something we normally learn within language-acquisition, by coming to master the use of 'X'.

As we have seen, empirical theories about mental properties, *presuppose* at least a certain *preconception* of what counts as a mental property. But this does not mean that one needs a cast-iron precise definition of these properties in advance of empirical theory-building, contrary to Socratism. Our concepts are tools which we fashion for our purposes, in science the purpose of describing, explaining and predicting phenomena. In scientific theory-building, definitions are to be read from *right to left*: we introduce labels for observed or postulated phenomena. What is correct is that such theory-building must be *accompanied* by a reflection on the possibly provisional understanding of the concepts that informs specific theories, experiments or lines of research. Without such reflection, the theories may simply miss their purported topic.

There is another respect in which the idea of philosophical anthropology as conceptual analysis requires modification. *Pace* Quine, the distinction between conceptual (a priori) and factual (empirical) questions and statements is both legitimate and important (see Glock 2003: ch. 3). Yet it may not be exhaustive. There is a sphere of *methodological* considerations that straddles or sits uneasily between the two.[18]

Among those sympathetic to a distinction between conceptual and factual issues and hence to the idea of philosophical anthropology as conceptual analysis some may be tempted to think that verification affords a direct link between meaning (concepts) and methodology. This temptation should be resisted, however. *Under what conditions* a term is applicable to something is part of its meaning. But *how* the (non-) application of a term is to be verified/falsified ('the method of verification') is not necessarily part of its meaning. For

---

[18]   Another possible addition to the dichotomy is the common sense certainties or hinge propositions highlighted by Moore and Wittgenstein or Collingwood's 'absolute presuppositions'.

it may depend on *factual* considerations of either a specific or theoretical kind.

Even if there is a link between meaning and verification, not all aspects of the method for verifying a proposition of its verification are part of its meaning, but only those which are linked to the way the relevant concepts are explained. Thus it is definitely wrong to suggest, for instance, that the fact that we can learn about who won the boat race by reading a newspaper goes some way to explaining the meaning of 'boat race'. Similarly, that the length of playing fields is measured through the use of tripods is a matter of physics, while to say that measuring involves the possibility of comparing the lengths of different objects is partly constitutive of the meaning of 'length'.[19]

Turning to the comparison between humans and animals, one methodological issue concerns the respective merits of experiment and observation. Should we set more store by observations in the field or by controlled experiments? The latter allow of more reliable corroboration and of systematically alternating the parameters of the situation. The former are more significant for biological purposes, notably the purposes of evolutionary theory and ecology. These are not straightforwardly empirical matters, since they concern what kind of empirical evidence should carry what kind of weight. But nor are they straightforwardly or exclusively issues of a conceptual kind. It is not part of the meaning of 'mind' or 'behaviour', for instance, that behaviour observed under natural conditions should reveal more about a subject's mental capacities than behaviour elicited as part of an experiment. Nonetheless the contrast carries a potential for anthropological puzzles and quandaries with a philosophical dimension. For one thing, while atypical behaviour by a specimen – e.g. symbol use by enculturated bonobos under experimental conditions – clearly evinces mental capacities, it is far from clear what the presence of these capacities shows about the nature of the species, in our case the proximity between bonobos and us (see sct. 6). For another, there is the following methodological dilemma. On the one hand, the more controlled and predictable animal behaviour, the more artificial and hence less significant are the findings. Ape-language studies are ecologically unsound, in so far as the symbolic systems acquired by enculturated apes are remote from their systems of communication in the wild. At the same time, rigorous procedures (e.g. duplication or 'double-blind

---

[19]   See H.J. Glock, *A Wittgenstein Dictionary* (Oxford: Blackwell, 1996), 382–5.

strategies') may simply undermine the subject's willingness to cooperate. On the other hand, the more unrestricted and spontaneous animal behaviour, the less rigorous the procedure and the more it relies on 'mere anecdotes'.[20]

In both ethology and developmental psychology, the use of anecdotes is hotly contested. This issue is obviously methodological, yet without being predominantly philosophical. Even if all philosophical problems concerning knowledge by testimony were resolved, there would remain empirical or theoretical questions concerning the reliability of field observation and episodic memory and the significance of individual cases to specific theoretical claims.

Another hot potato, which I shall touch only briefly in this context, is a well-known methodological principle of comparative psychology. According to 'Morgan's canon', we should only attribute higher mental capacities to a creature if this is the *only* explanation of its behavioural capacities.[21] In my view, Morgan's canon is heavy artillery indeed, and I propose to replace it by something more modest. Call it *Glock's canon* if you please, even though it's in fact more like a handgun. We should only attribute higher mental capacities to a creature if this is the *best* or most plausible explanation of its behavioural capacities. This weaker principle would put paid to the malpractice of explaining intelligent animal behaviour by reference to far-fetched feats of associative learning, for the sole purpose of avoiding reference to genuine planning or reasoning.[22] Irrespective of whether I am right on this, however, the controversies surrounding Morgan's canon once more defy a neat classification into the conceptual and the factual. Should something like parsimony ('Occam's razor') be the only or overriding methodological consideration? Or should other desiderata of scientific theories – explanatory power, simplicity, conservatism, modesty, precision, facility of computation, avoidance of perplexities – be given equal weight? One would suppose that the parameters of theory-building should depend at least partly on what works in what scientific field. And by what standards are associationist explanations more parsimonious than mentalistic ones in the first place? If by the standards of associationism, the reasoning is circular.

---

[20] See J. Dupré, *Humans and Other Animals*. Oxford: Oxford University Press, 2002), ch. 1.

[21] C. L. Morgan, *An Introduction to Comparative Psychology* (London: Walter Scott, 1894, 53–55).

[22] H.-J. Glock, 'Can Animals act for Reasons?', *Inquiry*, **52** (2009), 232–254.

Such issues are methodological and at least partly philosophical; yet in what sense are they conceptual?[23]

Finally, there are important *heuristic* connections between conceptual and factual investigations. One of them might be summed up by the scholastic principle *ab esse ad posse*. Even if for purely conceptual (philosophical) purposes it matters only what could be the case, we are well advised to look at actual cases. For these can alert us to possibilities we have ignored. Philosophical reasoning may be a priori in the sense of requiring an explication of our conceptual apparatus rather than the collection of novel facts; but it is not for that reason infallible.

5. The Anthropological Difference and Biological Continuity

In summary, I conceive of philosophical anthropology as a kind of impure conceptual analysis. Philosophical anthropology thus understood – namely as conceptual-cum-methodological reflection – complements and interacts with empirical or scientific anthropology, while nevertheless remaining *distinct* as concerns its particular contribution. In the remainder, I want to scrutinize the idea of an anthropological difference from this perspective. More specifically, I shall explore conceptual and methodological aspects of qualms about the very idea of an anthropological difference that are inspired by science.

Current debates about the mind are increasingly dominated by evolutionary theory and by naturalism. In its metaphilosophical capacity, naturalism is the idea that philosophy has no distinctive contribution to make over and above that of the special sciences. In this climate it appears that proponents of an anthropological difference are misguided 'human exceptionalists' who ignore the 'continuity across species' that has been discovered by evolutionary biology

[23] For discussions of various issues raised by Morgan's canon and Occam's razor in biology see: H. Kummer, V. Dasser and P. Hoyningen-Huene, 'Exploring Primate Social Cognition: Some Critical Remarks', *Behaviour* **112** (1990), 84–98; A. Baker, 'Occam's razor in science: a case study from biogeography', *Biology and Philosophy* **22** (2007), 193–215; S, Fitzpatrick, 'The Primate Mindreading Controversy' and E. Sober 'Parsimony and Models of Animal Minds' in: R.W. Lurz (ed.) *The Philosophy of Animal Minds* (Cambridge: Cambridge University Press 2009); H. Wilder, 'Interpretative Cognitive Ethology', in M. Bekoff and D. Jamieson (eds.), *Readings in Animal Psychology* (Cambridge/Mass.: MIT Press, 1996), 29–46.

and neurophysiology.[24] In this vein, various biological principles of continuity have been invoked to show that the differences between humans and animals can only be a matter of degree.[25] From this perspective, any attempt to draw qualitative distinctions between humans and animals appears deplorably anthropocentric and out of touch with natural science. This blanket charge is unwarranted. There is no gainsaying the empirical fact that there is both biological (in particular, genetic and neurophysiological) similarity and evolutionary continuity between us and certain non-linguistic animals. But it does not follow that they must approximate to our mental life.

According to evolutionary theory all of life derives from one or at most a few common origins, and we share a common ancestor with all the animals around us. But the extent to which evolution is uniformly a gradual process is controversial, as the debate over the possibility of punctuated equilibria shows, a debate which pits the gradualist mainstream against saltationists like Gould and Leontwin:[26]

Even if *natura non facit saltus*, moreover, continuity along lineages of evolutionary development does not settle the question of what mental capacities the animals around us possess. To suppose otherwise amounts to what one might call 'the evolutionary fallacy'. That fallacy is based on a mistaken picture of evolution, one which regards evolutionary development as a linear hierarchy and is summed up by the slogan that humans descended from apes. In fact, however, evolution results not in such a hierarchy, but rather in a branching tree. Although it is probable that our closest evolutionary *ancestors* without language shared many of our other mental capacities, these ancestors are extinct; and there is no guarantee that the biologically closest *extant species* is mentally close to us. If all vertebrates except *homo sapiens* had been vanquished by a wayward meteorite, it would be absurd to conclude that starfish and sea cucumbers must be mentally close to us.[27]

---

[24]   D. Jamieson, 'Animal language and thought', in E. Craig (eds.), *The Routledge Encyclopedia of Philosophy* (Routledge: London, 1998).

[25]   R. Crisp, 'Evolution and Psychological Unity', in Bekoff and Jamieson, op. cit. note 23, 309–23; C. Allen and M. Bekoff, *Species of Mind* (Cambridge/Mass.: MIT Press), xi.

[26]   S. J. Gould and N. Eldredge 'Punctuated Equilibria: The Tempo and Mode of Evolution Reconsidered', *Paleobiology* **3** (1977), 115–51.

[27]   For a parallel argument concerning the possession of language see S. Pinker, *The Language Instinct* (Penguin: Middlesex, 1994), 346.

It so happens that our closest extant relatives, the chimpanzees, share ca. 98% of our DNA. However, it does not follow that they share 98% of our mental life. If we set store by this 'DNA fallacy', we would also have to conclude that worms and flies share about 75% of our mental capacities. The trouble with this kind of reasoning is straightforward: small biochemical differences in genotype – roughly, the DNA sequence–may lead to significant differences in phenotype – the observable features, including not just morphology and physiology, but also behavioural repertoire.

In fact, this already holds at the level of neurophysiology. Although the brains of chimpanzees are made of the same matter, they are significantly smaller than those of humans (on average, 400 ccm to 1400 ccm), even if body-size is taken into consideration. And in addition to the anatomical there are also neurophysiological differences.[28] In any event, however, our mental vocabulary captures *neither* genetic *nor* neurophysiological differences, but differences in the kinds of behavioural and perceptual capacities we humans are interested in (as argued in sct. 3). To that extent, our mental concepts themselves may be anthropocentric; yet it does not follow that it is anthropocentric to insist that these concepts preclude application to non-linguistic creatures.[29]

A final question, which I can only broach here, is this. Does the biological continuity between human and non-human animals imply that both should be subject to the same kind of explanation? The answer is yes, in so far as explanations of the neuro-physiological preconditions of mental capacities, their ecological function and their evolutionary origin is concerned. But biological continuity does not militate against the idea that behaviour of a particular complexity and flexibility is subject to intentional or rational explanations – roughly, explanations by reference to a subject's intentions, beliefs and desires – that do not get a foothold with respect to more primitive forms of life.[30] Nor does it militate against the idea that such

[28]   G. Roth, 'The neurobiological basis of consciousness in man and animals', *Evolution and Cognition* **5** (1999), 137–148.

G. Roth and U. Dicke, 'Evolution of the brain and intelligence', *Trends in Cognitive Science*, **9** (2005), 250–257.

[29]   D. Davidson, *Subjective, Intersubjective, Objective* (Oxford: Oxford University Press, 2001), 96.

[30]   D. Dennett, *The Intentional Stance* (Cambridge and Massachusetts: MIT Press, 1987); H.-J. Glock, 'Can animals act for Reasons?', *Inquiry*, **52** (2009), 232–254.

Hans-Johann Glock

behaviour promotes, and is in turn promoted by, an evolution of a different, namely cultural rather than biological kind.[31]

6. Anti-Essentialism and the Biological Notion of a Apecies

As it stands, the quest for the anthropological difference is the quest to specify necessary and sufficient conditions for being human, features that, by necessity, all and only human beings possess. This quest seems to presuppose that human beings share a common nature or essence. And that idea has been challenged in both philosophy – in the wake of Dewey, Wittgenstein, Popper and Quine – and in science, in the wake of Darwin.

Darwin himself subscribed to the idea of mental continuity: 'there is no fundamental difference between man and the higher mammals in their mental faculties'. Yet he also wrote: 'Of the high importance of the intellectual faculties there can be no doubt, for man mainly owes to them his predominant position in the world'.[32] This tension notwithstanding, Darwin seems to have despaired of the attempt to identify something like an anthropological difference. He remarks that he once made a collection of attempts to pinpoint the distinguishing feature of humans and came up with over twenty: 'but they are almost worthless, as their wide difference and number prove the difficulty, if not the impossibility, of the attempt'.[33]

Some of his followers were even more vocal in their opposition. Ernst Haeckel coined the suitably ugly label 'anthropism' for 'the powerful and widespread syndrome of erroneous ideas which places the human organism in opposition to the whole rest of nature, and conceives of it as the premeditated goal of organic creation and as a god-like creature fundamentally distinct from the latter'. And he condemned the 'anthropistic theory of consciousness' which treats thought as a prerogative of human beings.[34]

---

[31]   M. Tomasello, *The Cultural Origins of Human Cognition* (Cambridge and Massachusetts: Harvard University Press, 1999).

[32]   Cp. Ch. Darwin *The Descent of Man*, in *So Simple a Beginning: the four Great Books of Charles Darwin*, ed. with an Introduction by Edward Wilson (New York: Norton, 2006), ch.III/798 and ch.V/868.

[33]   *The Descent of Man, and Selection in Relation to Sex*, 2nd Edn. (New York: Burt, 1874), 89.

[34]   E. Haeckel, *Die Welträtsel* (Bonn: Strauss, 1900), 14–15, 199). In a similar vein, W. Sombart called the idea that man is an entirely special creature

The Anthropological Difference

Before discussing the anti-essentialist objection, it is worth re-membering what is at issue in the debate. Both proponents and opponents of the idea of a human nature tend to agree on one point.[35] The pertinent notion of a *human being* is not a rich notion like that of a *person* (which has variously been construed as a meta-physical, moral, legal or forensic one); it is rather a *biological* notion – the notion of *homo sapiens*. This creates an obvious difficulty for pinpointing an anthropological difference. According to the tra-ditional conception of the essence of a kind of thing K is a set of fea-tures that eternally or *timelessly* characterize all and only things that are K and without which something could not be K. However, the Darwinist challenge goes, in so far as species are things that undergo *evolutionary change*, they cannot possess such essences.[36]

An essentialist might respond that species may be capable of chan-ging, yet only in their *accidental* (or contingent) not in their essential (or necessary) features. In that case, however, it would be impossible for one species to emerge from another, e.g. homo sapiens from homo erectus. For according to essentialism species differ precisely in at least one essential feature, their *differentia specifica*. Furthermore, es-sentialism maintains that all individuals can be unequivocally sorted into kinds – species in the biological case – namely according to their essential features. But the only determinate and clear-cut classifi-cations of individual organisms into species that are compatible with contemporary genetics and evolutionary theory are of a genea-logical or diachronic kind. They concern the different branches of the evolutionary tree.

In what follows I shall assume that 'species' signifies an interesting biological category in the first place.[37] If that assumption is false,

---

'hominism' and opposed it to 'animalism', for which humans are merely part of nature (*Vom Menschen*, (Berlin: Duncker & Humboldt, 1938), 89.

[35]   Hacker, op. cit., note 11, 4; D.L. Hull, 'On Human Nature', in: D.L. Hull & M. Ruse (eds.) *The Philosophy of Biology* (Oxford: Oxford University Press, 1998), 383–397.

[36]   Thus Hull asserts: 'if the human species has evolved the way that other species have evolved, then it cannot have a traditional "nature"' ('Historical entities and historical narratives', in C. Hookway (ed.), *Machines and Evolution: Philosophical Studies* (Cambridge: Cambridge University Press, 1984), 36). And R. de Sousa insists: 'the Darwinian revo-lution has made it impossible to take seriously ... the idea of a human essence' ('Learning to be Natural', in N. Roughley (ed.), *Being Human* (New York: de Gruyter, 2000), 292).

[37]   For a defence see J. Dupré, op. cit. note 20, ch. 4.

biological essentialism is in any event a non-starter. For reasons of space, I must also leave aside the 'ontological' question of whether species are sets, individuals or relations. Instead I shall concentrate on some currently popular definitions of species in biology that have direct implications for the tenability of essentialism.

The best-known definition of a species in contemporary biology has been the 'biological species concept' developed by Mayr.[38] According to this proposal, a species is a group of organisms with actual or potential reproductive links. The definition leaves an obvious lacuna, namely organisms that reproduce asexually. Furthermore, it has been notoriously difficult to specify what potential reproductive links amount to. And the criterion does not always coincide with the phenotypic classifications (the 'phenetic species concept') used in everyday life and much of biology. A related proposal is the 'cohesive species concept', which treats a species as the most inclusive group of organisms having the potential for genetic and/or geographic interchangeability. This suggestion has difficulties accommodating the genetic exchanges between species. And it no more allows for the definite assignment of each individual organism to a species than the biological species concept. This leaves so-called phylogenetic or cladistic species concepts, which treat *species* as a genealogical notion. A biological taxon is a temporally and geographically extended community of common decent; and a species is a separate branch of the evolutionary tree – a lineage of populations between two phylogenetic branch points (or 'speciation events', though that makes the definition sound more circular than it need be). Even this proposal faces objections.[39] But it holds a greater promise of determinately assigning individuals to biological taxa than any of its rivals. At the same time, given the fact of evolutionary development, it in no way guarantees that members of the same species are very similar in either phenotype or genotype.

In view of this situation, the most auspicious response for proponents of an anthropological difference is to concede the anti-essentialist point and to retreat from 'speciesism'. We should leave membership of a biological species to the – admittedly tender – mercies of genealogical (cladistic) taxonomies. Simplifying grossly, the biological definition of a human being should then run somewhat as follows:

---

[38]   E. Mayr, *Populations, Species and Evolution* (Cambridge, and Massachusetts: Belknap Press, 1970).
[39]   Dupré, op. cit., note 20, chs. 3–4.

anorganism *o* belongs to homo sapiens if and only if *o* is part of the same separate lineage of the evolutionary tree (a distinct chunk of the genealogical nexus) as we are.

Precisely where the separate human branch starts will be a matter for palaeontology to discover. Given human evolution, moreover synchronic and synchronic taxonomies, will *inevitably vary*. By itself, however, this does not rule out the idea of an anthropological difference, since that idea does or should concern *the present* first and foremost. The differences between us and our immediate ancestors are bound to be gradual. And the future course of evolution is at best a matter of tenuous speculation. What matters to *our self-understanding* first and foremost (not to mention our moral obligations) is the comparison between *us* and the animals *around us*. Accordingly, the task consists in establishing whether there are characteristic features that set extant humans apart from extant animals.

7. Responses to Anti-Essentialism: From Normality to Sociality

Even in that restricted capacity the anthropological difference faces plenty of obstacles. But at least we can confine ourselves to properties of individual organisms that are *synchronic* (non-genealogical). Standardly, two kinds of diachronic biological properties are distinguished, namely genotype and phenotype.[40]

Trying to locate the anthropological difference in the genotype faces the following dilemma. On the one hand, there is genetic variation in the human genome (although that variation is less pronounced than among chimpanzees, for instance). On the other hand, there is close genetic proximity between homo sapiens and the great apes.

[40] More recently, additional dimensions have been suggested. Thus E. Jablonka and M. Lamb (*Evolution in Four Dimensions*, (Cambridge/Mass.: MIT Press, 2005)) distinguish four dimensions of evolution: genetics, epigenetics, which includes all characteristics of cells and organisms that are heritable without being written into the genome, behaviour (social learning) and symbolic inheritance systems, including language. But our comprehension of epigenetics is still in its infancy; in any event, it appears improbable that there is a particular epigenetic system that characterizes all and only human beings. And the other two mechanisms of transmission and variation do not apply at the level of individual organisms on which we are currently focusing. The social dimension will be discussed in the next section.

Hans-Johann Glock

As mentioned above, small genetic differences may make for striking phenotypic differences. Nonetheless, the task of specifying a phenotypically anthropological difference proves to be far more vexing than one might initially suppose. One problem is familiar from debates in applied ethics, yet it has not received adequate attention in philosophical anthropology. There are *marginal cases*, members of our species which lack the allegedly unique features of human beings. This holds irrespective of whether these features be reproductive (ability to have offspring with other humans), morphological (possession of opposable thumbs) or mental (rationality, language); and it holds irrespective of whether the privations at issue are due to genetic, environmental or epigenetic factors.

An essentialist response to this difficulty is to invoke *potentiality*. Marginal cases possess the relevant features potentially, the story goes. Unfortunately, in severe cases that can mean no more than a counterfactual conditional of the following kind:

> had the individual had a different genetic make-up and been exposed to appropriate environmental conditions, it would have acquired the feature.

And in that emaciated sense members of other species posses the features as well. Indeed, in the present day and age this is no longer just a matter of what is *conceptually* conceivable. The developments of genetic engineering may turn the creation of an ultra-intelligent *Über-affe* into a physical possibility, something that may remain technologically unfeasible yet within the realm of decent science fiction.

A second equally well-known response to marginal cases is to invoke normality. The distinguishing feature is supposed to be possessed by all *normal* human beings, those who have followed a normal developmental pathway. The obvious difficulty is to spell out what *normal* means here. In discharging this obligation, one must avoid two pitfalls. One is myopia, namely to mistake merely local commonalities for anthropological constants. Thus Hull has complained that proponents of human nature tend to generalise 'a developmental pathway with which the speaker is familiar in recent, locally prevalent environments'.[41] As far as genetics is concerned, there is not one determinate developmental pathway connected with each species. Instead, there are only *reaction norms*, ranges of different developmental responses of a specified genotype to a

---

[41]   D.L. Hull, 'On Human Nature', in: D.L. Hull & M. Ruse (ed.) *The Philosophy of Biology* (Oxford: Oxford University Press, 1998), 591.

range of environments. Not just one lifecycle is possible, given the causal powers of the human genome. Indeed, in the human case the spectrum of possible life cycles is particularly wide.[42] The other pitfall to be avoided is circularity. The essentialist cannot lay down criteria for normal development which are based on potentially contentious ideas about anthropological universals and differences.

To be sure, there are some properties without which it is unlikely that individual humans can proliferate under any probable circumstances. But it is far from clear that they will be shared by all and only members of homo sapiens. For we also need to consider marginal cases at the animal end. Some animals – notably great apes, cetaceans and parrots – have acquired capacities that are often touted as anthropological differences. Most importantly, enculturated apes have acquired linguistic skills which display at least some of the features traditionally claimed to set language apart from more primitive systems of communication. The signs are conventional rather than natural or iconic; the users are capable of displacement, i.e. of communicating about objects beyond the immediately perceptible environment; and they also display a rudimentary syntax, i.e. different combinations of semantic elements are used to convey different messages.[43] Admittedly, no animal seems capable of acquiring linguistic skills that include semantic productivity and syntactic recursion. Yet this is cold comfort for proponents of an anthropological difference. First, turning this into a necessary condition of languagehood is stipulative; secondly, it rules out even more members of homo sapiens; thirdly, it hardly qualifies as the kind of anthropological difference which satisfies condition (c), something which is essential to our self-image. As Goodall remarked in a recent interview when she was confronted with the absence of syntactic recursion in chimpanzees: 'Why should that matter?'.

A somewhat less demanding response abandons essentialism and sets store by typicality rather than normality. We switch from a universal essence possessed by all and only humans to typical features. Evolutionary (cladistic) lineages tend to be associated with clusters of homeostatic properties; and all members of these lineages have at least some of these properties. These may include features that do

---

[42]   See Dupré, op. cit. note 20 and 'What is Natural about Human Nature', *Deutsches Jahrbuch Philosophie*, **3** (2010).

[43]   S. Savage-Rumbaugh S. Shanker and T. Taylor, *Apes, Language and the Human Mind* (Oxford: Oxford University Press, 1998;. S. Hurley and M. Nudds (eds.), *Rational Animals* (Oxford: Oxford University Press, 2006).

not play a role in the scientific explanation of human physiology and behaviour – by contrast to genetic or neurophysiological features, yet constitute a merely 'descriptive nature'. The crucial insight is this. There is nothing problematic about the idea that in contemporary circumstances humans typically develop in certain ways and hence have typical features and capacities. It is worth noting, however, that this amounts to a serious scaling down of the idea of an anthropological difference. By contrast to normality, typicality is a purely statistical rather than evaluative or normative notion. As a result invoking typicality will not deliver an anthropological difference of a traditional kind, namely one which sets all humans apart from all animals – in line with conditions (a) and (c).

For this reason I want to explore a different approach to the idea of an anthropological difference. This fourth reaction to the anti-essentialist objection is compatible with and complements the appeal to typicality, while being at once weaker and more ambitious. It abandons the commitment to the idea that each individual human being has an essence setting it apart from all animals, while seeking something that goes beyond a statistical regularity. The magic word is 'sociality'. We should turn from the individual to communities. Humans are first and foremost social animals, and are characterized by a unique kind of social organisation. The anthropological difference is to be sought in the area of capacities present in all extant human societies, yet absent in typical non-human specimen and in non-human societies.

8. 'Anthropological Difference light' and the Role of Language

Let me dissipate a few potential misunderstandings of this proposal. It is not simply the Aristotelian idea that man is a social animal – *zoon politikon* (*Politeia* 1253a 9–11; 1332b 3–8). Many species of animals are social. And even though only human societies may be rational in the way Aristotle envisaged, he regarded rationality as an essence inherent in all and only individual human beings – though in varying degrees. My aim, by contrast, is to avoid the difficulties with this idea by looking at preconditions of specifically human sociality. This kind of approach to the human – animal divide is close to the one pursued by Michael Tomasello and his research group.[44] But

[44]   M. Tomasello, *The Cultural Origins of Human Cognition* (Cambridge and Massachusetts: Harvard University Press, 1999).

they reached that destination by a very different route, one involving empirical comparisons between great apes and human infants rather than by methodological and philosophical reflections. And my take on the anthropological difference is not committed to any of their specific claims about the peculiarities of either the onto- or the phylogenesis of human beings.

My guiding questions are: What features and capacities, if any, are present in all human societies and absent in animal societies? Which capacities are prerequisite for the functioning of human societies? To state an obvious example, no human society comprised exclusively of severe autists would be viable.

In pursuing these questions, two points need to be borne in mind. First, it is imperative to distinguish features that are absent in some societies (cultural development) from capacities that typical humans . For instance, even if one dismisses some reports as inaccurate, prejudiced or romantic, there is no reason to accept that all human societies display progressive cultural development. At the same time, typical members of these societies are capable of participating and promoting cultural development, given a suitable social context. Secondly, we can disregard capacities that animals can acquire only through *enculturation*, such as the aforementioned symbolic skills. These are not part of their typical developmental pathways in the pertinent natural environment.[45]

Once we have taken what one might call (albeit reluctantly) 'the social turn' and acknowledged these points, a lot of candidates for an anthropological difference are back in the fray. The search for the anthropological difference turns on the optimal characterisation of what distinguishes contemporary humans/human societies from contemporary animals/animal societies. It remains an open question, however, of whether there is such a thing as *the* anthropological difference.

At first sight, there are no less than three striking features prevalent in all human societies and absent in animals or animal societies:

M. Tomasello, *Origins of Human Communication* ((Cambridge and Massachusetts: MIT Press, 2008). M. Tomasello and H. Rakoczy, 'What makes Human Cognition Unique?', *Mind and Language* **18** (2003), 121–47.

[45] One caveat. We may not know enough about the various channels of natural communication between cetaceans, in particular bottlenose dolphins, in order to decide how far they approximate linguistic communication.

Hans-Johann Glock

- a special and highly complex system of communication, namely language
- a special and highly complex kind of social relationships, one which involves social institutions, and hence cooperation, norms and values, and (possibly) division of labour.
- a special kind of *plasticity*: the capacity to adapt to highly diverse circumstances and environments through tools (technology) and rational deliberation (planning), a capacity which in turn depend on our *special cognitive powers*.

Within this syndrome, language has a special status. This point has been dramatically neglected within recent contributions to philosophical and non-philosophical anthropology. Ironically enough, this includes the contributions by Tomasello, notwithstanding both his ground-breaking scrutiny of the special qualities of human interaction (joint attention, shared intentionality, cooperation) and his investigations into the origins of language.[46] To be sure, diachronically language has evolved from non-linguistic forms of interaction and communication. But from a synchronic perspective, it enables and sustains the two other distinguishing features, for both conceptual and factual reasons.

The factual reasons are highly complex and diverse, yet they have been discussed at length from various perspectives, beginning with Vygotsky. And in the present context I can do no more than summarize the conceptual reasons. As I have argued at greater length elsewhere, ascribing thoughts—so-called propositional attitudes like belief and desire—makes sense only in the case of creatures capable of manifesting these thoughts in their behaviour.[47] And only a very restricted range of thoughts can be ascribed on the basis of non-linguistic behavioural capacities. The crucial result is this. The beliefs, desires and cogitative processes that can be ascribed on that basis are not nearly complex enough to sustain the kind of cooperative and complex interaction which can be sustained through linguistic communication.

Accordingly, if I were forced to name a single anthropological difference, my money would be on language. But I remain

[46] M. Tomasello, *Origins of Human Communication* ((Cambridge and Massachusetts: MIT Press, 2008).
[47] H.-J. Glock, 'Philosophy, Thought and Language', in: J. Preston (ed.), *Thought and Language* (Cambridge: Cambridge University Press, 1997), 151–169.

H.-J. Glock, 'Animals, Thoughts and Concepts', *Synthese* **119** (2000), 35–64.

unconvinced that naming such a single difference is the most illuminating way of characterizing the differences between humans and animals. This is decidedly not to deny the qualitative nature of the gap separating us from them. One only needs to look around to detect the vast differences between our technology and chimpanzee tools, or our societies and chimpanzee communities, for instance. Yet why should these differences have to be reducible to a single fundamental one? Indeed, why should we need to insist that the underlying differences are categorical, describable in terms of our thinking vs. their perceiving, our rationality vs. their intelligence, or our communicating vs. their signalling, for instance. Insisting that we think and communicate about a lot more and in a lot more complex fashion may just be enough. For in this case, a difference in quality may arise out of a difference in quantity. That at any rate is one Hegelian and Marxist idea which may be due for a revival.[48]

Glock University of Zürich
glock@philos.uzh.ch

[48] For help of a philosophical or editorial kind I should like to thank David Dolby, Anita Horn, Constantine Sandis, and Markus Wild. This essay has also profited from comments by audiences in Toledo, Grenada, Oxford, Waldshut and Zurich. Finally I should like to record my profound gratitude to the Hanse-Wissenschaftskolleg (Delmenhorst) for supporting this work through a fellowship.

Paul Broca and the Evolutionary Genetics of Cerebral Asymmetry

TIM J. CROW

1. Darwinian Gradualism and the Mueller-Huxley Challenge

In 1873, within two years of the publication of *The Descent of Man*[1], Friedrich Max Mueller wrote:

> There is one difficulty which Mr Darwin has not sufficiently appreciated ... There is between the whole animal kingdom on the one side, and man, even in his lowest state, on the other, a barrier which no animal has ever crossed, and that barrier is – Language ... If anything has a right to the name of specific difference, it is language, as we find it in man, and in man only ... If we removed the name of specific difference from our philosophic dictionaries, I should still hold that nothing deserves the name of man except what is able to speak ... a speaking elephant or an elephantine speaker could never be called an elephant.' and (quoting Schleicher) 'If a pig were ever to say to me, "I am a pig" it would ipso facto cease to be a pig'.[2]

What is the nature of a species? Darwin sought to establish continuity, and the links between species. In his 'Recapitulation and conclusion' to *The Origin Of Species*, he wrote:

> Hereafter we shall be compelled to acknowledge that the only distinction between species and well-marked varieties is, that the latter are known, or believed, to be connected at the present day by intermediate gradations, whereas species were formerly thus connected.[3]

[1]   Darwin, C., *The Descent of Man, and Selection in Relation to Sex* (London: J Murray, 1871), facsimile of original (New Jersey: Princeton University Press, 1981).
[2]   Mueller, F.M., 'Lectures on Mr Darwin's Philosophy of Language', *Fraser's Magazine vols 7 & 8*, in *The Origin of Language*. Reprinted in (ed.) R.Harris (Bristol: Thoemmes Press, 1873), 147–233.
[3]   Darwin, C., *On The Origin of Species By Means of Natural Selection: or, The Preservation of Favoured Races in the Struggle for Life* (London: John Murray, 1859).

doi:10.1017/S1358246112000070   © The Royal Institute of Philosophy and the contributors 2012
Royal Institute of Philosophy Supplement **70** 2012

Tim J. Crow

Thus gradualness of change and the principle that there is no difference other than a quantitative one between varieties and species were fundamental. But shortly after publication of *The Origin* T.H. Huxley wrote to his mentor that he hoped that Darwin had not loaded himself 'with an un-necessary difficulty in adopting Natura non facit saltum so unreservedly'[4]. Thus was initiated a division of opinion amongst evolutionists between those, on the one hand, who follow Darwin in strict gradualism, and those, on the other, who following Huxley take a saltational view of transitions, and therefore a more discrete and categorical view of the nature of species.

But what *is* a species? One attempt at a definition is the Biological or Isolation Species Concept: a species is a 'group of actually or potentially interbreeding natural populations that are reproductively isolated from other such groups.'[5] A more specific and functional definition of a species is 'the most inclusive population of individual bi-parental organisms which share a common fertilization system'.[6] Thus, according to Paterson, a species is defined by a 'specific mate recognition system'. I will argue that this concept is crucial to the question raised by Mueller and to the doubt that Huxley expressed to Darwin.

2. Saltations Modulated by Sexual Selection

The theory of punctuated equilibria[7] followed a history of challenges to the gradualist version.[8] Goldschmidt formulated the concept of the "Hopeful Monster" the outcome of a 'macromutation', doomed to

[4]   Cited in Gould, S.J., *The Structure of Evolutionary Theory* (Cambridge MA: Belknap Press, 2002).
[5]   Mayr, E., *Animal Species And Evolution* (Cambridge MA: Harvard University Press, 1963).
[6]   Paterson, H.E.H., *The recognition concept of species*, in *Species and Speciation*, ed. E.S. Vrba, (Pretoria: Transvaal Museum Monograph, 1985), 21–29.
[7]   Eldredge, N. and S.J. Gould, *Punctuated Equilibria: An Alternative to Phyletic Gradualism*, in *Models in* (ed.) T.M. Schopf, *Palaeobiology*, (San Franciso: Freeman Cooper, 1972), 82–115.
[8]   Bateson, B., *Heredity and variation in modern lights. From Darwin and modern science)*, in *William Bateson, Naturalist. His Essays and Addresses Togehter with a Short Account of His Life* (Cambridge: Cambridge University Press, 1928), 215–232; De, Vries, H., *Die Mutationstheorie.* (Leipzig: Verlag von Veit, 1901).

134

maladaptive failure that just occasionally might succeed.[9] The case for saltation has been argued at a macro-evolutionary level by Stanley on the grounds that the amounts of change seen within species and other taxa are simply insufficient to account for the overall pattern of evolutionary change that is seen over time.[10] All such general arguments come up against the difficulty that Goldschmidt's 'hopeful monster'[11] ran into: the greater the magnitude of the saltational change the less likely it is to have survival value, and the greater the difficulty the hopeful monster will have in identifying a mate. The possibility that the monster can identify an individual with the same mutation is clearly dependent on reproduction already having taken place, and even if this be assumed the new mutation is at a severe statistical disadvantage with respect to the existing population. Thus Goldschmidt's proposal, which challenged Darwinian gradualism and appeared to conflict with the principle of natural selection, has been widely disregarded.

But here Darwin's juxtaposition of *The Descent of Man*[12] and the theory of sexual selection introduces a new possibility. If sexual selection and speciation were in some way interdependent this might solve the problem of discontinuity and elucidate the significance of mate selection. Darwin himself made no specific proposal. A role for sexual selection in modifying a primary change in a sexually dimorphic feature to establish a new species boundary has been argued in relation to Hawaiian Drosophilid species by Kaneshiro[13] and Carson.[14] Similar arguments apply in the case of the prolific speciation of cichlid fishes in the lakes of East Africa[15] and in birds.[16]

[9]   Goldschmidt, R., *The Material Basis of Evolution* (New Haven: Yale University Press, 1940; rep. 1982).

[10]   Stanley, S.M., *Macroevolution: Patterns and Processes* (Baltimore: John Hopkins, 1998).

[11]   Goldschmidt, R., op. cit.

[12]   Op cit.

[13]   Kaneshiro, K.Y., 'Sexual Isolation, Speciation and the Direction of Evolution', *Evolution*, 1980. **34**: p. 437–444.

[14]   Carson, H.L., '*Sexual Selection: Driver of Genetic Change in Hawaiian Drosophila*', *J Hered*, 1997, **88**, 343–352.

[15]   Dominey, W.J., 'Effects of Sexual Selection and Life Histories on Speciation: Species Flocks in African Cichlids and Hawaiian Drosophila', in *Evolution of Fish Species Flocks*, (eds.) A.A. Echelle and I. Kornfield, (Maine: Orino Press, 1984), 231–249.

[16]   Price, T., 'Sexual Selection and Natural Selection in Bird Speciation', *Philos Trans R Soc Lond* [Biol], 1998, **353**, 251–260.

Tim J. Crow

What constitutes a saltation? By definition it is a genetic change of sufficient magnitude or novelty to account for a species difference. Goldschmidt considered that environmentally selected changes in genes were never sufficient to account for species differences. The latter he suggested were accounted for by chromosomal rearrangements, but chromosomal theories of speciation[17] have been criticized on the grounds that such rearrangements are frequent, often without phenotypic effect, and sometimes present as polymorphisms within a population.

Here it is argued that it is not chromosomal change *per se* that plays a role in speciation but change on the sex chromosomes. Such changes may be associated with sexual dimorphisms, that themselves are necessary to the construction of a mate recognition system, and are species specific. Furthermore non-recombining regions of X–Y homology have a special status in that they can account (as in the case of lateralization in humans, see below) for quantitative differences in a characteristic between males and females. Such dimensions of variation are plausible substrates for sexual selection.

The Y chromosome in mammals (like the W in birds) has a unique role, because it is not necessary for survival. While the X is the most stable chromosome across species (Ohno's law[18]) the Y is by far the most variable; it can be seen as a test-bed of evolutionary change. One possibility is that the primary change in speciation takes place on the Y, located in a region of homology with the X allowing correlated but independent change in the two sexes. Differing ranges of variation in a single variable have the potential to explain the type of runaway sexual selection envisaged by Fisher.[19] Thus a primary and saltational change on the heterogametic chromosome creates a target for selection by the other sex to define a new mate recognition system. A role for the gene prdm9 (that is involved in speciation and species differences in recombination[20]) in stabilizing the relationship between X and Y chromosomes has been suggested.[21]

[17] White, M.J.D., *Modes of Speciation*. (San Francisco: W H Freeman, 1978); King, M., *Species Evolution: the Role of Chromosome Change* (Cambridge: Cambridge University Press, 1993).

[18] Ohno, S., *Sex Chromosomes and Sex-Linked Genes* (Berlin: Springer-Verlag, 1967).

[19] Fisher, R.A., *The Genetical Theory of Natural Selection* (Oxford: Oxford University Press, 1930).

[20] Oliver, P.L., et al., 'Accelerated Evolution of the Prdm9 Speciation Gene Across Diverse Metazoan Taxa', *PLoS Genet*, 2009, **5** (12), e1000753.

[21] Crow, T.J., 'The Missing Genes: What Happened to the Heritability of Psychiatric Disorders?', *Molecular Psychiatry* 2011, **16**, 362–364.

In man the mate recognition system (the capacity for language) is defined by the dimension of asymmetry. Broca wrote "Man is of all the animals the one whose brain is most asymmetrical. He also possesses the most acquired faculties. The faculty of language distinguishes us most clearly from the animals".[22] The concept that asymmetry of the hemispheres is the defining feature of the human brain and the cerebral correlate of language is referred to as the Broca-Annett axiom – it implies that the genetic basis of this evolutionary innovation is the speciation event for modern *Homo sapiens*. To approach such predictions it is necessary that the cerebral dominance gene or right shift factor be identified.

The Genetics of Cerebral Dominance

An important clue to the location of the gene comes from sex chromosome aneuploidies. Individuals (present in the general population with a frequency of approximately 1 in 1000) who lack an X chromosome [XO, Turner's syndrome] have non-dominant hemisphere [spatial] deficits on cognitive testing. Individuals with an extra X [XXY, Klinefelter's, and XXX syndromes] have verbal or dominant hemisphere deficits (Table 1). A possible explanation is that an asymmetry determinant is present on the X chromosome. But then the question arises of why males, who only have one X chromosome do not have spatial deficits such as are seen in Turner's syndrome. The answer must be that the copy of the gene on the X chromosome is complemented by a copy on the Y i.e. that the gene is in the X/Y homologous class.[23] A hormonal explanation will not account for the similarity of the changes in XXY individuals, who are male, and XXX individuals, who are female. The case that the gene is present also on the Y chromosome is strongly reinforced by the verbal deficits/delays that are observed in XYY individuals.[24]

The hypothesis is further strengthened by evidence that Turner's and Klinefelter's syndrome individuals have corresponding deviations

[22] Broca, P., 'Rapport sur un memoire de M. Armand de Fleury intitul,: De l'inegalit, dynamique des deux hemisphŠres cer,braux', *Bulletins de l'Academie de Medicine*, 1877, **6**, 508–539.

[23] Crow, T.J., 'Sexual Selection, Machiavellian Intelligence and the Origins of Psychosis', *Lancet*, 1993, **342**, 594–598.

[24] Geerts, M., J. Steyaert, and J.P. Fryns, 'The XYY Syndrome: A Follow-up Study on 38 Boys', *Genet Couns*, 2003, **14** (3), 267–279.

Tim J. Crow

Table 1: Neuropsychological impairments associated with sex chromosome aneuploidies

	XX	XY	XO	XXY	XXX	XYY
No of sex chromosomes	Normal female 2	Normal male 2	Turner's syndrome 1	Klinefelter's syndrome 3	3	3
Verbal ability	normal	normal	normal	delayed	delayed	delayed
Spatial ability	normal	normal	decreased	normal	normal	normal

138

in anatomical asymmetry[25] and by the demonstration of a same sex concordance effect – the tendency for handedness and sex to be associated above chance expectation – the hallmark of X-Y linkage.[26] A role for an X-Y homologous gene is consistent with the presence of a sex difference – brain growth is faster[27] and lateralization to the right is stronger in females.[28] Females have greater mean verbal fluency and acquire words earlier than males.[29] These facts are related, and they inform us of the nature of the genetic mechanism: the gene is present on both X and Y chromosomes.

3. The Xq21.3/Yp Duplication

When we come to consider where on the X and Y such a gene might be located there is an important lead. A major chromosomal rearrangement took place in the course of hominin evolution. A 3.5 Mb contiguous block of sequences from the X chromosome was duplicated onto the Y chromosome short arm. That event is now dated at 6 million years.[30] It is therefore a candidate for the transition from a great ape/hominin precursor to Australopithecus. The homologous block thus created was subsequently subject to three deletions (small segments of the chromosome, that might influence the function of affected genes, are lost), and was split by a paracentric inversion (by a recombination, presently undated, of LINE-1

[25]   Rezaie, R., et al., 'The Influence of Sex Chromosome Aneuploidy on Brain Symmetry' Am J Med Genet (Neuropsychiatric Genet), 2009, **5** (150B(1)), 74–85.

[26]   Corballis, M.C., et al., 'Location of the Handedness Gene on the X and Y Chromosomes', American Journal of Medical Genetics (Neuropsychiatric Genetics), 1996, **67**, 50–52.

[27]   Kretschmann, H.F., et al., 'Human Brain Growth in the 19th and 20th century', Journal of the Neurological Sciences, 1979, **40**, 169–188.

[28]   Crow, T.J., et al., 'Relative Hand Skill Predicts Academic Ability: Global Deficits at the Point of Hemispheric Indecision', Neuropsychologia, 1998, **36** (12), 1275–1282.

[29]   Maccoby, E.E. and C.N. Jacklin, The Psychology of Sex Differences (Oxford: Oxford University Press, 1975); McGlone, J., 'Sex Differences in Human Brain Asymmetry: A Critical Survey', Behavioural and Brain Science, 1980, **3**, 215–263.

[30]   Williams, N.A., et al., 'Accelerated Evolution of Protocadherin11X/Y: A Candidate Gene-pair for Cerebral Asymmetry and Language', Am J Med Genet (Neuropsychiatric Genet), 2006, **141B**, 623–633.

Tim J. Crow

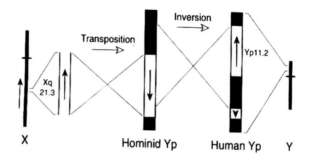

Figure 1. The Xq21.3/Yp duplication of 3.5 megabases from the Xq21.3 region of the X chromosome long arm to the Y chromosome short arm now dated at 6 million years, ie coincident with the separation of the chimpanzee, and hominin lineages. A second event (a "paracentric inversion") reversed the direction of most of the duplication, and some of the pre-existing Y short arm, but has not been dated.

element[31], a further re-arrangement of the structure of the chromosome, to give two blocks of homology in Yp11.2 (Fig. 1). Two regions on the human Y chromosome short arm thus share homology with a single region on the human X chromosome long arm (Xq21.3).[32] Genes within this region are therefore present on both the X and Y chromosomes in Homo sapiens but on the X alone in other great apes and primates.

An explanation for the retention of the duplicated block on Yp can be sought in its gene content. Three genes are known to be expressed within this region; PABPC5, a poly (A)-binding protein; TGIF2LX and Y, (homeobox-containing genes with testis-specific expression) and the ProtocadherinX (PCDH11X) and ProtocadherinY (PCDH11Y) gene-pair (all are located in the larger distal segment - Figure 2).

[31]   Schwartz, A., et al., 'Reconstructing Hominid Y Evolution: X-homologous Block, Created by X-Y Transposition, was Disrupted by Yp Inversion Through LINE-LINE Recombination', *Human Molecular Genetics*, 1998, **7**, 1–11; Skaletsky, H., et al., '*The Male-specific Regions of the Human Y Chromosome is a Mosaic of Discrete Sequence Classes*', *Nature*, 2003, **423**(6942), 825–837.

[32]   Lambson, B., et al., 'Evolution of DNA Sequence Homologies Between the Sex Chromosomes in Primate Species', *Genomics*, 1992, **14**, 1032–1040; Sargent, C.A., et al., '*The Sequence Organization of Yp/proximal Xq Homologous Regions of the Human Sex Chromosomes is Highly Conserved*', *Genomics*, 1996, **32**, 200–209.

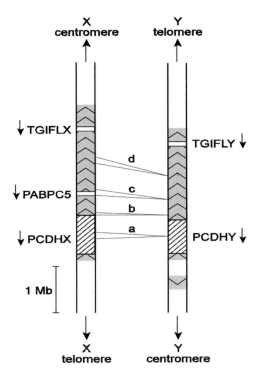

Figure 2. Alignment of the homologous regions on the X long arm and Y chromosome short arm to show four deletions (a to d) on the Y and the content of genes.

The Y gametologue of PABPC5 has been lost as a consequence of one of the deletions during hominin evolution (c in Figure 2), and TGIF2LY has been inactivated by a frameshift mutation. This leaves PCDH11X and PCDH11Y (each comprising seven extracellular cadherin motifs, a short transmembrane region and an intracellular cytoplasmic tail) that code for cell adhesion molecules of the cadherin superfamily as salient because both forms of the gene have been retained and are highly expressed both in fetal and adult brain[33] including the germinal layer of the cortex (T.H. Priddle, personal communication). The protein products of this gene pair are thus

[33]   Yoshida, K. and S. Sugano, 'Identification of a Novel Protocadherin Gene (PCDH11) on the Human XY Homology Region in Xq21.3', *Genomics*, 1999, **62**, 540–543; Blanco, P., et al., 'Conservation of PCDHX in Mammals: Expression of Human X/Y Genes Predominantly in the Brain', *Mammalian Genome*, 2000, **11**, 906–914.

Tim J. Crow

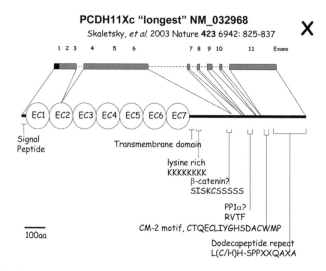

PCDH11Xc "longest" NM_032968
Skaletsky, *et al.* 2003 Nature **423** 6942: 825-837   **X**

Figure 3. Structure of the protocadherin *11X/Y* gene pair.

expected to play a role in intercellular communication perhaps acting as axonal guidance factors and influencing the connectivity of the cerebral cortex. This gene pair may thus have been subject to selective pressure throughout hominin evolution.[34]

The Y chromosome is described as consisting of strata revealing points in evolution at which blocks were added to the chromosome from the autosomes or the X [33]. For the reasons given above, it is suggested that the duplication from the Xq21.3 region of the X chromosome in hominins, and regions of XY homology in the mammalian radiation in general, have particular significance because they are relevant to sexual dimorphisms and the formation of mate recognition systems.

The structure of the ProtocadherinXY molecule (figure 3) reveals points of interest – 1) the ectodomain comprises seven Protocadherin repeats, structures that interact with the same features on the surface of another cell to generate adhesive forces, 2) a beta-catenin binding site is consistent with the report[35] that this molecule is involved in gyrification of the human cerebral cortex, 3) a protein phosphatase 1 alpha binding site indicates a role in axo-dendritic formation, 4)

---

[34] Williams, N.A., et al., op. cit.
[35] Chenn, A. and Walsh, C.A., 'Regulation of cerebral cortical size by control of cell cycle exit in neural precursors', *Science*, 2002, **297**, 365–369.

the dodecapeptide repeat motif is of unknown function, but is specific to this molecule. The protein coded by this gene is the only Protocadherin that includes both beta-catenin and protein phosphatase 1alpha binding sites. It is plausible that has a role in synaptogenesis, and as an axonal guidance factor.

The arguments for the Xq21.3/Yp duplication having critical relevance to hominin evolution can be summarized:

1) the timing at approximately 6 million years of the original duplication relative to the chimpanzee/hominin bifurcation.

2) the extent of change in the Protocadherin Y (16 coding changes), and particularly the Protocadherin X sequence (5 coding changes, including two to sulfur-containing cysteines) since the duplication. These changes appear fixed across populations.

3) the case that the genetic determinant of cerebral asymmetry is present on the X and Y chromosomes.

While the first argument relates to the Australopithecus speciation event, the third is concerned with the capacity for language in Homo sapiens. It may be implied that the presence of the homologous block on the Y-chromosome created a field for genetic innovation throughout the extent of the hominin lineage.

4. Species-specific Variation is Epigenetic

The salient issue is the nature of the transition to modern Homo sapiens, now considered to have taken place 160 thousand years ago. What was the critical change? Although not dated the paracentric version is a candidate.

In mammals genes on one X chromosome are subject to the process of X inactivation, but gene sequences that are also represented on the Y chromosome are protected from this influence. Such genes are expressed from both X and Y in males and from both Xs in females, a similar dosage thus being maintained in each sex. A possible mechanism is by epigenetic (modifications of gene expression without alteration of the DNA sequence itself; mechanisms include methylation of the DNA sequence, and modifications of the histone structures with which the DNA sequence is associated in the structure of the chromosomes) suppression of unpaired chromosomes in male meiosis.[36] Gene sequences

[36] Turner, J.M.A., 'Meiotic Sex Chromosome Inactivation', *Development*, 2007, **134**, 1823–1831.

that have been transferred from the X to the Y are in a new situation; a phase of epigenetic equilibration must be assumed. If X–Y pairing in male meiosis plays a role, the orientation of the sequence on the Y is also relevant. The paracentric inversion on the Y short arm could have been critical to the form of expression of the PCDH11XY gene pair.

A magnetic resonance imaging (MRI) investigation in monozygotic twins of handedness and asymmetry of the planum temporale[37] suggested an epigenetic influence on cerebral asymmetry, and this may account for the stochastic element incorporated in genetic theories.[38]

Epigenetic control of X and Y encoded sequences may have an even more fundamental role in embryogenesis. According to the hypothesis developed here the X and the Y chromosomes encode a pattern of genetic activity that encompasses the most recently acquired sexual dimorphism in a particular species. It seems worth considering that the primary function of "meiotic suppression of unpaired chromosomes" (MSUC) is to pass on to the embryo a genetic message that specifies those features that characterize the species. Such features are apparent in late ontogeny but may need to be imposed soon after fertilization in a sex-dependent way at a time when gene expression in general is suppressed.

The scenario has a further implication. If the mechanism of imposition of the message is by MSUC there is, particularly in Homo sapiens, scope for variability of pairing and thus variations in the epigenetic message. Such variation will be species-specific, in the case of Homo sapiens related to asymmetry and therefore to language. According to this theory species-specific variation including that relating to pathologies with a uniform incidence across populations is distinct from Mendelian variation and has its origin in meiosis and the transitions between species.[39]

---

[37]   Steinmetz, H., et al., 'Brain (A)symmetry in Monozygotic Twins', *Cerebral Cortex*, 199, **5**, 296–300.
[38]   Annett, M., *Left, Right, Hand and Brain: The Right Shift Theory* (London: Lawrence Erlbaum, 1985); McManus, I.C., 'Right-and Left-hand Skill: Failure of the Right Shift Model', *British Journal of Psychology*, 1985, **76**, 1–16.
[39]   Crow, T.J., 'The Missing Genes', op. cit.

Table 2: Summary of findings related to candidates for cerebral asymmetry.

	will account for a sex difference	expressed in germinal cell layer	cytogenetic change at 6MYA	subsequent change	selective pressure	No. of amino acid changes in hominid evolution	Radical change in protein structure
FOXP2[41]	no		no	no	+ve	2	none
PCDHXY gene pair[42]	yes	yes	Xq21.3 > Yp duplication	3 deletions on Y & a paracentric inversion (undated)	accelerated evolution	PCDHX 5 PCDHY 16	2 new cysteine residues added to PCDHX 1 closely related to 2 other changes in ectodomain 5
LM04[43]	no	yes	no	no	no	0	none
LRRTM1[44]	If imprinted	n/k	no	no	no	0	none

145

Tim J. Crow

5. Characteristic of Putative Cerebral Dominance Genes in Hominid Evolution

Other candidates for cerebral asymmetry have been suggested. On the basis of expression comparisons in foetal brain Sun et al. suggested LM04[40]. FOXP2 was proposed from family studies of language abnormalities, and also has been suggested as having a role in hominin speciation. LRRTM1was identified on the basis of an interpretation of linkage studies in handedness and psychosis. Table 2 summarizes the findings. It can be seen that the arguments for the Protocadherin XY gene pair are more numerous and some of them perhaps stronger than those of the other candidates, and that the timing of the initial duplication is more closely related to hominin evolution.

6. Conclusion

5 to 6 million years ago, 3.5 megabase of DNA duplicated from the long arm of the X to the short arm of the Y chromosome, an event that created a Hominin stratum on the Y. Consistent with a saltational account this genomic change is regarded as the speciation event for Australopithecus. Within the transposed block a gene pair – Protocadherin11X and Protocadherin11Y – has been subject to accelerated evolution, with 16 amino acid changes in the Y protein and five in the X. The latter are particularly significant in that they include the introduction of two sulphur containing cysteines, likely to have changed the function of the molecule, and are expressed in both males and females. Change on the Y is conceived as the initiating event in speciation, with change on the X representing the sexually selected phase of accommodation that establishes a new mate recognition system. The paracentric inversion, which has not been dated, is a candidate for the sapiens

[40] Sun, T., et al. 'Early Asymmetry of Gene Transcription in Embryonic Human Left and Right Cerebral Cortex', *Science*, 2005, **308** (5729), 1794–1798.
[41] Enard, W., et al., 'Molecular Evolution of FOXP2, A Gene involved in Speech and Language', *Nature*, 2002, **418**, 869–872.
[42] Williams, N.A., et al., op. cit.
[43] Sun, T., et al., op. cit
[44] Francks, C., et al., 'LRRTM1 On Chromosome 2p12 is a Maternally Suppressed Gene That Is Associated Paternally With Handedness and Schizophrenia', *Molecular Psychiatry*, 2007, **12** (8), 1–11.

speciation event as it has implications for XY pairing in male meiosis and epigenetic control of PCDH11XY gene expression. Cerebral asymmetry (the torque), according to Paul Broca the anatomical correlate of language, may have been introduced at this late stage in the hominin lineage.

University of Oxford
tim.crow@psych.ox.ac.uk

The Sad and Sorry History of Consciousness: being, among other things, a Challenge to the 'Consciousness-studies Community'

P.M.S. HACKER

1. Consciousness As a Mark of Modernity

The term 'consciousness' is a latecomer upon the stage of Western philosophy. The ancients had no such term. *Sunoida*, like its Latin equivalent *conscio*, meant the same as 'I know together with' or 'I am privy, with another, to the knowledge that'. If the prefixes *sun* and *cum* functioned merely as intensifiers, then the verbs meant simply 'I know well' or 'I am well aware that'. Although the ancients did indeed raise questions about the nature of our knowledge of our own perceptions and thought, and introduced the idea of an inner sense, they did not characterize the mind as the domain of consciousness. Aristotelians conceived of the mind as the array of powers that distinguish humanity from the rest of animate nature. The powers of self-movement, of perception and sensation, and of appetite, are shared with other animals. What is distinctive of humanity, and what characterizes the mind, are the powers of the intellect – of reason, and of the rational will. Knowledge of these powers is not obtained by consciousness or introspection, but by observation of their exercise in our engagement with the world around us. The mediaevals followed suit. They likewise lacked any term for consciousness, although they too indulged in reflections upon 'inner senses' – in the wake of Avicenna's distinguishing, arguably to excess, five such senses.

To us, this may seem extraordinary. How could the ancients and mediaevals manage to make sense of human nature and of the nature of the human mind *without* an *explicit* concept of consciousness? After all, is not consciousness the mark of the mental? Is it not consciousness that distinguishes us from mindless nature? Is it not precisely *because* we are conscious that there is something it is like to be us, and that there is not something it is like to be an automaton?

doi:10.1017/S1358246112000082   © The Royal Institute of Philosophy and the contributors 2012

Royal Institute of Philosophy Supplement **70** 2012

P.M.S. Hacker

This response is too swift. It presupposes the cogency of the early modern and contemporary *philosophical* conceptions of consciousness. If we attend carefully, we may well hear the ancients in the Elysian fields laughing at us moderns, wondering how *we* can possibly hope to make sense of human nature and of the nature of the human mind with the knotted tangle of misconceptions that *we* have woven into reflections on consciousness. For consciousness, as conceived by early modern and, rather differently, by contemporary, philosophers, is a mark, not of the mental, but of subtle and ramifying confusion. Of course, the laughter of the ancients may be a little wry – for they would have to admit that they had sowed the seeds of confusion. They had done so by their deeply misleading question: 'How do we know our own perceptions?' And they had made things worse by their confused answer, namely: that we do so by means of a 'common, or general, sense' (*koinê aisthêsis* (Aristotle), subsequently translated into Latin as *sensus communis*) or 'an internal sense' (*sensus interior* (Augustine)).

The English word 'conscious' is recorded by the OED as first occurring at the beginning of the seventeenth century, when, like the Latin 'conscius', it signified sharing knowledge with another or being witness to something. In its early forms, it occurred in phrases such as 'being conscious to another' and 'being conscious to something'. But sharing knowledge rapidly evolved into being privy to unshared knowledge, either about others or about oneself. So 'to be conscious to' quickly became a cousin to the much older expression 'to be aware of'. The form 'to be conscious to' was slowly displaced by 'to be conscious of'. 'To be conscious of something', of course, signified a form of knowledge. So like 'to know', 'to be conscious of something' is a factive verb – one cannot be conscious of something that does not exist or is not the case. Outside philosophy, there was no suggestion whatsoever that the objects of consciousness, i.e. that of which one can be said to be conscious, are restricted to one's own mental operations. One could be said to be conscious of *what* one perceived, or of some *feature* of what one perceived, of one's own or another's deeds – both good and evil, of a pertinent fact (the lateness of the hour, the merits of a case) and of one's own or another's virtues or vices, and so forth. It was not until the middle of the nineteenth century that 'consciousness' came to be used to signify wakefulness as opposed to being unconscious. Thenceforth one could speak of losing and regaining consciousness. The common or garden notions of self-consciousness, i.e. either being excessively aware of one's appearance (a usage now lapsed) or being embarrassingly aware that others are looking at one, is nineteenth-century vintage. Being class-conscious, money-conscious, or safety-conscious are twentieth century coinage.

2. The Early Modern Philosophical Conception of Consciousness

The expression 'conscious' was introduced into philosophy, almost inadvertently, by Descartes.[1] It does not appear in his work prior to the *Meditations* (1641), and even there it occurs just once. In the Third Meditation, it occurs not in relation to knowledge of one's 'thoughts' or 'operations of the mind', but in relation to awareness of the power to perpetuate one's own existence (AT VII, 49; CSM II, 34). It was only under pressure from objectors to this single remark that Descartes was forced, in his 'Replies to Objections', to elaborate his ideas on knowing our own 'thoughts'. His developed position in the *Principles* and late correspondence was unstable. The expression and attendant conception, caught on among Descartes' contemporaries and successors (Gassendi, Arnauld, La Forge) and among English philosophers (Stanley, Tillotson, Cumberland and Cudworth). But it is to Locke, almost fifty years later, that we must turn to find the most influential, fully fledged, *philosophical* concept of consciousness that was to dominate reflection on the nature of the human mind thenceforth. The attendant conception was to come to its baroque culmination (or perhaps nadir of confusion) in the writings of Kant and the post-Kantian German idealists.

Descartes used the terms *conscientia*, *conscius*, and *conscio* to signify a form of knowledge, namely the alleged direct knowledge we have of what is passing in our minds. What we are conscious of (which I shall call the 'objects of consciousness') are Thoughts, a term which Descartes stretched to include thinking (as ordinarily understood), sensing or perceiving (shorn of their factive force), understanding, wanting, and imagining. Because he held thinking to be the sole essential attribute of immaterial substances, he claimed that we are thinking all the time, waking or sleeping. He also held that consciousness of operations of the mind is indubitable and infallible. He argued that the mind is, as it were, transparent. For, he wrote (AT VII, 214; CSM II, 150), it is *self-evident* that one cannot have a thought and

---

[1]   It was already used by Bacon, initially in the form 'conscient' (1612), and then in the form 'conscious' (1625) to signify being privy to knowledge about one's faults. But the concept had no role in his philosophy.

not be conscious of it – although the thoughts we have in sleep are immediately forgotten.[2]

It is noteworthy that his position was equivocal and indecisive. He equivocated between taking consciousness of a thought to be reflective thought about a thought ('Conversation with Burman', CSM III, 335), and elsewhere holding it to be identical with thinking ('Replies to Bourdin', CSM II, 382). A corollary of this was that he equivocated between taking thoughts to be the objects of consciousness, i.e. that *of which* one is conscious, and taking thoughts to be species of consciousness in the sense in which seeing, hearing, smelling are species of perceiving ('Replies to Hobbes', AT VII, 176; CSM II, 124: all acts of thought 'fall under the common concept' of consciousness). Above all, he had no explanation for the possibility of this extraordinary cognitive power, which, unlike *all* our other cognitive powers, is *necessarily exercised upon its objects*[3], and is both *infallible* and *indubitable*. Within the confines of one's mind, this cognitive power is, as it were, godlike – omniscient. How can this be? As Thomas Reid later remarked, if one were to ask Descartes how he knew that his consciousness cannot deceive him, he could answer only that 'the constitution of our nature forces this belief upon us irresistibly' (*Essays on the Intellectual Powers of Man*, Essay VI, ch. vii).

Locke, writing almost half a century later, characterized consciousness not epistemically, in terms of indubitability and incorrigibility, but, as La Forge, Malebranche, and Cudworth had done, psychologically, comparing consciousness to an inner sense whereby we perceive that we perceive. 'Consciousness', he explained, 'is the perception of what passes in a Man's own Mind' (*Essay*, II-i-19). We attain knowledge of what passes in our minds by the exercise of an inner sense. We cannot perceive without perceiving that we perceive. Like Descartes, he held that one 'cannot think at any time, waking or sleeping without being sensible of it' (*Essay*, II-i-10). Unlike Descartes, he did not suppose that we must be thinking for the whole of our existence. Unlike Descartes, he did not limit the

[2] For the Cartesian investigations and reflections I am much indebted to Professor Hanoch Ben-Yami, with whom I spent five enjoyable days hunting together through Adam and Tannery and discussing the findings.
[3] It may seem that if acts of thought are species of consciousness, then it is obvious that if one thinks one must be conscious that one thinks, just as if one sees, one necessarily perceives. But that is a mistaken analogy. If one sees a tree, then what one perceives is not *that one sees it*, but *the tree*. However, Descartes requires that the object of consciousness be the act of thinking, not the object of the act of thinking.

objects of consciousness to the present or to the operations of the mind, since he held us to be conscious of our past mental operations and of our past and present actions.[4] Consciousness is the glue that binds together the fleeting perceptions of the mind into one persisting self-consciousness, and is a necessary condition for responsibility for our actions.

The eighteenth-century debate developed from these foundations. Let me summarize, in a *Galtonian picture*, the conception of consciousness that Kant, to his misfortune, inherited from the Cartesian and empiricist tradition. In this tradition, give or take a couple of points, consciousness is

i. The general form of Operations of the Mind, i.e. one cannot 'think' without being conscious of one's 'thinking';

ii. An *inner sense* – by the use of which we know how things are subjectively with us;

iii. Indubitable – one cannot doubt whatever one is conscious of;

iv. Infallible – one cannot make a mistake about what one is conscious of.

Furthermore

v. To think one is conscious of something does not differ from being conscious of something. So the mind is, so to speak, *transparent*, and what is in the mind is, as it were, *self-presenting*. So *mind is better known than matter*.

In addition, the objects of consciousness (what one is conscious of) are

vi. Limited to the operations of the mind;

vii. Temporally confined to the present;

viii. privately 'owned' (no one else can have my pains or do my thinking);

ix. Epistemically private – only I *really* know (because I have privileged access to) the operations of my mind.

Consequently, *the private is better known than the public*. Further,

x. One's consciousness of what passes in one's mind requires possession of ideas or concepts of mental operations.

---

[4] The latter is necessary for Locke because of the link he forged between consciousness, the concepts of a person and personal identity, and the idea of responsibility for one's actions.

These ideas or concepts have no logical relationship to behaviour, since they are applied to objects of inner sense
without reference to one's behaviour. To possess them requires no more than consciousness of the ideas
(Descartes)[5], or a private ostensive definition (Locke).[6]
And finally,

xi. Consciousness of the operations of the mind is *self-consciousness*: i.e. consciousness of how things are with one's self.

Points (viii) to (x) commit the early moderns and their followers to
the intelligibility of a logically private language. I shall not discuss
this fatal flaw here. Disagreements, which continued well into the
nineteenth century, turned largely on the questions of whether (a)
there are unconscious operations of the mind; (b) whether inner
sense is contemporaneous with, or subsequent to, its objects; and
(c) whether consciousness is or is not infallible.

3. Cracks in the Facade

Such was the conception of consciousness and self-consciousness that
plagued philosophy in the Cartesian/empiricist tradition. The whole
structure turns on two simple and correct thoughts. First, self-ascrip-
tion of *many* (but not all) psychological attributes is indubitable in
the following sense. If one feels a severe pain, one cannot doubt
that one is in pain. If one thinks that it is time to go, one cannot
doubt that one so thinks. If one is afraid of tomorrow's examination,
one cannot doubt that one is thus afraid. Secondly, in *many* cases, one
cannot be mistaken. So, for example, one cannot be mistaken that one
is in severe pain, or that one thinks that $2 + 2 = 4$ (and that one has not
misidentified one's thought with the thought that $2 + 2 = 22$).

[5] 'Thus it would be pointless trying to define, for someone totally blind,
what it is to be white: in order to know what that is, all that is needed is to
have one's eyes open and to see white. In the same way, in order to know
what doubt and thought are, all one need do is to doubt or to think. That
tells us all it is possible to know about them, and explains more about
them than even the most precise definitions.' *The Search after Truth*
(CSM II, 417f.; AT X, 524).
[6] 'Such precise, naked appearances in the mind [viz. 'abstract general
ideas'], without considering how, whence or with what others they came
to be there, the understanding lays up (with names commonly annexed to
them) as standards to rank real existences into sorts, as they agree with
these patterns, and to denominate then accordingly.' *Essay* II, ix, 9.

The Sad and Sorry History of Consciousness

It is all too easy to follow the Cartesian tradition in supposing that if one cannot doubt things to be so with oneself, and cannot be mistaken, therefore one must know, with complete certainty that they are so. But this seemingly innocuous move is precisely where one goes wrong. For we mistake the impossibility of doubt for the necessary presence of certainty, and the impossibility of mistake for the presence of infallible knowledge.

Doubt needs reasons. The possibility of doubting something may be excluded by realization of the eliminability of all genuine alternatives in the circumstances. Here possible doubt is excluded by the available evidence. In such cases, one may typically be quite certain that things are as one takes them to be. But doubt may also be excluded by purely *logical* or *conceptual* considerations: by the fact that *it makes no sense* to doubt the kind of thing in question, or that *it makes no sense* to doubt in such circumstances. Here doubt is excluded not *de facto*, but *de jure* – because no sense has been given to the words 'I doubt' as a prefix to the kind of empirical proposition in question, or in the circumstances in question. To give a few familiar examples of kinds of empirical proposition other than psychological self-ascriptions: it makes no sense to doubt whether one exists (if someone said 'I am not sure I exist' or 'I doubt whether I exist' we should ask him what on earth he meant); it makes no sense, in normal circumstances, as one walks through a wood of great oak trees, to doubt whether *this* is a tree or *this* is a tree, etc.; (if someone, as he touched each great tree, said 'I doubt whether this is a tree', we would think him deranged – or a philosopher). When doubt is excluded *de facto*, then it makes sense to speak of certainty. But when it is logically impossible to doubt – when it makes no sense to doubt, then it equally makes no sense to be certain either. The presence of certainty does indeed exclude all doubt, but if all doubt is *logically* excluded, there is nothing for certainty to exclude. So there is no room for certainty either – the logical space, so to speak, has vanished. Similar considerations apply to the exclusion of mistake. The logical impossibility of a mistake does not imply infallible knowledge, but the exclusion of knowledge *together with error*. So it is with anything that fits the bill for a Cartesian *cogitatio*. There is no logical space for ignorance, and hence too, no logical space for knowledge, no logical space for doubt, and hence too, no logical space for certainty. The utterance 'I know I am in pain' is not at all akin to 'I know he is in pain', and although I may be certain that he is in pain, I cannot (logically *cannot*) be certain that I am in pain – for there is no possibility of doubt that might be excluded by certainty.

P.M.S. Hacker

Why do we cleave so adamantly to the idea that we *know* with certainty that things are so with us? Because it is altogether natural to feel that if we *don't* know, then we must be *ignorant* of what we are being said not to know. And for sure, when one is in severe pain, one *is not ignorant* that one is in pain. Indeed! – But it does not follow that one knows (with certainty) that one is. It follows that one neither knows *nor is ignorant.* It is not that we don't know that things are thus-and-so with us – it is that there is no such thing as *not knowing* in these cases. But by the same token, *there is no such thing as knowing either.* The truth of the matter is that being mature language users, we can – in all the cases relevant to the early modern debate on consciousness – *say* how things are with us. Our saying so is constitutive (not inductive) evidence *for others,* for things being thus-and-so with us. Our sincere word therefore has a privileged status *for others.* Such constitutive evidence is defeasible, but if not defeated, *it stands firm.* But this does not show that we *know* that things are as we say they are – for there is *no such work* for the verb 'know' to do here (which does not mean that it cannot do *other* work here). It shows only that ignorance, *together with knowledge,* is here logically excluded.

Of course, if we assume, with the early modern tradition, that we know with certainty how things are ('subjectively') with us, then it is all too natural to ask *how* we know. Then we are strongly tempted to suppose that we do so by the exercise of a cognitive faculty. Moreover, since we can *say* how things are thus with us without any evidence, it is almost irresistible to suppose that this cognitive faculty is a form of perception – since to learn how things are by directly perceiving how they are involves no evidence either. So it seems that we know how things are with us *in foro interno* by means of an inner sense, which we then dub 'apperception', or 'introspection'. As William James put it so wrongly in 1890, introspection 'means, of course, the looking into one's own mind and reporting there what we discover' (*Principles of Psychology*, I, 185). It is by the use of this inner sense, it seems, that we perceive, or apperceive, or become conscious, of how things are with us. This inner sense is just like an outer sense, only

    (i)   Without a sense organ,
    (ii)   Its successful exercise is independent of observation conditions,
    (iii)   It never fails us, but always yields knowledge,
∴(iv)   We know the mind better than the material world (cp. Descartes, Brentano, Husserl).

But there is no such thing as a cognitive faculty that is miraculously immune to error, and no such things as a faculty of perception that enables us to perceive without any organ of perception and the successful exercise of which is independent of circumstances of observation. 'To perceive', as well as 'to see', 'to hear', etc. have a use as success verbs – but there is no such thing as succeeding if there is no logical possibility of failing. (It is, of course, noteworthy that 'to be conscious of' is not a *success verb* – one cannot try to become or succeed in being conscious of something – although it is a *factive verb*, since what one is conscious of being so is so.)

There is indeed such a thing as introspection – but, *pace* James, it is not a form of perception and involves no 'looking into' one's mind. It is a form of self-reflection, at which some people, like Proust, are better than others. It involves reflecting on one's actions and character traits, on one's springs of action, likes and dislikes. It is a route to self-knowledge, but also a highroad to self-deception. It is not exercised when one says that one has a headache or that one is thinking of going to London tomorrow. That a child has learnt to say 'Mummy, my head aches' does not show that he is becoming introspective. Nor does it show an advance in self-knowledge.

What is true is that if we are asked whether we are in pain, whether we want this or that, whether we are thinking things to be so, or thinking of something or other, we *can say so*. It is characteristic of Locke and his successors down to James, Brentano and Husserl, to confuse the ability to *say* how things are with one with the ability to *see* (by *introspection*) how things are with one. To be sure, when a human being who has mastered the use of language, has a pain, he can say so. If asked whether he is in pain, he can reply. It is tempting to think that he can say that he has a pain in his foot, because he feels, i.e. perceives the pain. But to feel pain is not a form of perception. To feel a pain in one's foot, for one's foot to hurt, just *is* to *have a pain* – not to have a pain and in addition to perceive it. Truthfully to say 'My foot hurts' is no more an expression of something one has *perceived*, *learnt* or *come to know* than is a groan of pain. Of course, one is not *ignorant* of one's foot's hurting either. Can one intelligibly *say* 'I know I have a pain'? In appropriate circumstances, of course. But all it means is that I *really do* have a pain, that *it is true* that I have a pain. It does not mean that I have evidence for it, nor does it mean that I perceive it directly.

A language-user can say what he is thinking. If asked 'A penny for your thoughts?', he can reply. So how does he know *that* he is thinking? Is it not by introspection? No. – Let us first ask how he knows *what* he thinks. Well, he has weighed the evidence, and decided that the weight of evidence is in favour of things being thus-and-so; so he says that things are so – that is what he has concluded is the case. If he regards it is a matter of opinion, or if he regards the evidence as not being decisive, he will affix an 'I think' to the sentence to indicate just that. So he says that he *thinks* things to be thus-and-so. 'I think' functions *here* as a qualifier signifying not a mental operation currently taking place, but as an indicator for others of the epistemic weight of the proposition to which it is affixed.[7]

Yes, but surely he *knows that he thinks what he thinks*! After all, do we not sometimes say 'I don't know what I think'? And if 'I don't know what I think' makes sense, then surely its negation 'I do know what I think' makes sense too! – It is true that we sometimes say 'I don't know *what* I think'. But not to know what one thinks is not: to think something and not to know what it is. If I don't know what I think about something or other, what I do is *not* 'peer into my mind' to find out. Rather, what I do is examine the evidence pertinent to the matter at hand, and make up my mind on the balance of evidence. 'I don't know what I think' is an expression of inability to judge ('I can't make up my mind', we say) – not of an introspective deficiency. It is a confession of not knowing *what to think*, which can be remedied only by looking again at the evidence.

All right; but still, we often proclaim that we don't know what we want. And here surely what we don't know is an operation of the mind! Don't we then quickly introspect and then say 'Now I know what I want'? – No. On the contrary: 'I don't know what I want' signifies *inability to decide* between desiderata. And finding out what one wants is not a matter of introspectively running over one's various desires, but rather of reflecting on the desirability characteristics of the available alternatives and choosing the most preferable. 'Now I know what I want!' means much the same as 'Now I have decided'.[8]

Now, let us to return to the ancients and their confused question: When we see something or see something to be so, *how do we know that we do*? Do we perceive our seeing by sight? Or do we perceive

[7] Of course, there are other uses of this verb. For detailed discussions, see G. Ryle, *On Thinking* (Oxford, Blackwell, 1979), A. R. White, *The Philosophy of Mind* (New York, Random House, 1969), B. Rundle, *Mind in Action* (Oxford, Clarendon Press, 1997), P. M. S. Hacker, *Wittgenstein: Meaning and Mind* (Oxford, Blackwell, 1990).

[8] One might, provocatively, say that these uses of 'I know' are non-epistemic, in the sense in which 'While you were with me, I forgot all my troubles' is not an epistemic use of 'forget' – it does not signify a failure of memory. So too, 'I know that I am in pain' or 'I know that I intend to go' do not signify the successful exercise of a cognitive faculty.

our seeing by a common or general sense? – Neither. There is no such thing as confusing seeing with hearing or tasting. If someone were to say 'I think there is a sound coming from the bush, but I am not sure whether I see it or taste it', we would not know what he meant. We exercise our senses and use our sense-organs in making judgements about things in our vicinity. According to the sense-qualities we apprehend, and to the sense organs we employ, we can affix an 'I can see . . .', 'I hear a . . .', 'I can smell . . .' to the expression of one's perceptual judgement. These prefixes indicate the sense-faculty and sense-organ by the use of which one takes oneself to have acquired information. There is no such thing as *mistaking* sight for smell, or hearing for tasting.[9] And if there is no room for *error*, and if there are no evidential grounds for saying 'I see a so-and-so' or 'I heard a sound from over there', then the question 'How do you know that you see (rather than hear or taste) something or other?' is to be *rejected*, not answered. One does not perceive that one perceives. Nor is one conscious *that one perceives*,[10] although one may be *conscious of what one perceives* – if it catches and holds one's attention. One can *say* what one perceives – but to be able to say *what one perceives* is not to *perceive that one perceives*. Roughly speaking, it is not that the 'I think' must accompany all my representations, as Descartes and Locke supposed. Nor is it even that it must be *possible* for the 'I think' to accompany all my representations, as Kant suggested. Rather, it must be possible for the 'I say' to accompany all my representations. Or, more perspicuously, it must be possible for me to say how things are 'subjectively' with me. And since I can say how things are thus with me, I can also reflect on things being so with me – which is something non language-using animals cannot do. But to reflect on things being thus-and-so with me is not the same as being conscious of thing's being thus-and-so, any more than reflecting on Julius Caesar's assassination is to be conscious of it.

In brief, consciousness is not an inner sense, and it is not a faculty for knowledge of the 'inner'. Roughly speaking, anything that

---

[9] Synaesthesia does not exemplify such an error, for the person who suffers from synaesthesia does not claim to hear the colours of objects, but vividly to associate sounds with colours. He does not shut his eyes and hear the colours of the flowers – indeed, there is no such thing. But when he sees the colours of the flowers, he associates sounds with them.

[10] Blindsight is not an exception to this conceptual truth. It is a confusion to suppose that the blindsighted see, but are not conscious of seeing. For detailed discussion, see J. Hyman, 'Visual experience and blindsight' in *Investigating Psychology: Sciences of the Mind after Wittgenstein* (London, Routledge, 1991), pp. 166–200.

P.M.S. Hacker

Descartes might, *with good reason*, wish to cite as an indubitably and infallibly known *thought* (*cogitatio*), everything 'inner' *for which truthfulness guarantees truth*, is something of which one *cannot* oneself be either ignorant or doubtful. By the very token of the *cannot*, one cannot know or be certain about it either. Consciousness, conceived as an inner sense with operations of the mind as its objects, is not a mark of the mental, but of thoroughgoing confusion.

4. The Contemporary Philosophical Concept of Consciousness

The concept of consciousness as moulded by the early moderns plagued philosophy well into the twentieth-century. However, it did not attract much interest among most early analytical philosophers (Moore is an exception), in the Vienna Circle, or among the dominant figures in the first decades of post-war analytic philosophy. This was due partly to the rise of behaviourism, partly to a decline of interest in philosophy of mind among analytic philosophers in the inter-war years, and partly to the post-war criticisms, launched by Wittgenstein and Ryle, of the early modern conception of the mind, of mental operations and of the relationship between mind and body. The subject of consciousness was awakened from its slumbers in the 1970s as a response to functionalism.

In a seminal article 'What is it like to be a bat?' (*Phil. Review* 1974), Thomas Nagel laid the groundwork for the next forty years of fresh confusion about consciousness. Nagel defended three salient theses:

1. *An experience is a conscious experience if and only if there is something it is like for the subject of the experience to have that very experience.*

What it is like for an organism to have a given experience is denominated 'the subjective character (or quality) of experience'. And this supposed consciousness – the 'what-it's-likeness' (as it is now called[11]) – of a given experience is dubbed 'phenomenal consciousness'.

2. *A creature is conscious or has conscious experience if and only if there is something it is like for the creature to be the creature it is.*

---

[11] See *The Oxford Companion to Consciousness* (Oxford, Oxford University Press, 2009), p. 665.

160

The Sad and Sorry History of Consciousness

So, we all know that there is something which it is like for us to be human beings – although it is very difficult to say what it is like. On the other hand, no one (other than a bat) can even imagine what it is like to be a bat.

3. *The subjective character of the mental can be apprehended only from the point of view of the subject.*[12]

Some clarification and elaboration is needed:

(a) Just as Descartes (and his successors) misguidedly extended the notion of Thought to include *seeming to perceive* in all its modes, *imagining*, and *wanting something*, so the new conception of Conscious Experience was misguidedly extended to include *thinking*[13] – which is no more an 'experience' than wanting is a species of thought.

(b) Each conscious experience was in due course argued to have its own qualitative character – its distinctive *phenomenal feel*.[14] The individual feel of an experience was dubbed a *quale*.[15] 'The problem of explaining these phenomenal qualities', Chalmers later declared,[16] 'is just the problem of explaining consciousness.' For what characterizes *any* conscious experience are the distinctive *qualia* that accompany it.

(c) It is of capital importance to realize that Nagel's claim that 'there is something which it is like to have a given conscious experience' is not a statement of *similarity*. That is, to ask: 'What is it like to walk fast?' is not a variant upon 'What is walking fast like, what does it resemble?' It is not to be answered by a comparison, such as 'Rather like running,

---

[12] This thesis is sketched in Nagel's 'Subjective and Objective' (repr. in his *Mortal Questions* (Cambridge University Press, Cambridge, 1979), and further developed in his book *A View from Nowhere*. For critical discussion of this misbegotten notion of 'point of view', see Bennett and Hacker, *Philosophical Foundations of Neuroscience*, 11.2.

[13] See J. R. Searle, *Mysteries of Consciousness* (London, Granta Books, 1997), p. 201.

[14] The notion of 'raw feels', subservient to a very similar muddled thought, was introduced much earlier by the behaviourist psychologist E. C. Tolman in his *Purposive Behaviour in Animals and Men* (New York, Appleton-Century-Crofts, 1932).

[15] The term was borrowed from C. I. Lewis, *Mind and the World Order* (1929) (New York, Dover, 1956).

[16] D. Chalmers, *The Nature of Consciousness* (Oxford, Oxford University Press, 1996), p. ix.

only one foot is always on the ground'. The question is not: What does it resemble? It concerns the subjective qualitative feel of the experience: what it feels like *for the subject*.

This novel analysis of consciousness, this attempt to save us from reductive physicalism or soulless functionalism, caught on like hot cross buns. It also made it possible for philosophers to hang on to the white coat-tails of cognitive neuroscientists. Consciousness studies became the all the rage.[17] Conferences proliferated, new journals were founded, a stream of articles and books on consciousness rapidly turned to a flood. A common article of faith among the self-styled 'consciousness studies community'[18] is that consciousness is essentially (some would grandly say 'metaphysically') characterized by reference to there being something that it is like to be a conscious creature, and that experience or 'phenomenal consciousness' is to be explained by reference to the fact that there is something that it is like to have it.

Once one has gone down this *cul-de-sac*, then a flood of apparently deep problems follow. What is consciousness for? What is the evolutionary advantage of consciousness? Why aren't there any 'zombies'? How can such a strange phenomenon as consciousness emerge from mere matter? How can one bridge the 'explanatory gap'[19] between neural activity and conscious experience? And so forth. I shall not try to answer these misconceived questions here –

[17]   Apparently a Google Scholar search in 2006 yielded over 600,000 books and articles with the word 'consciousness' in its title.
[18]   See M. Velmans and S. Schneider, *The Blackwell Companion to Consciousness*, Introduction, p. 1.
[19]   Curiously, this muddled idea is ascribed, as a grand new insight, to contemporary members of the consciousness studies community, in particular to J. Levine. But it is at least as old as Leibniz (see note 22 below), and was beautifully stated in the nineteenth century by Huxley and Tyndall. Huxley exclaimed 'How it is that anything so remarkable as a state of consciousness comes about as a result of irritating nervous tissue, is just as unaccountable as the appearance of Djin when Aladdin rubbed his lamp' (*Lessons in Elementary Psychology* (1866), p. 210). Tyndall remarked 'The passage from the physics of the brain to the corresponding facts of consciousness is unthinkable. Granted that a definite thought and a definite molecular action in the brain occur simultaneously, we do not possess an intellectual organ, nor apparently any rudiment of an organ, which would enable us to pass by a process of reasoning, from one to the other' (*Fragments of Science*, 5th ed. p. 420). It is striking that similar despair has been expressed in recent years by C. McGinn, who inferred, from the fact that *he* could not answer the question, that it is beyond the powers of the human mind to do

The Sad and Sorry History of Consciousness

I have already done so, together with my colleague Max Bennett, in *Philosophical Foundations of Neuroscience.*[20] What I should like to do is to make clear why the contemporary philosophical conception of consciousness that is embraced by the 'consciousness studies community' is incoherent – and to throw down a gage to members of that 'community'.

5. A Challenge to the Consciousness Studies Community

Why is it evidently so tempting to agree to this analysis of consciousness? I believe that four factors are in play. First is the persuasiveness of the claim that, as Davies and Humphreys declared, there isn't anything which it is like to be a brick, or an ink-jet printer, but 'there is, presumably, something it is like to be a bat or a dolphin and there is certainly something it is like to be a human being.'[21] For initially one is inclined to agree to this misconceived rhetorical statement. After all, you can ask someone what it was like for him to be a soldier, and you cannot ask an ink-jet printer anything. The second factor to benumb our linguistic sensibility is the relative unfamiliarity of the phrase 'there is something which it is like to', which involves second-level quantification over properties coupled with an unrecognized misuse of the interrogative phrase 'what is it like'. The third operative factor is the appeal of the idea of 'saving our humanity' – of providing a bulwark against the rising tides of reductionism and functionalism.[22] Finally, the appeal of mysteries, of facing the

---

so. For detailed critical scrutiny, see M. R. Bennett and P. M. S. Hacker, *Philosophical Foundations of Neuroscience* (Oxford, Blackwell, 2003), 11.3.

[20]   Of course, I am not suggesting that there are not numerous empirical problems about the various forms of consciousness. We should like to understand, not what consciousness is for, but rather what sleep is for. It is of interest to know the neural mechanisms involved in perceptual consciousness (i.e. of having one's attention caught by something in one's field of perception). It is important to discover how the brain maintains intransitive consciousness. And so on. My point is merely that the so-called 'hard problem' of consciousness, and the battery of related questions often cited by philosophers are merely conceptual confusions masquerading as empirical questions.

[21]   M. Davies and G. W. Humphries, eds. *Consciousness* (Oxford, Blackwell, 1993), p. 9.

[22]   Leibniz nicely observed: 'supposing that there were a machine so constructed as to think, feel and have perception, we could conceive of it

deepest and most difficult problem known to man, of being at the
Last Frontier of knowledge, is well-nigh irresistible. But in philosophy, *there are no mysteries* – only mystifications and mystery-
mongering.

I believe that the temptation must be resisted, and sober analysis
should take its place. I shall, very briefly, defend three antitheses.[23]

(1)   Experiences are not in general individuated by reference to
      what it feels like to have them but by reference to what they
      are experiences of. Most experiences have no qualitative char-
      acter whatsoever – they are qualitatively neutral.
(2)   There is not *something which it is like* to have an experience.
(3)   There is not *something which it is like* to be a human being or,
      for that matter, a bat.

Let me explain.

1a. It is true that being in severe pain is awful, that smelling the
scent of roses is pleasant, that the sight of mutilated bodies is horrify-
ing. These are qualitative characters of certain experiences.

1b. Every experience is a *possible* subject of attitudinal predicates,
e.g. of being pleasant or unpleasant, interesting or boring, attractive
or repulsive. But it is false that every experience is *an actual* subject
of such an attitudinal predicate. With respect to most experiences the
question 'What did it feel like to . . . ?' or 'What was it like to . . . ? is
correctly answered by 'It did not feel like anything in particular' and
'It was altogether indifferent'. To see the lamp posts as one walks
down the street or to hear the chatter in the class room feels neither
pleasant nor unpleasant, and is neither repulsive nor attractive.

1c. Experiences, which may indeed be the subject of the same attitudinal predicate, are not essentially distinguished by reference to it,

---

as enlarged and yet preserving the same proportions, so that we might enter
into it as into a mill. And this granted, we should only find on visiting it,
pieces which push one against another, but never anything by which to
explain a perception' (*Monadology*, §17). Here is the mystery and irreducibility of consciousness. It can be updated by replacing 'pieces that push' with
'neurons that fire'. The confusion remains the same.

[23]   For more detailed treatment, see P. M. S. Hacker 'Is there anything it is
like to be a bat?' in *Philosophy* **77** (2002), pp. 157–74, and M. R. Bennett and
P. M. S. Hacker, *Philosophical Foundations of Neuroscience* (Oxford, Blackwell,
2003) pp. 237–351. Space prevents a discussion of so called subjectivity – a
theme riven with incoherence. It is anatomized in *Philosophical Foundations*,
pp. 294–302. I shall use the term 'experience' in the broad and ill-defined
sense in which it is currently employed by students of consciousness.

but by their object. Smelling lilac may be just as pleasant as smelling roses, but the experiences differ despite sharing the same qualitative character. What distinguishes the experiences is not what it feels like to have them, but what they are experiences *of*.

1d. A persistent mistake among defenders of *qualia* is to confuse and conflate the qualities of what one experiences (e.g. the colour of the violets, the scent of the roses, the taste of the apple) with the qualities of the experiences (delightful, enjoyable, pleasant, revolting). *A perceptible quality is not a quality of a perception.* The colours of visibilia are not qualities of seeing them, but qualities of what one sees. The seeing of a red rose is not red, and the hearing of a bang is not loud, although it may be frightening.

1e. It is altogether misguided to stretch the term 'experience' to include thinking. But be that as it may, what differentiates thinking that $2 + 2 = 4$ from thinking that $3 + 3 = 6$ is not what it feels like to think thus but rather is *what is thought*. Even if, as Chalmers might suggest,[24] a binary whiff is associated with $2 + 2 = 4$, and a tertiary whiff with $3 + 3 = 6$, that is not what individuates the thinkings, as is obvious when one remembers that the tertiary whiff might become associated with the thought that $3 \times 3 = 9$. Or is the first whiff an additional whiff and the second a multiplicative whiff?

2. It is true that one can ask someone: 'What was it like for you to V?' (where 'V' signifies an 'experience'). Remember that this is not a request for a comparison, but for a description of the *felt character* of the experience. One may answer: 'It was quite agreeable (unpleasant, charming, repulsive, fascinating, boring) to V'. Then, if we wish to indulge in second-level quantification, we may say 'There was something that it *was* for A (or for me) to V, namely: *quite agreeable* (unpleasant, charming, etc.)'. What we *cannot* intelligibly say is: 'There was something it *was like* for A to V, namely quite agreeable'. That is, existential generalization requires the dropping of the 'like' – for the experience was not *like quite agreeable*, it *was* quite agreeable. This should be obvious from consideration of the answer to the question: 'What was it like for you to V?' For the answer (save among the illiterati) is not 'To V was like wonderful', but 'To V was wonderful'. And the existential generalization of that cannot yield the form 'There is something which it is like to V, namely wonderful'. The latter aberration is the result of a miscegenous crossing of the

---

[24]   Chalmers claims that his 'experience' of thinking about lions has a leonine whiff about it, so 'what it is like to think of a lion is subtly different from what it is like to think of the Eiffel tower' (see *The Conscious Mind*, p. 10).

existential generalization of a judgement of similarity with an existential generalization of a judgement of the affective character of an experience. The result is latent nonsense – which has now been rendered patent.

So, (i) it is simply ill-formed nonsense to suggest that a conscious experience is an experience such that *there is something it is like to have it*. (ii) Most experiences are qualitatively (affectively) characterless – they have no 'qualitative (attitudinal) character' at all. (If anyone were to ask us such questions as 'What is it like to see the buttons on my shirt?', 'What is it like to hear Jack say "and"?' or 'What is it like to feel the arm of the armchair?', we should be very puzzled at the questions, since such perceptual experiences are obviously qualitatively neutral in normal circumstances.)

Let us now turn to the third antithesis. It makes perfectly good sense to ask 'What is it like to be a doctor (a mother, an old-age pensioner, ill)?'. This is a request for a description of the pros and cons of a certain social role, or of being a V-er or of being in a certain condition. Such questions demand a specification of the qualitative character of the life of an X or the typical career of a V-er or of the condition of being F. That is precisely why this form of words was misguidedly chosen by modern consciousness students to explain what it is to be a conscious creature. Hence the statement: 'there is, presumably, something it is like to be a bat or a dolphin and there is certainly something it is like to be a human being.' But this statement is quite mistaken.

3a. Let me explain why, from the point of view of English grammar and of the devices of second-level quantification, there isn't anything it is like to be a bat, or to be a dolphin, and there certainly isn't anything it is like to be human. Sometimes there is no need, in a question of the form 'What is it like to be an X?', to specify the subject class, i.e to specify what it is like *for whom* to be an X. For it is often evident from the context. 'What is it like to be a doctor?' is restricted to adult human beings, 'What is it like to be a mother?' to women. But sometimes it *is* necessary, e.g. 'What is it like *for a woman* (as opposed to a man) to be a soldier?' or 'What is it like *for a teenager* (as opposed to someone older) to be the champion at Wimbledon?' And often the question is personal, as in 'What was it like *for you* to be a soldier in the Second World War?'

As in the previous cases of 'What is it like to V?', so too here the 'like' drops out in existential generalization. If you answer the question 'What is it like for a teenager to win at Wimbledon?' by saying 'It is quite overwhelming', then the existential generalization is not 'There is something which it *is like* for a teenager . . .', but rather

'There is something that it *is* for a teenager to win at Wimbledon, namely: quite overwhelming'. But this ineradicable flaw is not the worst of the ensuing nonsense.

3b. We can licitly ask 'What is it like for a Y – for a man, a woman, a soldier, a sailor, etc. – to be an X?' We can also licitly ask 'What is it like for you to be an X?' Note the general form of these questions. (i) The subject term 'Y' differs from the object term 'X'. (ii) Where the subject term is specified by a phrase of the form 'for a Y', then a principle of contrast is involved. We ask what it is like *for a Y*, as opposed to *a Z*, to be an X. (iii) There is a second principle of contrast involved in questions of the form 'What is it like for a Y to be an X?', namely with regard to the 'X'. For we want to know what it is like for a Y *to be an X*, as opposed to *being a Z*.

But the form of words that we are being offered by the consciousness studies community is 'What is it like for an X to be an X?' The subject term is reiterated. But questions of the form: 'What is it like for a doctor to be a doctor?' are awry. One cannot ask 'What is it like for a doctor to be a doctor *as opposed* to someone else who is not a doctor being a doctor?' for that makes no sense. Someone who is *not* a doctor cannot also *be* a doctor – although he may *become* one. The interpolated phrase 'for a doctor' is illicit here, and adds nothing to the simpler question 'What is it like to be a doctor?' – which is a simple request for a description of the role, hardships and satisfactions, typical experiences and episodes in the life of a doctor. *A fortiori*, questions such as 'What is it like for a human being to be a human being?', 'What is it like for a bat to be a bat?' and 'What is it like for me to be me?' are nonsense. For, they violate the condition of non-reiteration, and they transgress the two contrast principles. Gods and avatars apart, nothing other than a human being can be a human being; a human being cannot be anything other than a human being, for if a human being ceases to be a human being he thereby ceases to exist;[25] and it makes no sense to suppose that I might be someone else or that someone else might be me. So the pivotal question 'What is it like for a human being to be a human being (or 'for a bat to be a bat')?' collapses into the question 'What it is like to be a human being (or 'to be a bat')?' But now it is not clear what *this* question means — unless it amounts to no more than 'What is human life like?' If that *is* what it means – then although it is nebulous, there is no difficulty in answering it, e.g. 'Nasty, brutish and short' or 'Full of hope and fear'. Nor is there any

[25]   When Kafka turned Gregor Samsa into a beetle, which was Gregor Samsa, he transgressed the bounds of sense.

difficulty in answering the question 'What is the life of a bat like?' – any decent zoologist who studies bats can readily tell us. It is even more glaringly obvious that the supposition that there is something it is like for me to be me is sheer nonsense, for it is logically impossible (there is no such thing) for me to be anyone other than myself. Not only do *I* not know what it is like for me to be me – *there is nothing to know*. I do not know what it is like for me to be a human being either – for this is a form of words without any sense. It is not as if I might have been a cat or a dog, or a ink-jet printer. But I can, of course, tell you what my life has been like.

So, does anything come out of the mystification? Well, yes. What comes out is the following. One can ask a human being what it is like for him to fulfil the various roles he fulfils or to do the various things he does – and he can normally tell one. One cannot ask a brick what it is like for it to fill a hole in the wall or an ink-jet printer what it is like for it to run off twenty copies of one's paper. *For only sentient creatures have roles and have experiences, enjoying some, disliking others, and being indifferent to most.* – A meagre result for so much noise.

As far as I can see, these arguments are watertight. If that is correct, then the larger part of the multitudinous *philosophical* writings of the consciousness studies community, and a considerable number of neuroscientific writings, rest on fundamental conceptual confusions. So I herewith issue a formal challenge to the consciousness studies community: either show that these arguments are flawed, or retire from the field, admitting that consciousness studies *as the members of this community represent them* are sheer nonsense.[26]

St John's College, University of Oxford
peter.hacker@sjc.ox.ac.uk

---

[26] I am grateful to Hanoch Ben-Yami, Hanjo Glock, Hans Oberdiek and Herman Philipse for their comments on earlier drafts of this paper.

Human Nature and Aristotelian Virtue Ethics

ROSALIND HURSTHOUSE

Given that it relies on claims about human nature, has Aristotelian virtue ethics (henceforth AVE) been undermined by evolutionary biology? There are at least four objections which are offered in support of the claim that this is so, and I argue that they all fail.[1] The first two (Part 1) maintain that contemporary AVE relies on a concept of human nature which evolutionary biology has undercut and I show this is not so. In Part 2, I try to make it clear that Foot's Aristotelian ethical naturalism, often construed as purporting to provide virtue ethics with a foundation, is not foundationalist and is not attempting to derive ethics from biology. In Part 3, I consider the other two objections. These do not make a misguided assumption about Aristotelian ethical naturalism's foundational aspirations, nor question AVE's use of the concept of human nature, but maintain that some of AVE's empirical assumptions about human nature may well be false, given the facts of our evolution. With respect to these, I argue that, as attempts to undermine AVE specifically, they fail, though they raise significant challenges to our ethical thought quite generally.

1. Two Failing Objections

First Objection: No Human Essence

What is the Aristotelian connection between the virtues and human nature? We could locate it in the following claim (henceforth 'the Aristotelian claim about the virtues').

'(The) virtues arise in us neither (i) by nature nor (ii) contrary to nature, but (iii) nature gives us the capacity to acquire them and completion comes through habituation.'[2]

---

[1]   One of the objections comes from Bernard Williams. The other three are ones I have heard made at conferences over the last ten years or so, and occur in articles too numerous to be cited.

[2]   *Nicomachean Ethics*, translated and edited by Roger Crisp, Cambridge University Press, 2000, Book 2, Chapter 1.

doi:10.1017/S1358246112000094   © The Royal Institute of Philosophy and the contributors 2012

No significance should be attached to 'nature gives us'. An equally authoritative translation runs – '…neither by nature nor contrary to nature but because we are naturally able to receive them.'[3]

AVE accepts this claim, and the first objection consists of saying that it relies on the discredited concept of a human essence. Does it?

I accept that, although Aristotle was not the essentialist that Plato was, he certainly did believe some things about species essences which evolutionary biology undercuts. So he is, doubtless, alluding to such a human essence in the above claim. But we might just say, 'So what? Who cares?' The 19th century marine biologists had no difficulty in assessing Aristotle's observations in that field and (so I have read) finding most of them to be true; no-one said then, and no-one says now, post Darwin, 'Oh well, they have *all* been undercut by modern biology because we now know that there are no such things as the species essences that he assumed there were.' They just took the observations as being about the creatures they were obviously about and assessed them as true or false or worth exploring or whatever.

And we can do the same with his claim about the virtues. Modern Aristotelian virtue ethicists can take it as obviously about us, us humans, in the same way as human physiology is about us humans, and human psychology is about us humans and the human genome project is about us humans.

What is the claim saying? We can get a handle on it by thinking of a parallel claim to be made about human nature and language. The claim above is made up of three bits, and, in the case of language it goes (i) language does not arise in us by nature; each of us has to be taught to talk. But (ii) it does not arise in us contrary to nature either – our children lap up the teaching, Helen Keller thirsted for it – what could be more natural to human beings than language? And (iii) we suppose that, far from being blank slates as far as language acquisition is concerned, we are naturally able to receive language/have a natural capacity to learn a first language – any first human language – through initial training, and to complete the process ourselves. Given a training by our elders in our early years, we babble away, and after a time, we've got it.

---

[3]   *Aristotle Nicomachean Ethics*, translated by Christopher Rowe, philosophical introduction and commentary by Sarah Broadie, Oxford University Press, 2002.

Someone might want to say that the third bit regarding language – or indeed virtue – is very speculative or they might want to say that the claim about language is more plausible than the claim about the virtues – but surely no-one would want to say that the claim about language must be false or nonsensical because – as we have now realised, given evolutionary theory – there is no such thing as a human essence. So the same goes for the Aristotelian claim about the virtues. It may be false, but if so, this is not because there is no such thing as 'essential' human nature, rather that at least one of the three claims about us that make it up is false (the form of objection that will be considered in Part 3).

So, my conclusion regarding this objection is that Aristotelian virtue ethics is not undercut just because there is no such thing as a human essence, only (at the moment and for a few millennia back and for maybe not much longer in the future) the human species, or humans, or us.

Second Objection: No Concept of Health

Now we come to another, closely related, objection. The Aristotelian ethical naturalism which modern proponents of AVE promote relies heavily on the concept of health, claiming to find an analogy between the evaluations of members of other species as good, that is, healthy, members of their kind or defective in some way, and our ethical evaluations of ourselves. But modern biology, it is claimed, not only rejects the concept of an essential human (or any species') nature; it also, and perhaps thereby, rejects the concept of health (and related concepts such as those of defect and malfunction and abnormality).

That may well be true of evolutionary biology, but that is, after all, but one amongst many of the biological sciences, and it seems point-lessly foolish to deny that many of them do employ the concept of species-related health (and thereby the related ones of defect etc.). For, obviously, medicine, and veterinary science do.

In response, it may be pointed out that medicine and veterinary science are both primarily practical and professional rather than theoretical subjects, and hence a reflection of our interests and desires. They are aimed at being put into practice, at getting things in the world to go the way we want them to. So the concepts of human health, and domestic cat health pick out ways we want to be, or want our cats to be; they do not carve the world at the joints.

But then, one might say, what about human and animal physiology, with which the two practical/professional schools of study are so closely entwined? Medical and veterinary science are taught in universities as a mixture of both practical and theoretical, the list of the participating academics' research subjects is a mixture of both. True, medicine is distinct as an academic subject from human physiology, and veterinary science from animal physiology, because the former are primarily practical whereas human and animal physiology are not; they are not aimed at getting things in the world to go the way we want them to go, but to identify and explain the things there are. Nevertheless, physiology is primarily focussed on studying normal body function, where 'normal' is *not* just a statistical notion and human physiology gets defined as the science of the mechanical, physical, and biochemical functions of humans in good health, (their organs, and the cells of which they are composed.)

It may well be that human physiology first got going as an object of study only because of our interests in, or our valuing of, our living in certain ways; perhaps animal physiology got going for the same reason plus widespread prohibitions on human vivisection. Or perhaps we initially became interested in animal physiology because we valued domestic animals with certain properties – long life, large size, large reproduction (for their kind), resistance to external factors that inhibited any of these etc. And perhaps we first became interested in plant physiology because of our interest in agriculture.

Who knows. And again, who cares, because whether the just so story says that, or claims that the disciplines all began because we were struck with wonder about the world and wanted to know how all these bits of it worked – which was certainly what motivated Aristotle's marine biology – we wind up in the same place, with 'modern biology' as we have it now. Goodness knows how it evolved, but evolved 'it' certainly has, so that now we refer to 'it' as 'the biological sciences', using the plural to encompass its multiple branches, sub-disciplines and developments, which are quite beyond the ordering of a hierarchical taxonomy. We can classify the areas of study in different ways and I suppose two of the ways we could do so would be according to the extent to which they contributed to medical science or employed the 'evaluative' concept of health. But either grouping would have fuzzy edges.

The point of the above is not to try to set up the biological sciences as providing a suitably 'value-laden' foundation for ethics, but rather to draw attention to the fact that the ones that might be called value-laden or value-informed or to contain evaluations are not to be clearly distinguished from those that are not. We could regard medicine as applied biology but this is not to say that the other biological sciences are all value-neutral or non-evaluative and that values suddenly appear on the scene only when we do medicine. If evolutionary biology is indeed quite value-neutral, and has no use for concepts such as *health* or *malfunction* or *normal* (in its non-statistical sense) this presumably does not cut if off from the biological sciences of which that is not true – it gets material from at least some of them, and some of them get material from it. It is, as I said, but one biological science amongst many and not in any privileged position.[4]

So that evolutionary biology has no truck with the concept of health – or defect or malfunction or abnormality – has no bearing whatsoever on the fact that Aristotelian virtue ethics relies on those concepts.

To what extent does it indeed rely on them? Well, not to the point that some critics suppose, which brings me to the second part of the paper, which is a brief interlude on foundationalism and the Aristotelian biological analogy.

2. Aristotelian Ethical Naturalism is Not Foundationalist

A number of critics go to great lengths to illustrate why virtue ethics cannot be derived from evolutionary biology, or why evolutionary biology cannot provide it with a foundation. I am not going to discuss this form of objection because it is, simply, misplaced, but I will say something briefly about why it is misplaced, and what role the Aristotelian naturalism is playing if it is not a foundational one.

As we have just seen, it would be foolish to think that evolutionary biology would provide virtue ethics with its foundation; if any biological sciences did, it would be some of the other ones – the ones that provide medical science with its foundation – and ethology.

I take it that some of the biological sciences do provide medical science with a foundation in an obvious sense. They – and sometimes perhaps when one is talking about, say, pacemakers or laser surgery,

---

[4] Sterelny and Griffiths note that 'The contrast between polymorphic and monomorphic traits is standard in biology', defining monomorphic traits as traits that 'exist in the same form in every "normal" individual. Leg number is monomorphic in humans.' Kim Sterelny and Paul A Griffiths, *Sex and Death: An Introduction to Philosophy of Biology* (Chicago, University of Chicago Press, 1999) 346.

not only they but also some of the physical sciences – explain and justify a large number of medical claims. Where we still do not know how to do what we want to do (prevent cancer say, or cure chronic fatigue syndrome) because we do not know enough about how our bodies work, we are expecting that the biological sciences will tell us. Moreover, where we can justify but not explain, we are expecting the biological sciences to come up with the explanations. For example, we know (I think) that at least some acupuncture works – the sort that allows for open heart surgery on conscious patients – and it is very mysterious, but we expect some day western science will be able to explain it.

Now in this obvious sense in which biology provides medical science with a foundation, no Aristotelian ethical naturalist – including Aristotle on some authoritative interpretations – has ever supposed that it similarly provided a foundation for ethics. I certainly do not know of any modern virtue ethicist's work in which it is implied, let alone asserted, that ethics can be expected to become a branch of applied biology, as we might say medicine is, and I cannot think of any ethical claim of which any of us might want to say, 'Well we know that so and so is the case, and it's very mysterious why, but I expect one day biology will be able to explain it', the way we want to claim that about acupuncture and indeed hypnotism. Everyone who is taking the Aristotelian naturalist line takes it as obvious that they are not pretending to derive ethical evaluations of human beings from an ethically neutral human biology, but are already thinking about human beings in an ethically structured way.[5]

Perhaps thereby we divide ourselves from some of the proponents of the other sorts of normative ethical theories. Perhaps, amongst those proponents, there are still some stalwarts who believe they are, or who aspire to be, in the business of justifying their moral beliefs in some rational but ethically (and culturally) neutral way, whereas we virtue ethicists know we are not and are not even trying to be.

If we did think it was possible, we would surely avail ourselves of what was on offer. After all, it is obvious enough that, as far as justifying the claim that such and such a character trait is a virtue is concerned, there is no reason why virtue ethicists shouldn't make the same sorts of moves that proponents of the other normative theories make. We could spin the story that it is a character trait such that

[5]   Larry Arnhart, in *Darwinian Natural Right*, (New York: SUNY Press, 1998) might be an exception to this claim.

everyone's possessing it would have the best consequences; or the story that I can rationally will everyone's possessing it to be a universal law. If we thought one of these sorts of stories could provide a rational but ethically neutral foundation for virtue ethics – which biology clearly cannot – of course we would go for it. But, characteristically, we do not think that. So we think we would fare no better telling any of those sorts of stories.

'Well then', it might be said, 'if Aristotelian naturalism isn't seeking to provide ethics with a foundation in biology, what is it doing?' I think Bernard Williams came to give a good description.

Williams originally objected[6] to what he took Aristotelian naturalism to be, but he eventually conceded to Nussbaum[7] that there was a better way to read Aristotle, and he acknowledged (generous and honest man that he was) that most of his animadversions against it had been misplaced. (He retained one, which I shall consider in Part 3.) 'I grant' he said, 'that the Aristotelian enterprise may be seen in coherentist or hermeneutical terms'.[8] And, as far as the modern version is concerned, that seems a good description – it is offering a sort of coherentism – but a coherentism with a certain hermeneutical agenda.

Foot's Ethical Naturalism

After all, what you bring to a programme of achieving reflective equilibrium or coherence amongst your beliefs in a certain area is going to shape where you wind up, not least because it will affect what you take as relevant in that area. When Foot first began having her naturalistic thoughts, hardly anyone but her thought that they should work on getting their ethical and meta-ethical beliefs to cohere with a whole lot of other beliefs they had about good roots, good eyes, good cacti and so on, because they assumed those were irrelevant.

Taking Foot as the most influential ethical naturalist, it seems to me perfectly clear that what she takes herself to be doing is most

[6] Bernard Williams, *Morality* (Cambridge: Cambridge University Press, 1972) 'Moral Standards and the Distinguishing Mark of Man', and *Ethics and the Limits of Philosophy* (Cambridge, Mass.: Harvard University Press, 1985) chapter 3.

[7] Martha Nussbaum, 'Aristotle on Human Nature and the Foundations of Ethics', in J.E.J. Altham and R. Harrison (eds.), *World, Mind and Ethics*, (Cambridge: Cambridge University Press, 1995) 86–131.

[8] Bernard Williams, 'Replies', Op. cit. 200.

Rosalind Hursthouse

certainly not putting forward a foundation for ethics. She is a Wittgensteinian through and through, and hence anti-foundationalist, and she is doing what Wittgenstein says is the work of the philosopher namely assembling reminders for a particular purpose.[9] The general Wittgensteinian purpose is always to '*command a clear view* of our use of words'[10]; the particular purpose in Foot's case has always been to get clearer about our use of words when we are expressing or talking about our moral beliefs. When we evaluate someone as a good person, their action as right or wrong, their character as good or bad, what are we doing, what other uses of these words are these moral uses like?

When Foot first began objecting to the fact/value dichotomy, her opponents were quite sure they knew what the moral uses of 'good' and 'right' in assertions were like. They were like expressions of enthusiasm or disgust (the old boo hurrah stuff, remember). Or they were like commands – we saw more clearly what we were doing when we asserted 'John is a good man' when we saw our doing so as akin to our saying 'Be like John'. Or they were like self-addressed exhortations, 'Let me be like John!' And they were *not* like, were utterly unlike, 'John is a good thief' for example, because that was, obviously, a purely factual statement, as was 'That tree has good roots', and a different use of 'good' entirely.

Against these prevailing views, early Foot made at least two moves, just about the adjective 'good'. One was the old point that it is, at least for the most part, attributive, the way 'large' and 'small' are, and colour words, for the most part, are not. What that means is that, with a non-attributive adjective such as 'pink', you can say truly that something is pink without worrying about how you otherwise categorize the pink thing. It doesn't matter, for instance, whether you say it's a mouse or an animal, as long as it is, indeed, pink. But you can't do the same with 'large', because whether it's true that something being identified is large does depend on whether we categorize it as, for example, a mouse or an animal – one and the same thing is both a large mouse and a small animal. And so for 'good'; the good thief is the bad man, the good lover may, alas, be the bad husband, and so on.

Her second point was suggested by those examples. The adjective 'good' has a wide range of (as philosophers say) non-moral uses as well as moral ones. But we do not have any reason – such as a

---

9 *Philosophical Investigations* §127.
10 Ibid, §122.

distinction drawn in a language other than English, or a satisfactory philosophical account – to suppose that this philosophical distinction between the moral and non-moral uses can always be made.

Regarding Foot's early work, I think one could say that the programme was simply coherentist, intended to show the crude subjectivists around her the error of their ways – hence her readiness to discuss 'good' in relation to inanimate functional objects such as pens and knives. And one could say too, that the programme was successful, generating the vastly more sophisticated forms of subjectivism we have nowadays.

But what began as the assembling of many, varied, examples of the use of 'good' with the purpose of undermining the fact/value dichotomy, became, in her culminating work, the assembling of a narrower set, with a much more specific purpose – to show a likeness, an analogy, between our evaluation of aspects of the other animals and our ethical evaluations of ourselves. She was, she said, 'quite seriously likening the basis of moral evaluation to that of the evaluation of behaviour in animals'.[11]

The claim that there is a likeness or an analogy between two areas of talk distinguished by their subject matter (us and other animals that is) really is a pretty mild and one would think innocuous claim. If I stress that that is Foot's naturalist position – and mine, and I think Macintyre's – not that there is a foundation, not that there is any sort of primacy about the biological evaluations of the other animals, just that there is a likeness – it might be said, 'Well if that's all there is to it, what is all the fuss about?' That seems to me to be a good question. Why are people making such a fuss, trying to wipe virtue ethics right off the board?

It looks as though it really is Foot's analogy itself that is upsetting people, because they go on wanting to attack it even after we have belaboured the point that it is *not* an attempted foundation, for virtue ethics in particular, that the other theories would lack, but just an analogy. My suspicion is that, deep down, people don't like the analogy because, quite simply, it does not make human beings special enough as ethical agents; it does not keep us and our ethical thought and talk about ourselves properly insulated from any non-ethical thought and talk we have about the other animals. They want the difference in subject matter to make for lots of other differences, not to be told by Foot that they should be looking for similarities.

---

[11]   Philippa Foot, *Natural Goodness* (Oxford: Clarendon Press, 2001), 16.

Rosalind Hursthouse

Why go for the animal or biological analogy, they say, encouraging us to think of our ethical evaluations as being species-relative, when our ethical thought and talk about ourselves is about us as these very special beings, *persons*, which isn't a species-concept at all?

The response is – we go for the analogy in part to curtail our hubristic tendency to think of ourselves in that inflated way. The analogy puts us firmly in our place as something distinctly less than that special.

This does *not* rule out the significance of the fact that most of us are persons, that is, that we have a special sort of rationality. That would be odd, would it not, given that Foot's naturalism is Aristotelian and Aristotle is hardly an exemplar of a philosopher who downplays the point that our rationality distinguishes us from the other animals. That significant fact is present – it is us we are talking about after all – but in a species-relative way. Acquiring the rationality that makes *us* moral agents or persons fairly early in our development, and, if we are lucky, keeping it until we die, just is normal, healthy, human development. But, note, it is a stage in *human* development. The rationality and 'personhood' in question are human rationality and human personhood; the two concepts apply only to human beings, and thereby only to beings with certain biological properties, each of whom is, moreover, culturally and historically situated. We are not a whole different order of beings just because we spend most of our human lives being persons, and there is no reason to suppose, in advance of our encountering some promising candidates, that the concepts could also be applied, by family resemblance, to aliens or divine beings.

So one reason for heeding the analogy is that it helps us to shake off a bit more unwarranted Enlightenment optimism about what the Age of Reason will bring. Another reason is that we learn some interesting things about our ethical thought when we heed it.

Here is a little example of the sort of difference taking heed of the analogy can make. When, talking ethics, we are talking about good people and good lives, somewhere along the line we will probably come up against the problem presented by very different sorts of people and lives, all of which we are strongly inclined to say are good. Some of us incline to saying that there must always be an answer to which is best, it can't be indeterminate, and so search for some theoretical justification for ranking one over the other. Others find at least some of these attempts manifestly unsatisfactory, and accept the indeterminacy, saying that it reflects the Incommensurability of Values. We intend the capitals here, because we think of the incommensurability as being a significant feature of *moral* values, related to various features of us as Rational Beings – more capital letters – such as our autonomy, our integrity, the fact that we have personal values and so on.

However, if we follow Foot, we can recognise, agreeing with the second group, that the indeterminacy is certainly there, but not interpret the fact of its existence in such capitalised terms. Seen in the light of the analogy with the evaluation of other living things and how they are faring, all we are looking at is the sort of indeterminacy and 'incommensurability of values' – very much lower case – that we find right down at the level of plants, not something peculiar to ethics and our talk about ourselves as rational agents.

Here is a specimen of a particular sort of plant strikingly well-endowed in some respects, mildly defective in others, pretty good and healthy over all, and doing well in the way one would expect, given where it is growing. Here is another specimen, not as well-endowed in any respect, but without any corresponding defects; it is a good one too and also doing well. Is one better than another? Well, not according to any general criterion or standard. We might use a further criterion for a particular purpose; the showy well-endowed one may obviously be better for the village flower show competition. And we might invent a new criterion and make it general. But what would be the point when obviously the best description of the set up is to follow Aristotle and say that each is 'good with qualification'. The first is good despite-having-a-few-defects; the second is good though-with-nothing-outstanding-about-it.

A more general sort of difference that heeding the analogy can make is to encourage us to think about what empirical assumptions we make about ourselves as a kind of animal with a contingent nature when we talk about ethics and thereby to consider what would happen to that ethical thought and talk if the assumptions proved to be false.

In the remaining part of the paper I am going to do just that, through considering the second pair of objections.

3. Two Failing But Thought-provoking Objections

The objections considered in Part 1 took it that we Aristotelian virtue ethicists were talking old fashioned nonsense about the human essence. But a different set of critics have interpreted us rather more sensibly, allowing that we are, as I claimed in Part 1, talking about human nature in just the same way as, for instance, sociobiologists such as Wilson do when they say that human nature is ultimately selfish and philosophers of science such as Philip Kitcher do when they say no it isn't.[12]

Indeed, these critics want us to be talking sense about human nature, to be making straightforward empirical claims, because they think that evolutionary biology shows – well, no, not actually shows, but suggests – that some of these empirical claims are false; that the facts about human nature are, we may speculate, otherwise.

I will discuss two problematic putative facts about human nature allegedly suggested by evolutionary biology. I do not dispute that each of them, if it were a fact, would undermine one of the three bits of the Aristotelian claim about the virtues I cited at the outset. Nor do I dispute that they may well be suggested by evolutionary biology. My strategy will be to argue that, insofar as they are problematic for virtue ethicists, they are no more so than they are for most people who want to engage in ethical thought and talk.

Let us go back to the Aristotelian claim about the virtues. (The) virtues arise in us (i) neither by nature nor (ii) contrary to nature, but (iii) nature gives us the capacity to acquire them and completion comes through habituation.

It looks, does it not, as though it is not far off the obvious modern resolution of the nature/nurture debate; we become what we are because of the interaction of what we are 'born' with (saying 'conceived with' sounds too odd) and the environment. Take the first bit. It is obvious that we are not all born good, that virtue does not arise in us by nature, just as it is obvious that (contrary to Wilson) we are not all born selfish. (Of course, some people say that evolutionary biology shows that we are all born selfish, but this, if a fact, would so obviously be a problem for any ethical theory that I am not going to discuss it.)

But now take the third bit. It claims that there is a way in which we are born different from the other animals. Unlike them we can become virtuous because we are born with the capacities or propensities to acquire the virtues through habituation. The other animals cannot acquire *virtues*, which involve the recognition of certain considerations as *reasons* for acting because they do not, in the ethically relevant sense, recognise reasons *as* reasons at all. What 'habituation' covers in Aristotle is a lot. It begins in early

---

[12]   See, for example, his 'Comment' on de Waal in Frans de Waal, *Primates and Philosophers* (Princeton and Oxford: Princeton University Press, 2006).

childhood with an 'environment' which consists in being trained to behave in certain ways and gradually becomes something self-sustaining, i.e. you continue to act in those ways for reasons that you have made your own.

So there is one fairly straightforward empirical claim. We human beings are (for the most part) born with the capacities to acquire the virtues in this way.

Aristotle has also, in the second bit, made a point of saying that we do not acquire the virtues 'contrary to nature'. What is that claim doing? In part, it is just the denial of a picture that Plato, in his darker moments, draws. We would have the virtues contrary to nature if we were, psychologically, a battlefield for the irreconcilable forces of Reason and Passion (or Desire.) We would acquire the virtues if (and only if) Reason wins, but at a hefty price, our natural passions or desires destroyed, crippled, deformed, enslaved. And, according to the second bit, we are not like that. But this unfolds into much more.

Aristotle, and Plato more often than not, think that the passions are not insulated from reason, deaf to its suggestions. In so far as we are born with the capacities to experience, (Aristotle's examples) appetite, anger, fear, envy, joy, love, hate, longing, emulation and pity, we are born with the capacities to have these passions shaped by our upbringing and early experiences and later, by ourselves, by what we make of further experience and our reflections. Moreover, they think that, when the passions are shaped the right way by reason, they can come to be in perfect harmony with it.

Hence the famous Aristotelian distinction between virtue and mere continence which modern virtue ethicists sling at Kantians. If you tell the truth or pay your debts or help other people against inclination, because you think you should, that is mere continence and not good enough. You have more work to do on getting your passions into harmony with your reason. And when you have, you will find that, by and large, you enjoy doing what is virtuous; you will do it gladly; virtuous action –for the most part– gives pleasure to the virtuous. (In the terms of contemporary causal theories of action, your virtuous actions are overdetermined, caused both by the desire to do whatever it is and also by the belief that doing whatever it is is right plus the second order desire to do what is right.)

So there is a second empirical claim. We are all (pretty much) born to be such that we can bring our passions/desires into harmony with our reason and live happily and harmoniously together.

So we have two substantial empirical claims about human nature, about what (for the most part) is true of human beings.

i)   We are all pretty much born the same as far as those capacities or propensities that pertain to ethics – cognitive, affective, desiderative – are concerned. (I'll call them 'the ethically relevant capacities'.)

ii)   All (pretty much) of these ethically relevant capacities have a further feature; they can all be developed together, not at each other's expense.

So Aristotle's claim about the virtues, embodying as it does these two empirical claims, is up for refutation. So now let us look at the two obvious ways in which it can be false. They are the following two Putatively Problematic Facts, which are brought as the two further objections I shall now discuss.

PPF1 is that as far as the ethically relevant capacities are concerned, yes we are all born pretty much the same, but we are born a mess – the capacities cannot be developed together.

PPF2 is that as far as the ethically relevant capacities are concerned, we are not born pretty much the same but significantly varied.

Third objection: We Are An Ill-assorted Bricolage

That PP1 may well be a fact, and that this is suggested by evolutionary theory, is an objection to Aristotelian naturalism that has been pressed by Williams (I noted above that he had retained one of his objections it). We may well be, as he has memorably put it, 'an ill-assorted bricolage of powers and instincts'.[13]

Indeed, he thinks that evolutionary theory suggests that we are born as just such an ill-assorted mess. 'The most plausible stories now available about (our) evolution, including its very recent date …suggest that human beings are to some degree a mess, and that the rapid and immense development of symbolic and cultural capacities has left humans as beings for whom no form of life is likely to prove entirely satisfactory either individually or socially'.[14] We might note that this second quote is tentative – human beings are 'to some degree' a mess; they are beings for whom no form of life is 'likely' to prove 'entirely' satisfactory. But if we take that tentativeness seriously, the claim, as something aimed at Aristotelian

---

[13]   'Replies' in J.E.J. Altham and R. Harrison (eds.), *World, Mind and Ethics* (Cambridge: Cambridge University Press, 1995) 199.

[14]   'Evolution, Ethics and the Representation Problem', in *Making Sense of Humanity* (Cambridge: Cambridge University Press, 1995) 109.

naturalism, is just too weak to touch it, and hence not interesting. None of us thinks – do we? – that democracy, as a social form of life, is entirely satisfactory. After all, it brought in Hitler and, after a fashion, Bush. But we think it's the best practicable one. And that's good enough; it gives us something to aim at socially, in the global village. *Eudaimonia*, or a flourishing life, the life of virtuous activity, which is what Aristotle thinks we can each individually live when we get our passions into harmony with our reason, does not have to be thought of as entirely satisfactory. In fact, Aristotle himself rather suggests that it is, in a way a kind of second best – our rational aspect ('the divine element within us') would be better satisfied if we lived the divine life of reflective activity. But it is the best practicable option for us, because we are human not divine. (I'm not endorsing any of that of course – it's the funny stuff from Book 10. I'm just mentioning it to make it clear that even for Aristotle, let alone a modern virtue ethicist, 'the good life' for human beings doesn't have to be roses all the way.) And that's good enough; it gives us something to aim at individually.

So to make the objection interesting, I think we have to take it as something rather stronger. Then it appears as, basically, an old idea – old enough to be present, at least to some extent, in Plato, as I noted earlier – namely that our unique combination of some set of affective/desiderative capacities not very different from those of some of the other animals plus a set of tricksy cognitive capacities unique to us (as a set) in the animal kingdom, makes us seriously at odds with ourselves – to the extent indeed that there is no likelihood that living *this* way, say, ethically, will be more satisfying or fulfilling or make us happier than living some other way. On the contrary, it is unlikely that any one of us will live a satisfying life, fulfilling our nature, given each of us is a mess, and if it turns out that some of us actually do, this will just be luck, no indication that anyone would be well-advised to take us as a model in the hope of winding up in the same happy state.

As the Platonic parallel to this gloomy picture reminds us, there corresponds to this old version of the idea, an old way to deal with it, namely aim at the life hereafter. Yes, it is agreed, the combination of the spirit and the fleshly desires is most unfortunate, the two never to be reconciled, so the only thing worth doing is preparing your spirit for its release in either the Western or the Eastern ways. Less familiar is another Eastern way of dealing with the problem which recommends dismantling or reshaping (according to one's favoured interpretation) one's cognitive and cultural powers to return to the state or condition of small children.

Rosalind Hursthouse

What should be noted about these ways of responding to the idea that we human beings are a mess is that they are responding in *the only practical way*, that is, by finding something substantial and long term for practical reason to aim at. Because that's the problem that the speculation presents us with which has to be addressed. And it is a problem not just for virtue ethicists, but *everyone*.

If there is no such thing as a predictable form of *eudaimonia*, or happiness or well-being for us humans, if any individual who winds up leading a satisfying life does so just by chance – then how can we make rational long term decisions about what to do? What is there for practical reason to do? I rely on being able to take the well-being of others as an end whether I am a virtue ethicist, a Kantian or a consequentialist.

Moreover, even if I am an egoist, I rely on being able to take my own well-being as an end. If it is not a practicable end, I could exercise my practical rationality in keeping alive (just in case I might be one of the lucky few) and in securing short term enjoyments and freedom from pain, but as for any more long term goals, I might just as well flip a coin to decide whether or not to go for them, and if so how. For, like everyone else, I am a mess of irreconcilable powers and instincts and there is no form of life that is at all likely to be satisfying to me.

So, I would say, the idea that Aristotle's more optimistic view is completely misplaced, and that we are all just a mess is, indeed, a very disturbing idea, but it is no more disturbing to Aristotelian virtue ethics than it is to any other position, including egoism. As I have noted, it is hardly a new idea, and why the facts of our evolution should be thought to give it a new plausibility is unclear to me, but I think we should all cross our fingers and hope that this is not so or we are all in trouble.

Fourth Objection: We Are Not Born Pretty Much The Same, But Varied

There are at least two ways in which we are not *all* born *exactly* the same which were (perhaps) recognised by Aristotle and which should be distinguished from the second Problematic Putative Fact that evolutionary biology is claimed to suggest.

One is very obvious; he classifies some people as 'brutish', noting that brutishness can arise 'through disease and disability' and asserting that such people possess neither virtue nor vice. On a charitable reading (ignoring some typically dreadful remarks about the condition being mostly found amongst non-Greeks) he is noting a familiar variation in human cognitive abilities, namely that some humans are born severely 'mentally handicapped' as we say. And he is excluding them from the category of people who are up for ethical assessment, as we all do today.

Many people find the second way he seems to recognise variation more disconcerting. In a tantalisingly brief passage in Book 6, he apparently introduces the idea of natural virtue, what you are born with, in contrast to full virtue, which is the set of character traits you wind up with after many years of dedicated habituation and the acquisition of practical wisdom. On one way of reading the passage, in saying we are born with natural virtue, he is just saying again what he said in the claim I began with – that we are all (pretty much) born naturally able to acquire the virtues. But on another way of reading it, he is noting what might well have seemed to him to be a fact, as it may to us, namely that some of us – only some of us – are lucky enough to be born much more able to acquire the virtues than others. After all, it often looks as though some babies are just born happy, amenable, and sweet-tempered and that, as toddlers, they display vestigial courage and self-control long before any training has had a chance to kick in, whereas others are born unhappy, cranky, difficult and timorous.

All right, so let us suppose, with Aristotle interpreted this way, that this is a fact. It entails that, as far as becoming good people is concerned, we do not start on a level playing field; some of us are likely to find it easier than others. Is that problematic for virtue ethicists? Well, it doesn't seem to bother Aristotle and I do not see it as a problem for any of us moderns. It is not a major qualification on the claim that we are all (for the most part) naturally able to acquire virtue. When we recognise virtue as a threshold concept, all we need is that, born with natural virtue or without, we are all, for the most part, born naturally able to reach the threshold. That some of us are bound to find it easier than others and get there more quickly, that within life's short span, some of those born without natural virtue can never get to be as good as some of those who started with that natural advantage, is just how things are. There are greater and lesser grades of virtue which are not in any way under the control of their possessors, just as there are greater and lesser grades of intelligence similarly beyond their possessors' control.

So this particular way in which there may be variation in the human population does not seem to be problematic for virtue ethics at all. I think myself that one advantage of going back as far as Plato and Aristotle for one's philosophical ethics is that one goes back to something so manifestly un-Christian, so untouched by the idea that a just and loving god creates us all equal, with an equal chance of becoming good. Aristotle's view of natural virtue, and Plato's serene assumption in the Republic that we are born as guardians or not are clearly untouched by it, as is their taking as obvious the enormous effect of nurture on whether we turn out good or bad.

It does not seem to me so obvious that proponents of the other ethical theories, if they incline to some sort of equality we all have as persons, can shrug off this sort of unfairness in life so readily. Maybe they can, because, after all, everyone nowadays accepts that being born into a certain sort of family and/or social milieu gives you a substantially greater or lesser chance of becoming good than being born into a different sort. But one still sometimes encounters an unwillingness to admit that A is a better person than B, notwithstanding some rather nasty emotional reactions that B has carried over from her unfortunate upbringing and that A is virtuously without, when B has, *ex hypothesi*, done 'everything she could' to extirpate them.

Be that as it may, the modest amount of variation perhaps implied by Aristotle's idea of natural virtue is not, as I said, a problem for Aristotelian virtue ethicists. But that we are able to accommodate some such inequality does not show we can tolerate a lot more, and it is, theoretically, on the cards, that we are born much more varied than Aristotle's sketchy idea of natural virtue allows.

This brings me to what, I take it, those who appeal to evolution are really after. Sterelny and Griffiths say

> '(So) no general biological principle suggests that human moral feelings, mental abilities, or fundamental desires should be any more uniform than human blood type or eye color. On the contrary, human cognitive evolution seems likely to have involved an evolutionary mechanism that produces variation within a population ...'.[15]

I take it their thought is that, as far as the ethically relevant capacities are concerned, we are varied in really serious ways.

Since we have no idea whether or not this is so, thinking about it involves a thought experiment and the obvious one that springs to mind is: What if it turned out to be the case that about 10% of the population, say, were born psychopathic. (In so far as I have

[15]   Kim Sterelny and Paul E.Griffiths, op.cit note 3, 8.

grasped the distinction between that and sociopathy, I really do mean psychopathy.) Given we are not quite clear about what psychopathy is, we have to make the story up as we go along, but what I am imagining – and the people I have found bringing this objection forward are clearly imagining – is that, assuming some of us are born this way, there would be something biologically identifiable very early on with fairly clear cut edges. I mean something which, although there are very occasionally borderline cases, is otherwise an all or nothing matter. And given that it is psychopathy that we are imagining, what we are also imagining is that the presence of this identifiable whatsit is a very reliable, though certainly not infallible indicator of seriously immoral behaviour in adulthood. (Fill in for yourself whatever you take to be the prime examples of immoral behaviours to be.)

This sort of example tends to be brought up to frighten virtue ethicists, but it seems to me that it ought to frighten the living daylights out of anyone who is serious about ethics, or at least that we should all find it very problematic. Again, it is not a new threat or a new idea. It is just the old idea that some significant group of us are born irredeemably (for the most part yet again) wicked or amoral – or rather, predisposed to become wicked or amoral. You might think that the modern pseudo scientific version gives an especially threatening twist to the idea by introducing the point that, *ex hypothesi*, we would be able to identify these people, when or even before they are born, but that really is not so – that is part of the old idea too. We have a lamentable history of some group of us believing that another group of us is born irredeemably wicked; it is mostly a history of the assumption that the bad sort can be spotted before or at birth because mostly it is simply the history of racism (well, and sexism too of course.)

No doubt because of that history, our modern sensibilities are not at all attuned to taking this idea on board in our ethical thought. If we really did discover such a thing, what on earth would we do and how would we justify whatever we did in ethical terms, *whichever* normative theory we appealed to? I can imagine that some particularly hardline act utilitarians, and some of the redneck fundamentalists might cheerfully say oh well we'll kill 'em off at birth, and justify this in their usual ways, but I would say the rest of us are in real trouble.

So this is another speculation with respect to which I think we all, not just the virtue ethicists, had better cross our fingers and hope it is not so. That is as far as I have got in my exploration of the idea that our being varied, rather than pretty much the same as far as ethically relevant capacities are concerned, would present a serious problem

187

Rosalind Hursthouse

for virtue ethics. And so far my conclusion is, in some versions it would not present any problem (though in the case of 'natural virtue' it might be awkward for some egalitarians or people who believe in fairness) and in the some-of-us-might-be-born psychopathic version, it would present a serious problem for any of us, whatever normative ethical theory we espouse.

4. Conclusion

Overall my conclusion is that, pending further efforts, neither evolutionary biology nor armchair speculations about what it suggests might yet be revealed about human nature pose any threat to virtue ethics as such, though the two speculations I have discussed above would indeed be problematic for ethics as we know it.

The University of Aukland
r.hursthouse@auckland.ac.nz

Doubt and Human Nature in Descartes's *Meditations*[1]

SARAH PATTERSON

La première Méditation n'est plus une théorie à comprendre, c'est un exercice à pratiquer.   Étienne Gilson[2]

1. Introduction

Descartes is well known for his employment of the method of doubt. His most famous work, the *Meditations*, begins by exhorting us to doubt all our opinions, including our belief in the existence of the external world. But critics have charged that this universal doubt is impossible for us to achieve because it runs counter to human nature. If this is so, Descartes must be either misguided or hypocritical in proposing it. Hume writes:

> There is a species of scepticism, antecedent to all study and philosophy, which is much inculcated by Des Cartes and others, as a sovereign preservative against error and precipitate judgement. It recommends an universal doubt, not only of all our former opinions and principles, but also of our very faculties... The Cartesian doubt, ...*were it ever possible to be attained by any human creature (as it plainly is not)* would be entirely incurable; and no reasoning could ever bring us to a state of assurance and conviction upon any subject (*Enquiry* 12.3; emphasis added).[3]

Hume thinks that this antecedent or methodological scepticism is simply a dead end; if we could achieve Descartes's universal doubt, we could never escape from it. But there is a more fundamental

[1] This paper draws on research carried out during leave funded by a Birkbeck College Research Grant and by a Mind Fellowship, and I am grateful to the College and to the Mind Association for their support. I would also like to thank Constantine Sandis for helpful comments on an earlier draft.

[2] Etienne Gilson, *Etudes sur le rôle de la pensée médiévale dans la formation du système cartésien* (Fourth Edition. Paris: Vrin, 1975), 186.

[3] David Hume, *An Enquiry Concerning Human Understanding*, edited by L.A. Selby-Bigge, 3rd ed. revised by P.H. Nidditch (Oxford: Clarendon Press, 1975). References by section and paragraph number.

doi:10.1017/S1358246112000100   ©The Royal Institute of Philosophy and the contributors 2012
Royal Institute of Philosophy Supplement **70** 2012   189

problem with Descartes's method, and that is that the doubt he recommends is so contrary to human nature that it is unattainable by any human creature. In particular, Hume regards Cartesian doubt about the existence of the corporeal world as impossible. The sceptic 'must assent to the principle concerning the existence of body', because 'Nature has not left this to his choice'.[4] As he famously says, 'Nature by an absolute and uncontroulable necessity has determined us to judge as well as to breathe and feel'[5] and 'Nature is always too strong for principle'.[6]

Reid is another critic who regards it as impossible for us to genuinely doubt the existence of the external world, as the First Meditation enjoins us to do. 'The perception of an object', Reid writes, 'implies both a conception of its form, and a belief of its present existence'[7]; and it is not in our power to 'throw off this belief of external objects', any more than it is in our power to free ourselves from the natural force of gravity.[8]

If our nature compels us to believe in the existence of external things when we perceive them, then it seems that Descartes must be either deluded or disingenuous when he claims to doubt the existence of the corporeal world. Indeed, the fact that he manages to navigate that world successfully would seem to prove it. Reid tartly remarks:

> I resolve not to believe my senses. I break my nose against a post that comes in my way; I step into a dirty kennel; and after twenty such wise and rational actions, I am taken up and clapt into a mad-house...If a man pretends to be a sceptic with regard to the informations of sense, and yet prudently keeps out of harm's way as other men do, he must excuse my suspicion, that he either acts the hypocrite, or imposes upon himself.[9]

Hume and Reid agree that Descartes's injunction to doubt our senses is impossible to carry out, because our nature as human beings compels us to believe that we sense external bodies. They also agree

[4]   David Hume, *A Treatise of Human Nature*, edited by L.A. Selby-Bigge, 2nd ed. revised by P.H. Nidditch (Oxford: Clarendon Press, 1978), 187.

[5]   Op. cit. note 4, 183.

[6]   Op. cit. note 3, section 12, paragraph 23.

[7]   T. Reid, *Inquiry into the Human Mind on the Principles of Common Sense* (1801) in *Thomas Reid's Inquiry and Essays*, eds. R. E. Beanblossom and K. Lehrer (Indianapolis: Hackett, 1983), 84.

[8]   Op. cit. note 6, 85.

[9]   Op. cit. note 6, 86.

that if we could manage to overcome nature and attain Cartesian doubt, we would gain nothing. Descartes, then, must be misguided, hypocritical or both in exhorting us to doubt our senses and all our former opinions.

Many contemporary readers of Descartes will respond that these criticisms are based on a misunderstanding of the aims of Cartesian scepticism. They may agree with Hume and Reid that it is not humanly possible for us to disbelieve our senses to the extent of walking into posts or stepping into ditches, still less to do so as a result of reading the First Meditation. But this is irrelevant, the response goes, if Descartes is not aiming to induce such disbelief. Descartes himself says that 'the sceptics who neglected human matters to the point where friends had to stop them falling off precipices deserved to be laughed at'[10], and that no sane person has ever seriously doubted that material things exist.[11] Indeed, the fact that he describes the reasons for doubt he presents as 'slight, and, so to speak, metaphysical'[12] and as exaggerated[13] suggests that he does not expect them to generate genuine doubt. What, then, is his aim in advancing reasons to doubt? Well, the response goes, when Descartes asks how we know that we are not dreaming or deceived by an evil demon, or contemporary epistemologists ask how we know we are not brains in a vat, they are not trying to get us to withhold assent to our ordinary beliefs, but challenging us to provide a positive account of our justification for holding them. Since the doubts are advanced for theoretical ends, they can have a theoretical payoff. This also provides a response to the second charge, that the doubt has no value.

This response may paint an accurate picture of some contemporary uses of sceptical argument, but I believe that it is not an accurate interpretation of the *Meditations*. There is strong textual evidence that Descartes wants his readers to engage in genuine doubt – that is, that he wants us not just to accept that there is theoretical reason to doubt our opinions, but actually to withhold assent from them. The Preface states that he wants no readers except those who are able and willing to meditate seriously and 'to withdraw their minds

---

[10]   References by volume and page number to C. Adam and P. Tannery (eds.) *Oeuvres de Descartes*, 11 vols. (Paris: Vrin, 1904), and J. Cottingham, R. Stoothoff and D. Murdoch (eds.) *The Philosophical Writings of Descartes*, Vols. I and II (Cambridge: Cambridge University Press, 1984) (AT 7 351, CSM 2 243).

[11]   AT 7 16, CSM 2 11.

[12]   AT VII 36, CSM II 25.

[13]   AT VII 89, CSM II 61; AT VII 226, CSM II 159.

Sarah Patterson

from the senses and from all preconceived opinions'.[14] Descartes writes in the Fifth Replies:

> When I said that the entire testimony of the senses should be regarded as uncertain and even as false, I was quite serious; indeed this point is so necessary for an understanding of my *Meditations* that if anyone is unable or unwilling to accept it, he will be incapable of producing any objection that deserves a reply.[15]

'Regarding the testimony of the senses as uncertain' might sound like taking a theoretical stance towards such testimony, rather than genuinely doubting it. But Descartes continues by pointing out that this attitude towards the senses should not be extended to everyday life, but should be reserved for the investigation of the truth. It is here that he remarks that the ancient sceptics deserved to be laughed at. But this suggests that he finds those sceptics ridiculous not because they doubted their senses, but because they extended the doubt to everyday life instead of reserving it for meditation. It is precisely because the disbelief in the senses is genuine that it is dangerous to extend it to the actions of everyday life; if we do so we will fall off precipices and walk into posts. While we are meditating, though, it is vital that we withdraw our minds from the senses. The importance of this process is emphasised at the start of the Second, Third and Fourth Meditations, and it is clear that it is a process that we as meditators are meant to carry out.

So the questions pressed by Hume and Reid arise afresh. How can Descartes think it humanly possible for us to genuinely doubt our senses, to doubt that material things exist? And what benefit could possibly be gained by doubting our senses? In this paper I offer an account of Descartes's use of doubt in the *Meditations*, particularly doubt about the senses. On the interpretation I favour, Descartes uses doubt as a tool for cognitive reform.[16] This reform is needed

---

[14] AT VII 9, CSM II 8.

[15] AT VII 350, CSM II 243.

[16] For other interpretations stressing the importance of cognitive reform in the *Meditations*, see J. Carriero's *Between Two Worlds: A Reading of Descartes's* Meditations (Princeton: Princeton University Press, 2009), as well as D. Garber, '*Semel in vita*: The Scientific Background to Descartes's *Meditations*' and G. Hatfield, 'The Senses and the Fleshless Eye: The *Meditations* as Cognitive Exercises', both in A.O. Rorty (ed.) *Essays on Descartes's* Meditations (Berkeley: University of California Press, 1986). Garber traces what he sees as a dialogue between Descartes and common sense in the *Meditations*; I would suggest that what he calls 'common sense' is what Descartes regards as prejudice. Carriero stresses

to overcome the legacy of childhood errors. Descartes stresses the fact that we begin life as infants, dependent on the senses, and form beliefs and habits of thought before we can make correct use of the natural light of reason. We regard the cognitive dispositions so formed as *natural* because of their familiarity. In Descartes's view, however, they are merely *habitual*; thus habit usurps the place of nature. Doubting the senses can free us from these habitual errors and restore our nature to us, Descartes believes, but only if the doubt is not merely theoretical.

2. Reasons to Doubt in the First Meditation

Let us briefly review the sequence of doubts that begin the *Meditations*. When Descartes looks for reasons to doubt the senses, he first notes that the senses sometimes deceive, and that those who deceive even once are not worthy of trust. But though they sometimes deceive us about things which are very small or very distant, we would surely be insane, he says, to doubt the evidence of our senses when we see our hands in front of our faces. Then he reflects that dream experience can seem as evident; dreams may trick us into believing that we are sitting by the fire when we are asleep in bed. Finally, he suggests that an omnipotent God could have brought it about that there is no earth, no sky, no extended thing, no shape, no size, no place, while ensuring that these things appear to us to exist just as they do now.[17]

Does Descartes seriously expect us to doubt our senses on the basis of these considerations? He describes his conclusion that all his former beliefs are subject to doubt as 'based on powerful and well thought-out reasons', and continues:

(1) So in future I must withhold assent from these former beliefs just as carefully as I would from obvious falsehoods, if I want to discover any certainty.[18]

Descartes's disagreements with Scholastic Aristotelian epistemology. Since Descartes regards this as grounded in childhood prejudices (see e.g. footnote 6 below), our approaches are not incompatible.

[17] AT VII 21, CSM II 14. The supposition that we are deceived by an evil demon is not included here because Descartes does not introduce it as a reason to doubt our existing opinions. Instead, he introduces it to ensure that we do not assent to opinions we have found reason to doubt (AT VII 22-3, CSM II 15).

[18] AT VII 21, CSM II 14.

Sarah Patterson

Descartes here presents suspension of belief as the rational response to his sceptical arguments. Surely Hume and Reid are right to regard it as psychologically impossible, not to speak of irrational, not to believe our senses on these grounds.

Maybe so, but is this what Descartes intended? We must read him carefully. The resolution expressed in (1) is conditional: *if* he wants to discover any certainty (the French translation adds, 'in the sciences'), *then* he must withhold assent from his former beliefs. This suggests that suspension of belief is the rational response to his sceptical arguments under certain conditions, the conditions depicted in the opening paragraphs of the *Meditations*. Call the person in these conditions 'the meditator'. In his guise as meditator, Descartes earlier says:

> (2) Reason now leads me to think that I should hold back my assent from opinions which are not completely certain and indubitable just as carefully as I do from those that are patently false.[19]

For the meditator, reason dictates that assent should be withheld from beliefs that are subject to any doubt at all. Consequently, suspension of belief is the meditator's rational response to the sceptical arguments. But why is it rational for the meditator to withhold assent from beliefs that are in any sense dubitable, as (2) claims? Notice that the meditator says 'Reason *now* leads me to think...'. This suggests, again, that there is something about the meditator's specific conditions that makes it rational to withhold assent from anything dubitable. What are these conditions? The *Meditations* begins thus:

> (3) Some years ago I was struck by the large number of falsehoods I had accepted as true in my childhood, and by the highly doubtful nature of the whole edifice that I had subsequently based on them. *I realized that it was necessary*, once in the course of my life, to demolish everything completely and start again right from the foundations *if I wanted to establish anything at all in the sciences that was stable and likely to last*.[20]

The later reference to certainty in (1) presumably alludes to this aim of establishing something stable and lasting in the sciences. Passage (3) tells us that stable certainties can be established in the sciences only if we demolish our existing beliefs and start afresh. This demolition is necessary, Descartes says, because our beliefs constitute a

[19] AT VII 18, CSM II 12.
[20] AT VII 17, CSM II 17, emphasis added.

194

doubtful structure based on falsehoods accepted in our infancy. Taken together, passages (2) and (3) tell us that *if* we seek to demolish a belief structure based on falsehoods accepted in childhood in order to establish stable certainties in the sciences, *then* it is rational for us to withhold assent from beliefs about which any doubt can be raised. Only in the context of this project of demolition and reconstruction, then, does Descartes claim that the meditator should withhold assent from the senses on the basis of his sceptical arguments.

What are the implications of this for the objection that Cartesian doubt about the senses is both impossible and fruitless? Firstly, it implies that the sceptical arguments are not expected to induce suspension of belief all on their own, as it were. The role of the sceptical arguments is simply to show that our beliefs are 'in some sense doubtful', as Descartes puts it. It is only in the context of the resolution to demolish our existing beliefs and start afresh that it is rational to suspend belief in whatever is in some sense doubtful. Secondly, it means that the feasibility and value of suspension of belief in the senses depends on the feasibility and value of the project of demolishing our existing beliefs in order to establish something lasting in the sciences. What reason does Descartes give to persuade us that this project of demolition and reconstruction is necessary?

At first sight, the motivation Descartes offers for the project seems slender. He says that he was struck by the large number of falsehoods he had accepted as true in his childhood. Presumably we can all think of some falsehoods we accepted as true in childhood; perhaps, as children, we believed that Father Christmas brought us presents, or that monsters lived under the bed, or that babies are delivered by storks, or some such. But the fact that we now recognise these falsehoods as such means that we no longer accept them, so it is hard to see how they could render other beliefs we have dubious. Presumably we are all modest enough to accept that we have some unrecognised false beliefs, some of which may well have been acquired in childhood. But this commonplace observation hardly seems to necessitate what Descartes describes as the 'enormous task' of demolishing all our beliefs and starting again from the beginning. If some of our beliefs are false, why not identify and correct them piecemeal, instead of attempting to reject all our opinions at once?

The fact that the rationale for the project of demolition and reconstruction seems so slight fuels the suspicion that Descartes has another agenda, such as a particular conception of knowledge or of enquiry, or a preoccupation with indubitability. Descartes does have an agenda that cannot be revealed to the reader at this initial stage, if only in the sense that he knows what the outcome of the project will be, while the reader does not. But this point is compatible with many different views of what that agenda is, of what Descartes aims to achieve through the use of doubt. I suggest that we should take Descartes at his word when he says that the reason we should demolish and rebuild our beliefs is that they are founded on falsehoods accepted in childhood. On this more literal reading of the aim and motivation for the project of doubt, it is precisely because we are subject to these founding falsehoods that cognitive reform is needed.[21] Let us see what can be said for this for this more literal reading of Descartes's agenda.

3. The Consequences of the Errors of Childhood

The ill-formed, ill-founded character of our early beliefs and the consequent necessity of starting afresh is a frequent theme in Descartes's work. The earlier *Discourse* compares our beliefs to an unplanned city that has grown up through the haphazard addition of buildings, the unfinished *Search After Truth* compares them to a picture badly drawn by a young apprentice, and the Seventh Replies compares them to a barrel of sound apples contaminated by rotten ones. In all three cases the defective character of our beliefs is connected to their childhood origin. Descartes writes:

> I reflected that we were all children before being men and had to be governed for some time by our appetites and our teachers, which were often opposed to each other and neither of which, perhaps, always gave us the best advice; hence I thought it impossible that our judgements should be as unclouded and firm as they would have been if we had had the full use of our reason from the moment of our birth, and if we had always been guided by it alone.[22]

[21] I believe that a stronger claim can be made out: that (with one exception) the project of cognitive reform through doubt is (a) feasible and (b) necessary only for those who are subject to the founding errors of childhood. An exception is needed to allow for those whose beliefs are subject to major error and distortion *independent of* these founding errors. Descartes would not of course deny that there could be such people, nor that they could undergo and benefit from a further round of demolition and reconstruction. But for most human beings, Descartes believes, reform of the errors and biases originating in childhood is necessary and sufficient to remove the main cause of error in our beliefs.

[22] *Discourse* II, AT VI 13, 14, CSM I 117.

...Our senses, inclinations, teachers and the intellect are the
different artists who may work at this task [sc. of tracing ideas
on a child's imagination], and among them the least competent
are the first to take part, namely our imperfect senses, blind instincts and foolish nurses. The most competent is the intellect,
which comes last...[23]

...those who have never philosophized correctly have various
opinions in their minds which they have begun to store up
since childhood, and which they therefore believe may *in many
cases* be false.[24]

Descartes uses these comparisons to recommend the demolition of
the city, the erasure of the drawing, the emptying of the barrel; the
city is to be rebuilt according to a plan, the picture redrawn by the
master artist, the barrel refilled with sound apples. Similarly,
the opinions acquired since childhood should be cleared away, so
that they can be replaced with better ones:

...regarding the opinions to which I had hitherto given credence,
I thought I could not do better than undertake to get rid of them
all at one go, in order to replace them afterwards with better ones,
or with the same ones once I had squared them with the standards of reason.[25]

...[the master] painter would do far better to make a fresh start on
the picture; rather than wasting time correcting the lines he finds
on the canvas, he should wipe them off it with a sponge.
Similarly, as soon as a man reaches what we call the age of dis-
cretion, he should resolve once and for all to remove from his
imagination all traces of the imperfect ideas that have been
engraved there up till that time. Then he should begin in
earnest to find new ideas, applying all the strength of his intellect
so effectively that if he does not bring these ideas to perfection, at
least he will not be able to blame the weakness of the senses or the
irregularities of nature.[26]

...in order to separate out the true ones, it is best to begin by
rejecting all our opinions and renouncing every single one; this
will make it easier, afterwards, to recognise those which were

[23]   *Search After Truth*, AT X 507, CSM II 406.
[24]   Seventh Replies, AT VII 481, CSM II 324; emphasis added.
[25]   *Discourse* II, AT VI 13, 14, CSM I 117.
[26]   *Search After Truth*, AT VII 508, CSM II 406.

true (or discover new truths), so that we end up admitting only what is true.[27]

The architectural metaphors used in the *Discourse* and *Search* indicate the instability of childhood opinions as a foundation for our beliefs. The passages from the *Search* and the Seventh Replies emphasise the magnitude of the falsity to be found in opinions formed in childhood. The *Discourse*, *Search* and *Principles* link the falsity of these beliefs to the fact that the intellect or reason is not fully developed in childhood; the *Search* and *Principles* also implicate the senses in these errors. The description of our predicament in the *Search* is particularly striking:

> The intellect is like an excellent painter who is called upon to put the finishing touches to a bad picture sketched out by a young apprentice. It would be futile for him to employ the rules of his art in correcting the picture little by little, a bit here and a bit there, and in adding with his own hand all that is lacking in it, if, despite his best efforts, he could never remove every major fault, since the drawing was badly sketched from the beginning, the figures badly placed, and the proportions badly observed.[28]

Here the faults in the image sketched by the apprentice are so extensive and so fundamental that it is necessary for the master to erase it and begin again; the picture cannot be corrected piecemeal. The message of the simile is that the errors in the opinions acquired in childhood via our senses, instincts and teachers are so extensive and so fundamental that the intellect, the master, cannot correct them one by one. This message is most explicit in the opening words of the later *Principles*:

> *The seeker after truth must, once in the course of his life, doubt everything, as far as is possible.* Since we began life as infants, and made various judgements concerning the things that can be perceived through the senses before we had full use of our reason, *there are many prejudices that keep us from knowledge of the truth.* It seems that the only way of freeing ourselves from these opinions is to make the effort, once in the course of our life, to doubt everything which we find to contain even the smallest suspicion of falsity.[29]

---

[27] Seventh Replies, AT VII 512, CSM II 349.
[28] AT VII 507–8, CSM II 406.
[29] AT VIIIA 5, CSM I 193, emphasis added.

This passage also mentions a further problem: the opinions acquired in childhood are not just false, they are also obstacles to the knowledge of the truth.

It is clear from these texts that the project of demolishing and reconstructing our opinions is not motivated simply by the banal observation that we acquire the occasional false belief in childhood. In Descartes's view, the mistakes we make in childhood are so fundamental and so pervasive that piecemeal correction is hopeless; that is why we must 'demolish everything completely and start again right from the foundations'.[30] When he begins the *Meditations* by speaking of the 'large number' of falsehoods accepted in childhood, and the 'highly dubious' character of the beliefs based on them, he is perfectly sincere.

4. The Need to Doubt the Senses

What is the nature of these fundamental childhood errors? When Descartes sets to work to undermine the edifice of belief, he targets the senses: 'whatever I have up till now accepted as most true I have acquired by or through the senses'.[31] The implication is that the many basic falsehoods taken as true in childhood are acquired through reliance on the senses. That this is his considered view is plain from Descartes's explicit descriptions of our early cognitive development, as well as his frequent references to the prejudices of the senses.[32] The later *Principles* states that 'the chief cause of error arises from the prejudices of childhood'.[33] Our infant reliance on the senses imbued our minds with 'a thousand prejudices'; and in later childhood, 'forgetting that they were adopted without sufficient examination', we regarded these prejudices as 'known by the senses or implanted by nature, and accepted them as utterly true and evident'.[34]

How do these prejudices 'keep us from knowledge of the truth', as Descartes claims they do? He explains in the Second Replies that the reason it is difficult for us to perceive the primary notions of metaphysics clearly and distinctly is that they conflict with 'many prejudices derived from the senses which we have got into the habit of

---

30 AT VII 17, CSM II 12.
31 AT VII 18, CSM II 12.
32 See, for example, AT VII 158, CSM II 112.
33 AT VIIIA 35, CSM I 218.
34 *Principles* I.71, AT VIIIA 36, CSM I 219.

holding from our earliest years'.[35] He writes in the earlier *Discourse* that

> many are convinced that there is some difficulty in knowing God, and even in knowing what their soul is. The reason is that they never raise their minds above things that can be perceived through the senses; they are so used to thinking of things only by imagining them (a way of thinking especially suited to material things) that whatever is unimaginable seems to them unintelligible.[36]

As this passage shows, Descartes believes that our childhood reliance on the senses entrenches a habit of thinking in terms of what can be sensed. The soul is thought of, if it is thought of at all, as a kind of attenuated body, a wind or ether permeating the limbs.[37] Things that do not affect the senses, such as God and the soul, are regarded as difficult to know. Conversely, bodies are regarded as easy to know, since they are assumed to resemble our sensory perceptions completely.[38] For example, distant stars are taken to be small, because that is how they appear to our senses; space where we sense nothing is taken to contain nothing corporeal; bodies are taken to possess heat, colour and other sensible qualities wholly resembling our sensory perceptions.[39]

In contrast to what he regards as the widespread conviction that it is difficult to know God and the soul, Descartes believes that our own minds and God are 'the most certain and evident of all possible objects of knowledge for the human intellect'. That, he says, is the one thing he set himself to prove in the *Meditations*.[40] This remark testifies to the importance Descartes attaches to overcoming the prejudices of the senses and learning to appreciate 'the certainty that belongs to metaphysical things' such as God and the soul.[41]

[35]   AT VII 157, CSM II 111.

[36]   AT VI 37, CSM I 129.

[37]   Second Meditation, AT VII 26, CSM II 17.

[38]   Third Meditation, AT VII 35, CSM II 25; Sixth Meditation, AT VII 75, CSM II 52.

[39]   These are not the only effects of the founding error. Thanks to our infant reliance on the senses and the vividness of sensory ideas, we form the belief that nothing is in the intellect that was not first in the senses, a tenet of Scholastic Aristotelian epistemology (AT VII 75, CSM II 52).

[40]   Synopsis, AT VII 16, CSM II 11. This last remark about the aim of the *Meditations* should be taken with a pinch of salt, given Descartes's confession to Mersenne that the work contains all the foundations of his physics (see AT III 298, CSM III 193).

[41]   AT VII 162, CSM II 115.

Doubt and Human Nature in Descartes's *Meditations*

Thanks to the continuing effect of the habitual prejudices of the senses, 'only those who really *concentrate* and *meditate*, and *withdraw their minds from corporeal things*, so far as is possible, will achieve perfect knowledge' of metaphysical things.[42] The 'greatest benefit' of the First Meditation doubt, Descartes says, is precisely that it both frees our minds from prejudices, and provides a way to draw the mind away from the senses.[43]

In effect, the *Meditations* attempts to correct the effects of the process that occurred in childhood, when our minds were stocked with beliefs acquired through reliance on the senses, and the intellect exercised little or no critical scrutiny. Hence Descartes writes,

> the only opinions I want to steer my readers' minds away from are those which they have never properly examined – opinions which they have acquired not on the basis of any firm reasoning but from the senses alone.[44]

These long-standing opinions based on the senses are to be eradicated, and our minds are to be re-stocked with opinions subjected to the scrutiny of the intellect and based on firm reasoning. If this is Descartes's plan, it is clear that it can proceed only if we really do renounce our old opinions and cease to trust our senses, so far as we can. So the questions raised by Hume and Reid press with particular force. How can we do this if we could not doubt our senses without falling into danger? How can we do this if we are psychologically incapable of doubting our senses?

Precisely because he is so insistent that his readers should genuinely withdraw their minds from their senses, Descartes is sensitive to these questions of practicality. He stresses that the meditator should have 'a clear stretch of free time'[45], and that the task of meditation 'does not involve action but merely the acquisition of knowledge'.[46] If the meditator is sitting quietly, engaged only in meditation, the danger of walking into posts is minimal. But of course there is no such danger if it is psychologically impossible for us not to trust our senses. What is Descartes's response to this charge?

---

[42] AT VII 157, CSM II 111; emphasis added. It is because of the importance of attentive meditation, Descartes explains, that he wrote 'Meditations' rather than 'Disputations' or 'Theorems and Problems' (AT VII 157, CSM II 112).

[43] AT VII 12, CSM II 19.

[44] AT VII 158, CSM II 112.

[45] AT VII 18, CSM II 17.

[46] AT VII 22, CSM II 15.

Descartes holds that trust in the senses is both habitual and natural for us. It is natural because we have, he believes, a strong natural propensity to believe that we perceive material bodies when we sense. It is habitual because we are in the habit of believing that the senses are the source of certainty and truth. Having decided in the First Meditation that he must withhold assent from his existing opinions, he finds that these habitual opinions 'keep coming back, and despite my wishes, they capture my belief, which is as it were bound over to them as the result of long occupation and the law of custom'.[47] The existence of these natural and habitual tendencies to belief means that a special measure is needed to enable the meditator to withdraw the mind from the senses and suspend belief in the existence of bodies, so far as possible.[48] The measure Descartes uses is the pretence of falsity. He resolves to deceive himself by 'pretending for a time that these former opinions are utterly false and imaginary'; and he resolves to do this until 'the weight of prejudice is counter-balanced and the distorting influence of habit no longer prevents my judgement from perceiving things correctly'.[49] As he says here, the pretence of falsity is needed to counteract the effect of the prejudices ingrained since childhood, the habits that distort our judgement and prevent us from perceiving clearly and correctly. Although it is a pretence, it serves the purpose of counteracting our natural and habitual tendencies towards belief in the sensible world. Before we examine how the pretence of falsity is put to use, it will be useful to clarify the character of the fundamental error of childhood.

5. The Nature of the Founding Error

Is our fundamental error an error of the senses, or an error of judgement? On the one hand, when Descartes sets out to undermine the foundations of our existing opinions in the First Meditations, he

---

[47]   AT VII 22, CSM II15.

[48]   It is particularly difficult for us to doubt the existence of our own bodies because we are taught by nature that we are intermingled with them to make one thing. Presumably that is one reason that Descartes explicitly discusses the feasibility of doubting the existence of our hands and bodies in the First Meditation. At first he suggests that only the insane could do this; then he points out that in dreams we believe false things about our own bodies (AT VII 18–9, CSM II 13).

[49]   AT VII 22, CSM II 15.

targets the senses, saying that 'whatever I had accepted as most true I had accepted by or through the senses'.[50] And we have already seen that he attributes our childhood errors to a preoccupation with the senses. On the other, Descartes invokes the pretence of falsity to counteract prejudices or pre-judgements, and to correct the effect of habits that distort our judgement.

Descartes finally identifies our fundamental error regarding the senses in the Sixth Meditation. It is that of misusing sensory perceptions by treating them as reliable guides for immediate judgements about the essences of external bodies, without waiting for the intellect to examine the matter.[51] In doing this, he says, we habitually pervert the order of nature.[52] The proper purpose of our sensory perceptions is to inform the mind of what is beneficial or harmful for the mind-body composite, the human being. When we use them as touchstones for immediate judgements about the essences of the external bodies we sense, we use them for an unnatural and improper purpose.

It is clear from this diagnosis that the founding error is an error of judgement, rather than of the senses proper. The character of the error fits Descartes's description of the predicament of the human mind in infancy. Our earliest judgements, he believes, are governed by our desire to survive. As a result, in childhood 'the mind judged everything in terms of its utility to the body in which it was immersed'.[53] Since our capacity for sensory perception is given to us by Nature as a guide to what is beneficial and harmful to us as embodied creatures, it is not surprising that the infant should rely on sensory perceptions for survival. As Descartes explains in the Sixth Replies,

> From infancy I had made a variety of judgements about physical things in so far as they contributed to preserving the life which I was embarking on…But at that age the mind employed the bodily organs less correctly than it now does, and was more firmly attached to them; hence it had no thoughts apart from them and perceived things only in a confused manner…Now *I had never freed myself from these prejudices in later life*, and hence there was nothing that I knew with sufficient distinctness, and nothing I did not suppose to be corporeal.[54]

---

[50] AT VII 18, CSM II 12.
[51] AT VII 82–3, CSM II 57–8.
[52] AT VI 83, CSM II 57.
[53] AT VIIIA 36, CSM I 219.
[54] AT VII 441, CSM II 297, emphasis added.

The founding error becomes entrenched when the confused judgements made in childhood become habitual, instead of being revised in later life.

Descartes's claim that we pervert or overturn the order of nature might be taken to mean that we allow the senses to usurp the place of the intellect. But that would suggest that the senses and the intellect compete for the control of judgement, and that is not how he views the matter. For Descartes, the senses and the intellect are faculties of perception; they do not make judgements. Judgement occurs only when we affirm or deny the content of a perception by an act of will. Our errors of judgement stem from our misuse of our free will (as it must do, given that the author of our nature is not responsible for them). We use our wills incorrectly whenever we affirm something without perceiving its truth with sufficient clarity and distinctness; and this is what we do habitually when we draw conclusions about the nature of external bodies from sensory perceptions without adequate intellectual examination. Such judgements are erroneous in Descartes's specific sense of the term: they involve the incorrect use of free will that is, for him, the essence of judgement error.[55]

Mistaking the epistemic role of the senses, we treat sensory perceptions as the source of certainty. The founding error, then, is an error of judgement that becomes habitual. In particular, we habitually judge that external things wholly resemble our sensory perceptions. Worse still, we fail to recognize our responsibility for these judgements; we regard our habitual view of the world as implanted by nature or known by the senses, as he puts it in the *Principles*.[56] This mistake is reinforced by the fact that we fail to recognize the role of judgement in what we call 'sensing'. The senses do not make judgements, but the final stages of what we call sensing are the product of judgement, the work of the intellect and will. There is no falsity in the sensory perceptions of external objects that occur in our minds when our sense organs are stimulated.[57] Descartes does describe these perceptions as materially false, but this simply means that they provide material for false judgements.[58] Because these ideas are obscure and confused, we are liable to misjudge their objects.[59] In particular, we are liable to judge that they represent

---

[55] AT VII 60, CSM II 41.
[56] I.71, AT VIIIA 36, CSM I 219.
[57] AT VII 438, CSM II 295–6.
[58] AT VII 234, CSM II 164.
[59] AT VII 233, CSM II 163.

qualities in objects which they wholly resemble, as happens when we judge that heat in a body is something wholly resembling the idea of heat that is in us.[60] Sensory perceptions of heat are given to us by nature to inform us of the potential of other bodies to help or harm our own, and as such they are sufficiently clear and distinct.[61] Sensory perceptions also carry information about the essential natures of these bodies, but in an obscure form.[62] That is why careful thought is needed if we are to make true judgements about the corporeal world on the basis of such perceptions. In Descartes's view, we are solely responsible for the mistakes we make when we judge without such careful thought; the sensory ideas themselves are not the source of our errors.

This point is worth stressing because it is so often missed. It is easy to miss, because Descartes himself obscures it by his talk of the errors and prejudices of the senses. When he speaks in this way, Descartes is speaking colloquially, attributing to the senses what is actually the result of judgement.[63] His considered view is that we do make fundamental errors because of our reliance on the senses, but these errors are not due to our reliance on a faculty that is by nature unreliable, erroneous or otherwise faulty. Our benevolent creator would not, indeed could not give us such a faculty. Instead, the errors are due to our misuse of a faculty of sensation that is perfectly in order, and indeed testifies to the power and goodness of God.[64] We err when we misuse sensory perceptions by assigning them a role for which nature (i.e. God) did not intend them.

6. Correcting the Founding Error

Let us now begin to map out the way in which the *Meditations* uses doubt about the senses to correct the founding error. As we saw, Descartes directs us to pretend that our long-standing opinions are false, that our senses delude us, to ensure that we do not slip back into our errors. The pretence of falsity is put into effect using the device of the evil demon. We are to suppose that we are being deceived by a demon of the utmost power and cunning, who not only supplies us with delusory experience but also deludes us about the

---

60 AT VII 82, CSM II 56.
61 AT VII 83, CSM II 57.
62 AT VII 83, CSM II 58.
63 AT VII 437–8, CSM II 295; see also AT VII 32, CSM II 21.
64 AT VII 87–8, CSM II 60.

very existence of bodies. This supposition is intended to disrupt our habitual trust in the senses and to draw our minds away from their preoccupation with sensible things.

Pursuing this supposition, Descartes begins the Second Meditation by supposing that everything he sees is spurious (*falsa*), that his memory lies, that he has no senses, that body, shape, extension and place are chimeras.[65] The first fruit of this rejection of the sensible is a conception of the self as 'a mind, or intelligence, or intellect, or reason – words whose meaning I have been ignorant of until now'.[66] This grasp of the self as a thinking thing does not depend on the grasp of anything corporeal; in fact, it is arrived at by supposing the non-existence of anything corporeal. This being so, Descartes argues, the mind must be 'most carefully diverted' from sensory images of corporeal things 'if it is to perceive its own nature as distinctly as possible'.[67]

Despite having been introduced to this intellectual grasp of the self as a mind, the meditator 'cannot stop' thinking that corporeal things, which can be sensed and imagined, are known more distinctly than the mind, which cannot.[68] Descartes confronts this childhood prejudice directly through the examination of the piece of wax. The essential nature of the wax is grasped not by the senses, which perceive only its outward forms, nor by the imagination, which can form only a limited number of images, but by the intellect, when we understand that the wax is a body capable of being extended in an infinity of different ways. Even what we call 'seeing with our eyes' involves an act of judgement, Descartes argues. We *judge* that the wax is there before us when we perceive its colour and shape, just as we *judge* that there are men in the square below us when we see hats and coats. Hence we not only perceive what the wax is using the intellect, by conceiving of it as an extended body; we also perceive the wax itself using the intellect when we do what we ordinarily call 'sensing' it.

This claim that what we call 'sensing' involves an intellectual act is elaborated in his discussion of the three grades or stages of sensing in the Sixth Replies. The first stage consists of physical motions in the bodily organs, the second of the immediate mental effects of these, 'including perceptions of pain, pleasure, thirst, hunger, colours, sound, taste, smell heat, cold and the like' (AT VII 437, CSM II 294). Sensing proper ends with these. The third stage includes 'all

---

65 AT VII 24, CSM II 16.
66 Second Meditation, AT VII 27, CSM II 18.
67 AT VII 28, CSM II 19.
68 AT VII 29, CSM II 20.

the judgements about things outside us which we have been accustomed to make from our earliest years' (AT VII 437, CSM II 295); but 'when from our earliest years we have made judgements, or even rational inferences, about the things that affect our senses', we do not distinguish these judgements from simple sense-perception. Descartes writes:

> We make the calculation and judgement at great speed because of habit, or rather, we remember the judgements we have long made about similar objects (AT VII 438, CSM II 295).

Thus we refer these judgements to the senses because they are so habitual that they have become, in effect, an automatic part of the process set in train by the stimulation of our sense organs.

The realisation that much of what we call sensing is in fact the work of the intellect is of key importance for Descartes's project of challenging the 'prejudices of the senses'. It marks the meditator's first step on the path to exposing the founding error. The second step is taken in the Third Meditation, when Descartes identifies

> something which I used to assert, and which through habitual belief I thought I perceived clearly, though I did not in fact do so. This was that there were things outside me which were the sources of my ideas and to which they were wholly similar [*omnino similes*].[69]

Why, he asks, do we believe that external things are wholly similar to our sensory ideas? (Notice that the accent is on the resemblance claim, rather than the existence claim.) Firstly, nature has apparently taught us to think this; that is, we have a spontaneous impulse to believe it. But our natural impulses have led us astray in the past, so this is not a good enough reason. Secondly, we think that our sensory ideas come from something outside us, because their occurrence is not under our control; and the most obvious judgement for us to make is that these external things transmit their likenesses to us. But this is not a good enough reason either. These ideas might come from a source within us, as they do when we are dreaming; and even if they come from external things, that does not entail that they must resemble them. Here Descartes points out that we have two incompatible ideas of the sun. One, derived from what we call sensing, represents it as small; the other, derived from astronomical observation and reasoning, represents it as many times larger than the Earth. The sun cannot

[69] AT VII 35, CSM II 25.

Sarah Patterson

resemble both ideas, and in this case we judge that the first idea is the one it least resembles.[70]

Descartes concludes that it is 'not reliable judgement but merely some blind impulse' that has made us believe up till now that there are external things which transmit their likenesses to us through the senses.[71] As we have seen, the belief that external bodies wholly resemble our sensory perceptions is one of the most entrenched prejudices of childhood (as well as a cornerstone of Scholastic Aristotelian epistemology). This habitual belief now appears far more dubious than it did after the arguments of First Meditation. There habitual beliefs were still regarded as being highly probable opinions, ones it is much more reasonable to believe than deny.[72] By this point in the meditator's progress, this habitual belief seems to be without justification.

The belief in the existence of external bodies wholly resembling our sensory perceptions is finally reassessed in Sixth Meditation, in the light of the knowledge of own nature and its creator that has been gained through meditating. Descartes's reasoned proof of the existence of body appeals to the fact that God has given us a 'great propensity' to believe that our sensory perceptions are caused by material things, and no faculty for recognizing any other source. The impulse to believe that sensory ideas are *caused* by external bodies is thus legitimated as a natural propensity bestowed by a veracious creator. Now that we know that our creator is not a deceiver, we can say that

> There is no doubt that everything I am taught by nature contains some truth. For if nature is considered in its general aspect, then I understand by the term nothing other than God himself, or the system of created things established by God. And by my own nature in particular I understand nothing other than the totality of things bestowed on me by God.[73]

Descartes claims that our God-given nature teaches us that we have bodies to which we are united, and that our bodies are surrounded by other bodies that vary in ways corresponding to the variation in our sensory perceptions.[74] But the impulse to believe that external

---

[70]   AT VII 39, CSM II 27.
[71]   AT VII 40, CSM II 27.
[72]   AT VII 22, CSM II 15.
[73]   AT VII 80, CSM II 56.
[74]   AT VII 81, CSM II 56.

bodies *wholly resemble* sensory ideas is *not* legitimated as a teaching of nature. Descartes writes:

> There are, however, many other things which *I may appear to have been taught by nature*, but which in reality I acquired not from nature but from *a habit of judging without consideration*, and therefore it may easily turn out that these are false. Cases in point are the belief that any space in which nothing is occurring to stimulate my senses must be empty; or that heat in a body is something exactly resembling the idea of heat that is in me; or that when a body is white or green, the same whiteness or greenness which I perceive through my senses is present in the body; or than in a body that is bitter or sweet there is the same taste which I experience, and so on; or, finally, that stars and towers and other distant bodies have the same size and shape which they present to my senses, and other examples of this kind.[75]

The beliefs listed here are childhood prejudices, beliefs acquired through a habit of making judgements without due consideration that dates back to our earliest years. Since they all reflect the assumption that external bodies wholly resemble our sensory perceptions, that assumption too is a prejudice of childhood. The impulse to believe that external things resemble sensory ideas is revealed as an acquired tendency masquerading as a teaching of nature.

Teachings of nature and childhood habits are easily confused, since long-standing habits are so familiar that they seem natural to us. But their provenance, and hence their epistemic status, is completely different. Teachings of nature come from a God who cannot deceive, so they are guaranteed to contain some truth.[76] Habits of judgement acquired in childhood are most likely to be false. In childhood, as we saw, we are reliant on sensory perceptions for survival, and we come to treat them as infallible guides to truth, a role they were never intended to play. Descartes explains this in an important discussion in which he clarifies what he means by a teaching of nature. Our nature as embodied minds teaches us to avoid external bodies that cause painful sensations, since these are signs of potential

---

[75] AT VII 82, CSM II 56–7, emphasis added.

[76] Why is what our nature teaches only guaranteed to contain *some* truth? We learn later in the Sixth Meditation that our inner sensations sometimes deceive. This occasional deception of the senses is a natural and unavoidable consequence of our composite nature as human beings, so it is compatible with the perfection of our creator (AT VII 88–9, CSM II 62).

Sarah Patterson

harm, and to seek out ones that cause pleasant sensations, since these are signs of potential benefit. It is here that he says that the proper purpose of the sensory perceptions given to us by nature is simply to inform the mind of what is beneficial or harmful to the mind-body composite. But our nature as composites of mind and body

> does not appear to teach us to draw any conclusions from these sensory perceptions about things located outside us before waiting until the intellect has examined the matter, for knowledge of the truth about such things seems to belong to *the mind alone*, not to the combination of mind and body.[77]

This is a crucial passage. Descartes claims that knowledge of the truth about external bodies belongs to the mind alone, and that is why intellectual examination is required before we make judgements about such things on the basis of sensory perceptions. Of course we made such judgements without intellectual examination in childhood, before we had full use of our reason. But we are at fault because we have continued to make them ever since, even though we now have the capacity to correct them.[78] Through our failure to correct them, we are

> in the habit of perverting the order of nature. For the proper purpose of the sensory perceptions given me by nature is simply to inform the mind of what is beneficial or harmful for the composite of which the mind is a part...But I misuse them by treating them as reliable touchstones for immediate judgements about the essences of the bodies located outside us; yet this is an area where they provide very obscure information.[79]

We misuse sensory perceptions when we make them the basis for precipitate judgements about external things without waiting for the intellect to examine the matter.[80] This is the founding error of childhood, which we are now in a position to correct.

This is the final step on the path to correcting the prejudices of the senses. It makes essential use of the lesson learned at the first step, in the Second Meditation, when the meditator discovered that bodies

---

[77] AT VII 82–3, CSM II 57.

[78] The fact that our creator is not a deceiver guarantees that any falsity in our opinions is correctible by some faculty that is part of our natural endowment (AT VII 80, CSM II 55–6).

[79] AT VII 83, CSM II 57–8.

[80] AT VI 83, CSM II 57–8.

such as the wax are known not by the senses but by the mind alone. This lesson is applied when the meditator reasons that knowledge of the truth about external bodies belongs to the mind alone, not the mind-body composite. Our natures as composites teach us to avoid things that cause pain and seek out what causes pleasure, but it does not teach us to draw conclusions from sensory perceptions about external things 'without waiting until the intellect has examined the matter'.[81] Our tendency to do this is not natural, as we take it to be, but habitual. By nature, knowledge of the truth about external things 'belongs to the mind alone', and that is why we must examine and interpret sensory perceptions before we make judgements about the natures of external bodies.[82] Our failure to do this is the source of the founding error that perverts our nature.

7. The Role of Doubt About the Senses

What role does doubt about the senses play in the process of correcting the founding error? One might think that it operates only at the outset, that it simply helps to wipe the slate clean, to free our minds from our old beliefs or prejudices, so that the process of reconstruction can begin. But such an interpretation would obscure the process of active doubting in which Descartes wants us to engage as the *Meditations* progresses. As we have seen, Descartes states in the Synopsis that the greatest value of the First Meditation doubt is that it frees our minds from prejudices and lays down the easiest route by which the mind may be drawn away from the senses.[83] But he describes the *actual* withdrawal of the mind from the senses as occurring in the Second Meditation, in which the mind uses the freedom it has gained to suppose the non-existence of things perceived through the senses, and thereby becomes aware of its own nature for the first time.[84] He claims in the Second Replies that although many writers had said that the mind must be drawn away from the senses in order to understand metaphysical matters, no

---

[81]   AT VII 82, CSM II 57.
[82]   AT VII 82, CSM II 57
[83]   AT VII 12, CSM II 9.
[84]   AT VII 12, CSM II 9. The Synopsis states that 'this exercise [sc. of doubting the existence of all things, especially material things] is also of the greatest benefit since it enables the mind to distinguish without difficulty what belongs to itself...from what belongs to body' (AT VII 12, CSM II 9).

one had shown how this could be done. He, Descartes, has provided the correct – and, he claims, unique – method of doing this in the Second Meditation.[85]

As we saw, Descartes begins the Second Meditation by supposing that everything he sees is spurious (*falsa*), that his memory lies, that he has no senses, that body, shape, extension and place are chimeras.[86] The pretence of deception by the demon is invoked several times (AT VII 24–6, CSM II 17–8), reinforcing the thought that sensory images are no more than dreams (AT VII 28, CSM II 19). By disregarding sensory images and denying that anything material exists, we learn to distinguish what belongs to an intellectual nature from what belongs to corporeal things (AT VII 131, CSM II 94).

This direction of mental attention away from sensory perceptions and towards the objects of the understanding is a reversal of the direction it has had since childhood. So it is not surprising that Descartes warns that 'protracted and repeated study' of the Second Meditation is required 'to eradicate the lifelong habit of confusing things related to the intellect with corporeal things, and to replace it with the opposite habit of distinguishing the two'.[87] It takes effort to withdraw attention from sensory images and concentrate the mind on things that cannot be sensed.[88] We have to learn to exercise 'the intellectual vision which nature gave [us], in the pure form which it attains when freed from the senses; for sensory appearances generally disturb and obscure it to a very great extent.[89]

By the start of the Fourth Meditation, the meditator can declare that

> During these past few days I have accustomed myself to leading my mind away from the senses…The result is that I now have no difficulty in turning my mind away from imaginable things and towards things which are the objects of the intellect alone and are totally separate from matter.[90]

---

[85] AT VII 131, CSM II 94.
[86] AT VII 24, CSM II 16.
[87] AT VII 131, CSM II 94.
[88] Descartes explains in the *Principles* that 'our mind is unable to keep its attention on things without some degree of difficulty and fatigue; and it is hardest of all for it to attend to what is not present to the senses or even to the imagination' (AT VIIIA 37, CSM I 220).
[89] AT VII 162–3, CSM II 115.
[90] AT VII 53, CSM II 37.

Doubt and Human Nature in Descartes's *Meditations*

The meditator now understands that our own minds and God are 'the most certain and evident of all possible objects of knowledge for the human intellect', as Descartes puts it in the Synopsis.[91]

This realisation corrects one of the prejudices of childhood, the belief that God and the soul are difficult to know because they cannot be sensed. But how does withdrawing the mind from the senses in the Second Meditation enable us to correct our erroneous beliefs about things that *can* be sensed? At the start of the Third Meditation, the meditator realises that the habitual judgement that there are things outside us wholly resembling our sensory ideas is not based on clear perception, and may be false. What puts us in a position to realise this? The realization follows the acknowledgement that we 'previously accepted as wholly certain and evident many things which [we] afterwards realized were doubtful', namely, the earth, sky, stars, and everything that we apprehended with the senses.[92] Presumably these things were realized to be doubtful in the First Meditation. But now the meditator is able to isolate why it is that these things we apprehend through the senses are doubtful. That we have sensory ideas of such things is not in doubt. But the claim that there are external things that wholly resemble our sensory ideas of earth, sky, stars and so on is now recognized as being doubtful because we do not clearly and distinctly perceive that it is true. If we were as certain of this as we are that we are thinking things, we would not be able to doubt it; or, rather, we would be able to doubt it only by doubting the truth of clear and distinct perceptions.

Withdrawal from the senses, as practiced in the Second Meditation, contributes to this discovery in two ways. Firstly, withdrawal from the senses enables us to learn what clear and distinct perception is like. Through discounting sensory images and denying that any body exists, we are able to form 'a concept of the soul which is as clear as possible and is also quite distinct from any concept of body'.[93] We are also able to form a clear and distinct intellectual conception of the piece of wax as an extended thing. Secondly, withdrawal from the senses enables us to understand the limitations of the senses, through the examination of the piece of wax. It reveals that what we call 'sensing' a particular body involves intellectual judgement, and it reveals that the senses grasp the outward forms of extended things. We judge that the wax is there from the colour and shape that we

---

[91]   AT VII 16, CSM II 11.
[92]   AT VII 35, CSM II 24.
[93]   Synopsis, AT VII 13, CSM II 9.

perceive; knowledge of the wax comes from the scrutiny of the mind alone, not from what the eye sees.[94] But this means that the judgements that the wax is there, and that the wax is thus-and-so, require reasons. If we perceived the existence of the wax as clearly and distinctly as we perceive our own existence, we would be as certain of the former as we are of the latter. However, our claims about the existence of external bodies are not based on clear perception, so we are able to doubt their existence despite our natural propensity to affirm it.

The Second Meditation thus plays a key role in exposing the prejudices of the 'senses' and revealing the standard of clear intellectual perception to which they are to be compared. This fact helps to explain an aspect of Descartes's procedure which might otherwise be puzzling. Descartes believes that our assumption that there are bodies resembling our sensory perceptions is a prejudice, a judgement made without clear rational support. So why does he not launch straight into the critique of the grounds for this judgement at the start of the *Meditations*? Why postpone it until the Third Meditation?

The judgement that we perceive material things through the senses is one that Descartes thinks we have a strong natural propensity to make, so it is not easy for us to withhold assent from it. That is why we need the arguments of the First Meditation to give us reason to withhold assent from it, and the pretence of deception by the demon to enforce the withholding of assent. The belief that external things wholly resemble sensory ideas is not natural, but it is strongly fixed in our minds by habit, so similar measures are needed to loosen our allegiance to it. Our attachment to the senses is so deep-rooted that we are unable to achieve clear intellectual perception until it is loosened; and we need to experience the certainty that attaches to clear and distinct perception in order to realize that the belief is not genuinely certain, but only seems certain because of its familiarity.[95]

So, the First Meditation doubt about the senses, carried forward by the pretence of deception, introduces the meditator to clear intellectual perception in the Second Meditation. This prepares the way for the Third Meditation critique, which introduces deeper and more theoretically significant reservations about the senses than

---

[94] AT VII 32, CSM II 21.

[95] The confusion of the two is readily explained within Descartes's framework. Clear and distinct perception inclines the will to assent (AT VII 59, CSM II 41), but so does a habit of assenting.

were mooted in the First Meditation. The Third Meditation critique introduces worries about the reliability of teachings of nature, as distinct from worries about clear and distinct perceptions. Since our natural impulses have lead us astray when choosing the good, it seems that we cannot trust our impulse to believe that there are bodies outside us that resemble our sensory perceptions. This worry is finally resolved in the Sixth Meditation, as we have seen. To resolve it we need to know not only that our nature is the gift of a non-deceiving God, but also which impulses derive from that nature and which are due to habit. The impulse to believe that we perceive material things through our senses is natural, and therefore trustworthy. The impulse to believe that those material things wholly resemble our sensory perception derives from a habit of misusing sensory perceptions as guides to the essential natures of external bodies. It is the intellect, not the senses, that grasps the truth about the bodies we perceive, as we learned in the Second Meditation; and we should not make judgements about the bodies we perceive without proper intellectual examination. Here, finally, the meditator is in a position to expose the founding error of childhood, and to correct the habits of bad judgement that perpetuate it.

8. Responding to Hume and Reid

Hume and Reid charge that Cartesian doubt, particularly doubt about the senses, is so unnatural as to be impossible; and they charge that if it could somehow be achieved, it would be of no benefit. Descartes agrees that it is natural for us to believe that we perceive material things when we sense; that is something our nature teaches us. But he also believes that much of what we think we perceive through the senses is simply the result of habits of judgement. If we seek firmer foundations for the sciences than the prejudices of childhood, we must suspend these natural and habitual tendencies to judgement by pretending that we are deceived by an evil demon. By reversing our long-standing preoccupation with sensible things, this process enables us not only to achieve clear intellectual perception, but also to understand our own natures. In particular, it enables us to expose and correct our erroneous beliefs about the purpose of the senses.

In a sense, then, Hume and Reid are right. They are right that the Cartesian meditator does not doubt the existence of the external world in everyday contexts, since the doubt is practiced only during meditation. The withholding of assent is an artificial exercise,

215

pursued through the pretence of falsity. But Hume and Reid are wrong to claim that Descartes is hypocritical or disingenuous in enjoining us to doubt. The *Meditations* is a manual for cognitive reform, designed for practical use. If the work is to have the psychological effects Descartes wants to achieve, if his readers are to genuinely reform their ways of thinking, they must genuinely withdraw their minds from the senses and treat their old opinions as false. Nothing less will serve to reverse the bad habits of a lifetime and restore us to our true nature as cognitive agents. Moreover, it is precisely because so much of our thinking is grounded in habit rather than nature that it is possible for us to change it. This marks one of Descartes's most fundamental disagreeements with Hume. For Hume, habit is a manifestation of nature; our most basic beliefs, such as our belief in causal connections, are acquired through the influence of habit on the imagination. For Descartes, nature and habit are in conflict. Our habit of reliance on sensory images obscures the natural light of intellectual perception and leads us to confuse habits of bad judgement with genuine teachings of nature.

If the interpretation of the *Meditations* sketched here is along the right lines, there is one final challenge that should be addressed. If the errors we make in childhood are as numerous and as pervasive as Descartes claims, how is it that they have so little practical impact on us? Without the corrective exercise of the *Meditations*, Descartes believes that most people live and die without ever achieving a distinct perception.[96] But most people are not noticeably disadvantaged by this; they still manage to live successful lives. How can this be so? And, if it is so, what advantage could we expect to gain from the arduous task of reversing long-standing beliefs through meditation?

Presumably the errors in question have little everyday impact because they are errors in our beliefs about the underlying structure of the world. Not surprisingly, given their natural purpose, sensory perceptions are a good enough guide to the corporeal world to serve in our daily dealings with it. They tell us where neighbouring objects are and enable us to distinguish them from one another. The fact that we have a confused grasp of the nature of God and the soul has little practical impact. Presumably Descartes thinks that even if we find these metaphysical things hard to understand, we can still know them well enough to do our duty and hope for salvation. Why, then, is it so important for us to correct these errors? Descartes has, I think, at least two answers to this question. Firstly,

[96]   AT VIIIA 37, CSM I 220.

Doubt and Human Nature in Descartes's *Meditations*

if we seek to understand the hidden structure of the corporeal world, if we want to understand it well enough to create new technologies in mechanics or in medicine, we must correct our fundamental childhood misapprehensions. In this way, the correction of these errors is necessary for practical advances. Secondly, we will not understand the truth about our own natures and our relationship to God and the corporeal world unless we correct these fundamental mistakes. We will not achieve the clear intellectual perception that is God's gift to the human mind until we correct the habits of thought that block our way. For both these reasons, we cannot set the sciences on a firm foundation until we correct these habitual errors. For Descartes, the aim of the seemingly artificial process of Cartesian doubt is to reverse the distortions of habit and to show us how to use our faculties as nature intended.

Birkbeck College
s.patterson@bbk.ac.uk

The Sceptical Beast in the Beastly Sceptic: Human Nature in Hume

P.J.E KAIL

1

David Hume's most brilliant and ambitious work is entitled *A Treatise of Human Nature*, and it, together with his other writings, has left an indelible mark on philosophical conceptions of human nature. So it is not merely the title of Hume's work that makes discussion of it an appropriate inclusion to this volume, but the fact of its sheer influence. However, its pattern of influence – including, of course, the formulations of ideas consciously antithetical Hume's own – is an immensely complex one, subtle and incredibly difficult to decode. In all probability 'Hume's' presence in contemporary thinking of human nature is to likened to the end product of a historiographical game of Chinese whispers, whereby 'Hume's' view on x and y is now inflected with interpretations his work – or, more accurately, selected parts of it – that are in turn filtered by thinkers and traditions with different focuses and interest from Hume's own. I am not equipped even to begin to trace this line of influence, a lack compounded by my relative ignorance of the present state of the debate on human nature. Nevertheless various 'humean' doctrines still orient debate (even if they aren't labelled as such) and I guess these claims include the idea that causation is a matter of instantiating a universal regularity, that normativity can understood causally, that motivation is a matter of belief plus some independently intelligibly 'attitude', that a self is best conceived as a collection of independent states that (somehow) combine to yield a self and so on.

It may or may not come as a surprise that, within the narrow confines of Hume scholarship, much of what is taken to be central 'humean' doctrine has been probed, debated, questioned and sometimes rejected. I don't, however, propose to become embroiled in the nitty-gritty of these exegetical issues (though inevitably what I say will be informed by my own views). Instead I shall make some remarks about how the author of *A Treatise of Human Nature* conceives of human nature. I shall do this by considering the relation

doi:10.1017/S1358246112000112   ©The Royal Institute of Philosophy and the contributors 2012

Royal Institute of Philosophy Supplement **70** 2012

between aspects of Hume's philosophy and the age-old sceptical trope of drawing comparisons human thought and behaviour with animal thought and behaviour. This trope has both descriptive and evaluative dimensions. The descriptive dimension is that human beings and animals are not, cognitively speaking, radically different in kind and so human nature and animal nature, are, in the relevant respects, the same. The evaluative aspect concerns the presumptuousness, as it were, of the idea that humans and the beast are in fact different in kind. The cognitive superiority of humans is then presumed to show a difference in kind that partly places us in a morally superior position. But this is a pretension the sceptic seeks prick. Human beings are actually in an inferior position in key respects and treated less well by the hand of nature than dumb beasts. Our misguided view of our own superiority expresses only a vanity that is to be exposed by the sceptic. Hume at one participates in this tradition and transforms it, signalling his alignment with the descriptive claim but rejecting the evaluative view of human nature.

2

We begin with Hume's essay 'Of the Dignity or Meanness of Human Nature', published in 1741.[1] In this essay Hume discusses two sects, which, for want of a better pair of terms, I shall call the 'optimists' and the 'pessimists'. The former 'exalt our species to the skies, and represent man as a kind of human demigod, who derives his origin from heaven, and retains evident marks of his lineage and descent', whilst the pessimists 'insist upon the blind sides of human nature, and can discover nothing, except vanity, in which man surpasses the other animals, whom he affects so much to despise' (*EMPL* 80–81). The contrast echoes what Hume identifies as the common but false view of the relation of reason and passion, where the 'pre-eminence' of the former owes to its 'divine origin', in contrast to the 'blindness, unconstancy, and deceitfulness of the latter' (*T* 2.3.3.1; SBN 413),[2] and a careless thought would be that, since Hume sides

---

[1]   All page references to *David Hume: Essays, Moral, Political and Literary*, ed. Eugene Miller, rev. ed. (Indiana: Liberty Press, 1995). Henceforth *EMPL*.
[2]   References to Norton and Norton (eds.) *A Treatise of Human Nature* (New York: Oxford University Press, 2000), following the convention of book, part, section and paragraph numbers. Page references to *A Treatise*

with the passions, he sides with the 'mean' view of human nature. But matters are far more subtle, as we shall see.

'Of the Dignity or Meanness of Human Nature' begins to navigate these two camps by noting that in 'forming our notions of human nature, we are apt make a comparison between men and animals, the only creatures endowed with thought that fall under our senses' (*EMPL* 82). The vast differences in cognitive achievement between them and us show that there 'comparison is favourable to mankind' (*EMPL* 82). Animals are far more limited, cognitively speaking, than human beings. Those stressing human nature's meanness seek to 'destroy this conclusion' by a) 'insisting only upon the weakness of human nature' and b) by 'forming a new and secret comparison between man and beings of the most perfect wisdom' (*EMPL* 82–83). The optimist is mistaken.

It is not difficult to suppose that Hume is here thinking of Michel de Montaigne. In his longest essay, 'An Apology for Raymond Sebond', one finds a sustained deployment of the sceptical trope I mentioned in section I, namely a comparison of human and animal achievements. Montaigne thinks that humans are in many ways inferior and appearances suggest that we differ from beasts only in vanity. The work itself is ostensibly a defence of the eponymous Spanish 'theologians' claim that human reason is impotent without divine illumination, though what its real aim is a vexed issue (rather like what Bayle's real purposes are in his uses of scepticism). It is easily read as a pessimist text, however, where the comparison is unfavourable to humans. First, Hume's allusion to a 'secret comparison between man and beings of the most perfect wisdom' is not hard to find. The vanity of man 'makes him equal himself to God; attribute to himself God's mode of being; pick himself out and set himself apart from the mass of other creatures' (505). Montaigne's sceptical piety means that whilst he will officially reject the idea that we are like God, his attitude of humility is fuelled by the presumption of an infinitely greater being that the human. We are then offered pages and pages cataloguing claims, anecdotes, ranging from dancing elephants (519)[3] and a merciful tiger (535), and (occasionally) arguments to show that the human 'is the most blighted and frail of all creatures and, moreover, the most given to

---

of Human Nature ed. L. A. Selby-Bigge, revised by P. H. Nidditch (2nd ed., Oxford: Clarendon, 1978) (SBN).

   [3]   *Michel de Montaigne: The Complete Essays*, translated M. A. Screech (London: Penguin, 1991).

pride' (505). Animals instantiate virtues and show more fidelity to them than humans do (516).[4] They have instincts that constitute a greater sensitivity to features of the world than mere human reason. Thracians, reports Montaigne, use foxes to determine whether it is safe to walk on ice, showing the animal's superior detective capacity (515). We can also credit animals with reason. Since their behaviour resembles ours in key respects, then from 'similar effects we should conclude that there are similar faculties. Consequently, we should admit that animals employ the same method and the same reasoning as ourselves when we do anything' (514). Chrysippus's apparently reasoning dog makes an appearance in this connection.[5] On a road that branches into three forks, the dog, hunting his prey, sniffs the first two forks, and, having failed to pick up the scent on the first two, moves immediately down the third road. Surely Fido is reasoning disjunctively (517). In line with his Pyrrhonist temper,[6] Montaigne does not draw a final conclusion that it is *true* that human and animal cognitive capacities are of the same kind, but only that appearances do not support the presumed superiority.

Where there *are* apparent differences, they support a view of humans as inferior to animals. Human beings have a reflective capacity, 'the freedom to think', but this provides 'little cause to boast about it, since it is the chief source of the woes which beset' humanity (514). The freedom to think breaks us away from the rest of sentient creatures whom 'Nature clasps….in a universal embrace; there is not one of them which she has not plainly furnished with all means necessary to the conservation of its being' (509). At best, the freedom to think helps to show that humanity is 'lodged down here, among the mire and shit of the world, bound and nailed to the deadest, most stagnant part of the universe…the lowest category of animate creatures' (505).

[4]   For a discussion of the history of this particular trope, see Peter Harrison 'The Virtues of Animals in Seventeenth-Century Thought', *Journal of the History of Ideas*, **59** (1998), 463–484

[5]   For a fascinating account of the historical uses of this animal, see Luciano Floridi, 'Skepticism and Animal Rationality: The Fortune of Chrysippus' Dog in the History of Western Thought', *Archiv für Geschichte der Philosophie*, **79** (1997), 27–57.

[6]   How can man '…from the power of his own understanding, know the hidden inward motivations, of animate creatures?' (505). For a discussion of Montagine and Pyrrhonism, in connection with naturalism see Jessica Berry 'The Pyrrhonian Revival in Montaigne and Nietzsche', *Journal for the History of Ideas* **65** (2004), 497–514. She uses this to draw interesting lessons about Nietzsche's naturalism.

3

A lot of water passed under many bridges between Montaigne and
Hume of course, and the differences between the two emerge from
a confluence of many streams. In the intervening period Descartes
became notorious for his view that animals are mere machines. He
thought they lacked feeling and reason. One reason for this was
what Descartes saw as their lack of language. But this is not a novel
claim, and indeed Montaigne devoted some of his essay to showing
that animals do have a form of language.[7] Second, Descartes
refused to see the analogies between human and animal behaviour
as holding any epistemic weight.[8] But Descartes's views were not,
to put it mildly, met with universal approbation. John Locke and
Henry More resisted them and this resistance was to continue well
into the eighteenth century in British thought. Descartes' refusal to
take analogies between human and animal behaviours seriously was
lampooned. Thus Mandeville wrote in the *Fable of the Bees*

> Look on the trembling and violent convulsions of his [the
> animal's] limbs; see, while his reeking gore streams from him,
> his eyes become dim and languid, and behold his strugglings,
> gasps and last efforts for life, the certain signs of his approaching
> fate. When a creature has given such convincing and undeniable
> proofs of the terrors upon him, and the pains and agonies he feels,
> is there a follower of *Descartes* so inured in blood, as not to refute,
> by his commiseration, the philosophy of that vain reasoner?
> (181).[9]

Ironically, Descartes' mechanical programme for animals was taken
up by others and applied to human beings. His claims in part encour-
aged a closer look at the structure of animal anatomy and physiology,
and the discovery of deeper similarity between humans and animals
pushed against Descartes' cleavage between man and beast. La
Mettrie's notorious *Man A Machine* was published in 1747, and in
the year Hume published the first two books of the *Treatise*
Jacques de Vacuason's mechanical duck took its first bite of grain

[7] For the context of this argument see Richard Serjeantson 'The passions and animal language', *Journal for the History of Ideas*, **62** (2001),
425–444.
[8] For a discussion of this, seen Harrison 'The Virtues of Animals in
Seventeenth-Century', p. 480.
[9] Page references to *The Fable of the Bees; or Private Vices, Publick
Benefits* ed. Kaye (Indianapolis: Liberty Fund, 1988), Vol. 1.

and 'defecated', pressing home the idea that the 'inner workings' and as well as 'external workings' of all creature could be given a mechanical gloss.[10]

Hume embraces analogical argument and its application to animal cognition. His confidence in analogy is expressed in his approval of those anatomists who 'join their observations and experiments on human bodies to those on beasts, and from the agreement of these experiments...derive an additional argument for any particular hypothesis.' (T 2.1.12.2; SBN 325) In key places in the *Treatise* (and elsewhere) Hume draws explicit comparisons between humans and animals in order to emphasize commonalities. Both the *Treatise* and the first *Enquiry* include sections entitled 'Of the reason of animals' arguing for the conclusion (which he takes to be evident anyway) that 'beasts are endow'd with thought and reason, as well as men' (T 1.3.16.1; SBN 176). The long *Treatise* discussion of pride and humility (the indirect passions central to humean moral psychology) is capped with a section entitled 'Of the pride and humility of animals' (T 2.1.12), making much of various examples of animal comportment which suggest pride, such as 'the port and gait of a swan' and the 'vanity and emulation of nightingales' (T 2.1.12; SBN 326). Correlatively, Hume concludes his long discussion of love and hate in the second part of book II with 'Of the love and hatred of animals' (T 2.2.12). Note, first, the significant *placement* of these sections: each comes at the end of long discussions on reason, pride and humility and love and hatred. They function, in effect, as conclusions for those discussions that show that we differ from animals in degree and not kind.[11] Second, Hume takes the continuities between humans and animals in these sections to be 'evident'. Third, his deep-seated commitment to naturalism is expressed in his claim that respecting such continuities is a 'touchstone' against which any philosophical system is to be tried (T 1.3.16.2; SBN 176). Fourth, Hume takes these commonalities to express the view that in the 'whole sensitive creation...[e]very thing is conducted by springs and principles, which are not peculiar to man, or any one species of animals' (T 2.2.12.1; SBN 397). This amounts to a large-scale view that the mechanisms (in the non-technical sense of 'mechanism') underlying human thought and behaviour are no different in

[10] For a fascinating discussion of this topic, see Jessica Riskin, 'Eighteenth-Century Wetware', *Representations*, **83** (2003), 97–125.
[11] One serious difference may turn on the fact that animals are not moral agents – for discussion, see A E Pitson 'The Nature of Humean Animals', *Hume Studies*, **19** (1993), 301–316.

kind from those underlying animal behaviour. So if we take 'human nature' to mean the fundamental 'spring and principles' that guide thought and behaviour then 'human nature' is no different in kind from 'animal nature'.

Hume's philosophy is explanatory in its aspirations – he seeks to explain human cognitive processes and the presence of certain distinct areas of thought – but his account is shot through and through with sceptical layers which display affinities with Montaigne.[12] The first thing to note is that basic materials Hume uses in his explanation – impressions, ideas, association, force, vivacity-are not his own invention (though he puts his own peculiar stamp on them). All this vocabulary stretches at least as far back at Hobbes and what is significant for our concerns is such vocabulary was employed in the explanation animal behaviour, and whilst some human behaviour owes itself to these origins, our cognitive lives are not exhausted by such materials and processes. What is different about Hume is that he seeks to extend this vocabulary to explain *all* our mental live in its terms.

Pressed into the service of this task is a sceptical argument. Hume's positive conclusion that causal reasoning is to be identified fundamentally with associational mechanisms that drive the beasts is effected by an argument that alternative accounts of what constitutes such reasoning are faulty. Consider this claim of Leibniz's.

> Beasts pass from one imagining to another by means of a link between them which they have previously experienced....In many cases children, and for that matter grown men, move from thought to thought in no other way but that. This could be called 'inference' or 'reasoning' in a very broad sense. But I prefer to keep to accepted usage, reserving these words for men and restricting them to the knowledge of some reason for perceptions' being linked together. Mere sensations cannot provide this: all they do is to cause one naturally to expect once more the same linking that has be observed previously.[13]

For Hume, 'knowledge of some reason for perceptions' being linked together' amounts either to awareness of necessary connections, the powers and forces that maintain the course of nature, or the grasp

---

[12]   For a fuller discussion, see my 'Leibniz Dog and Humean Reason' in Emilio Mazza and Emanuele Ronchetti (eds.) *New Essays on David Hume* (Milan: Angeli, 2007), 65–80.

[13]   *New Essays on Human Understanding* ed. Remnant and Bennett (Cambridge: Cambridge University Press, 1996), 143.

of some reason to think the future will resemble the past. Hume however thinks that neither is possible. His scepticism about whether we are 'determin'd by reason' to draw an inference from cause to effect issues in a 'naturalism' whereby our reasoning is 'brute' both in the sense that it is not caused by our capacity to grasp reasons in its favour *and* that the causal mechanism is the same as that which guides animals. In effect, Hume argues that the narrow sense of 'reasoning', which Leibniz claims as the accepted usage does not exist and so it is the very broad sense of 'reasoning' which Leibniz extends to animals that governs us too. So Hume deploys the sceptical trope that seeks to undermine the differences between animals and humans on reasoning used by from Sextus through Montaigne, Charron and others by arguing against particular inflationary accounts of the nature of human inference and modelling our practice on that which is taken to be operative in the beasts.

Hume of course recognizes differences between humans and beasts. He recognizes that many animals are governed by peculiar behavioural routines (like nest building) that he calls 'original instincts'. With respect to causal inference, the differences between us and the animals resolve themselves into higher-order association relations operating on lower-order ones. Hence in 'Of the dignity or meanness of human nature' Hume notes the superiority of human reason over animals but doesn't imply any difference in kind, and in a long footnote to *Enquiry* 9 'Of the reason of animals' he lists the different ways in which reasoning capacities can be extensive or limited.

So far so good. However, there are two puzzles about Hume's overall project of explaining human cognition with animal materials. One is that he doesn't discuss the 'demonstrative reasoning' (roughly, inferences based on conceptual relations) when talking about the reason of animals. So it seems left out of the account. The second puzzle is altogether nastier. In a notorious footnote to an essay entitled 'Of National Characters', Hume wrote 'I am apt to suspect the Negroes to be naturally inferior to the whites. There scarcely ever was a civilized nation of that complexion, nor even any individual eminent either in action or speculation...In JAMAICA, indeed, they talk of one negroe as a man of parts and learning; but it is likely he is admired for slender accomplishments, like a parrot, who speaks a few words plainly.' (*EMPL* 208n) Hume's claim is quite incredible, and not merely for its evident offensiveness. It is further incredible because Hume feels that the alleged 'uniform and constant difference' between the cognitive achievements of whites and non-whites marks 'an original distinction between breeds of men'. But the whole tenor of Hume's naturalizing philosophy and his emphasis on continuity with animals is set against the invocation of original distinctions regarding cognitive achievements.[14] It seems to me that not only is Hume is guilty of being racially offensive but also in a way that seems to go entirely against the thrust of his philosophy.

4

Hume rejects the pessimists' conclusion of the 'meanness' of human nature. For one thing, he is set against the 'secret comparison between man and beings of the most perfect wisdom' (*EMPL* 82–83). The kind of despairing asceticism that he takes to infect conceptions of morality stems from this religious presupposition that Hume thinks we should dispense with. The pessimists also held that humans are those that are least adapted to the environment. Now, there is much to suggest that Hume takes animal nature to be adaptive (though he refuses to give any religious interpretation to it). All the interlocutors in the *Dialogues Concerning Natural Religion* agree that there is a 'curious adapting of means to ends, throughout all nature'[15], but disagree about its implications. This adaptive strand appears in Hume's account of human nature too, and it is one of the strands upon which Norman Kemp Smith's naturalist reading alights: he suggests, for example, that the so-called natural beliefs are 'wonderfully adapted as any of the animal instincts'.[16] There is certainly textual evidence for this reading too. In both the *Enquiry*

---

[14]   Emmanuel Eze tries to explain what in Hume's theory of mind might be behind this claim, and how Hume might be think of "negro" minds as closer to animal minds. But I think this fails to address that fact that Hume talks of an 'original' distinction, which he treatment of the differences between humans and animals in no way countenances. See Eze 'Hume, Race and Human Nature', *Journal for the History of Ideas* **61** (2000), 691–698. It is worth noting that Hume was anti-slavery – see his essay 'Of the populousness of ancient nations'.

[15]   J C A Gaskin (ed.) *David Hume, Principle Writings on Religion* (Oxford: World Classics, 1993) 45.

[16]   'The Naturalism of David Hume (I)', *Mind* **14** (1905), 149–173, 155. Kemp Smith takes Hume's earlier work to be informed by a 'half-heart-ed...theistic view of nature' (*The Philosophy of David Hume: A Critical Study of its Origins and Central Doctrines* (London: MacMillan, 1941) 563. I think that is unwarranted claim. For discussion see John P. Wright 'Kemp Smith and the Two Kinds of Naturalism in Hume's Philosophy' in Emilio Mazza and Emanuele Ronchetti (eds.) *New Essays on David Hume* (Milan: Angeli, 2007) and Louis Loeb 'What is Worth Preserving

Concerning Human Understanding and the *Enquiry Concerning the Principles of Morals* there are statements that seem to go just that way. Thus in connection with causal inference he writes of a

> ...pre-established harmony between the course of nature and the succession of our ideas; and though the powers and forces, by which the former is governed, be wholly unknown to us; yet our thought and conceptions have still, we find, gone on in the same train with the other works of nature. Custom is that principle, by which that correspondence has been effected; so necessary to the subsistence of our species and the regulation of our conduct. (*EHU* 5.21; SBN 54–55)[17]

This is followed in the next paragraph with a reference to 'the ordinary wisdom of nature' (*EHU* 5.22; SBN 55). In the *Enquiry Concerning the Principle of Morals* he writes of the standard of moral sentiment 'arising from the internal frame and constitution of animals', each of which has its 'peculiar nature' (*EPM* Appendix 1, 21; SBN 294).[18]

I don't want pursue this issue any further here. Let me instead note that one reason that Montaigne held the human condition to be wretched is that human beings are less well adapted to their environment than our dumb friends. This is something with which that other pessimist, Mandeville, agrees. In the 'wild State of Nature, those creatures are fittest to live peaceably in great numbers [are those] that discover the least of Understanding and have the fewest Appetites to gratify' (41). Hume echoes this view of the pre-social human condition. He writes

> Of all the animals, with which this globe is peopled, there is none toward whom nature seems, at first sight, to have exercis'd more cruelty than towards man, in the numberless wants and necessities, with which she has loaded him, and in the slender means,

---

in the Kemp Smith Interpretation of Hume?', *British Journal for the History of Philosophy* **17** (2009), 769–797.

[17] References to Beauchamp (ed.) *An Enquiry Concerning Human Understanding* (Oxford: Oxford University Press, 1999) by section and paragraph number. Page numbers to L. A. Selby-Bigge (ed.) rev. Nidditch *Hume's Enquiries* (Oxford: Clarendon Press, 1975) (SBN).

[18] References to Beauchamp (ed.) *An Enquiry Concerning the Principles of Morals* (Oxford: Oxford University Press, 1998) by section and paragraph number. Page numbers to L. A. Selby-Bigge (ed.) rev. Nidditch *Hume's Enquiries* (Oxford: Clarendon Press, 1975) (SBN).

which she affords to the relieving these necessities (T 3.2.2.2; SBN 484).

Both Mandeville and Hume think that the human animal can transcend its ill-suited natural state by the imposition of society. Both thinkers also offer genealogical accounts of how the human animal establishes society. These accounts differ in a number of ways, but two are relevant for our concerns. The first is that whereas Mandeville holds that human nature is constant both within and without society, Hume takes society to be transformative of that nature. The second is that Mandeville's view of human nature echoes the pessimist conception of it that Montaigne espoused and Hume rejects.

Mandeville, like Montaigne, maintains that the only way in which humans are relevantly different from animals is in terms of our susceptibility to flattering self-conceptions. Just as Montaigne wrote that the human 'is the most blighted and frail of all creatures and, moreover, the most given to pride' (505), Mandeville's *Fable of the Bees* maintains that of man 'the most perfect of Animals', pride is 'inseparable from his very Essence (however cunningly soever some may learn to hide or disguise it)' (44–5). It is this feature of human beings that is central to the establishment of society. It is through this 'bewitching engine' (43) that others can be manipulated by an 'artful form of flattery' (43) to conceive selfless actions as expressions of estimable virtue. Persons act in line with the interest of others because such flattery helps to 'buoy them up in mortifying what was dearest to them'. Their natural disposition to be 'led by the sensual dictates of nature' is kept in check because they are 'asham'd of confessing themselves to be those despicable wretches...so little remov'd from Brutes' (44–5). So for Mandeville, like Montaigne, a false pride is what divides us from the rest of the brutes and though it helps to establish a conception of ourselves that motivates actions that are beneficial to society, it leads to a false conception that alienates us from our first-order nature. Human nature is mean all along.

Hume's solution is different. He thinks that our characters can be changed by the social environment. His clearest statement of this idea is in the essay 'Of National Characters' where Hume enters in the eighteenth-century dispute regarding the extent to which differing manners and characters of nations are determined by the climate, and more generally, physical environment in which human creatures are placed. Such 'physical causes' Hume defines as 'qualities of air and climate...supposed to work insensibly on the temper, by altering the tone and habit of the body' (*EMPL* 198), which probably picks up on the theories of John Arbuthnot and Abbé Du Bos. Hume rejects such accounts,[19] siding with those who hold that such differences are accounted for by the action of 'moral causes', though adding to this theory an account of cultural transmission which makes much of sympathy and imitation, the latter he takes to be a marked feature of the human animal. What is important for our concerns is how he characterizes a 'moral cause' and what its effects can be. Moral causes are 'those circumstances which are fitted to work on the mind as motives or reasons and which render a particular set of manners habitual to us' (op. cit.). Moral causes then are circumstances (and our conception of them) that we perceive as having practical salience, which in turn change our character dispositions. He adds a given moral cause 'alter[s] even the [character] disposition that …[we] receive from the hand of nature' (op. cit). He illustrates this by arguing that the peculiar circumstances attaching to the professions of the soldier and the priest does not merely constrain some fixed character of the persons occupying that role but changes their character.

With this in mind, let us now consider how Hume thinks humans transcend their given nature. What he seeks to explain in his account of the 'artificial virtues' are, roughly speaking, moral norms that govern impartial interpersonal relations, including respect for property and fidelity to promises. There are a number of senses in which these are 'artificial', and a key idea that Hume thinks there is no natural psychological motive linked to the relevant behaviour. It makes sense to credit humans with other-regarding behaviour – such as care for their children – that is not motivated by a grasp of its being morally required. But being honest or keeping one's promises are motivations that are *ipso facto* moral motivations. So Hume proposes an account of how conventions that produce and govern such behaviour emerge. His account begins with a conjecture that, prior to the institution of property, human animals inhabit family groups and this makes them sensible of the advantages of co-operative behaviour. Awareness of co-operative behaviour leads to a convention to establish property rights whose normative force derives from awareness of the fact that they serve one's own non-moral interests. At this stage, Hume's picture of co-operative behaviour produces an artifice – a convention – but an artifice that does not involve the imposition of a false view of human nature. It is simply enlightened

---

[19] Except, perhaps, in the case of the northern propensity for strong liquor and the southern propensity for love and women (again, we are not showing Hume in his best light). Even here Hume seems ambivalent about physical causes.

self-interest, and so in 'so sagacious an animal, what necessarily arises from the exertion of his intellectual faculties may justly be esteemed natural' (*EPM* Appendix 3.9; SBN 307).

For many commentators this is the whole of Hume's account of the emergence of co-operative behaviour. Justice is a complex convention the normative force of which rests on long-term self-interest (long self-interest being turned to check more short-term self-interest). There are two reasons to think that this is incorrect. The first is that Hume thinks that our hardwired disposition to approve morally of certain dispositional features becomes extended, *via* sympathy to the convention itself. Second, there is every reason to think that the establishment of the convention feeds back into the motivational dispositions of human nature.[20] Through education respect for the conventions becomes part of the motivational dispositions of human creatures ('changeableness is essential' to 'human nature' Hume writes earlier in the *Treatise* (*T* 2.1.4.3; SBN 283). Thus sentiments of justice take on such 'firmness and solidity, that they may fall little short of those principles which are the most essential to our natures, and the most deeply radicated in our internal constitution.' (*T* 3.2.2.26; SBN 501) Our motivational patterns are changed and, unlike Mandeville's view, human beings become sincerely motivated and integrated creatures. Human nature might be animal but its capacity for second-nature does not make for its meanness.

St Peter's College, University of Oxford
peter.kail@philosophy.ox.ac.uk

---

[20] For two accounts of this which the present discussion relies upon, see Michael Gill *The British Moralists on Human Nature and the Birth of Secular Ethics* (Cambridge: Cambridge University Press, 2006) and Rachel Cohon *Hume's Morality: Feeling and Fabrication* (New York: Oxford University Press, 2008).

Human Nature and the Transcendent

JOHN COTTINGHAM

1. Human Restlessness

Let me start with the enigmatic dictum of Blaise Pascal: *'l'homme passe l'homme'* – 'man goes beyond himself'; 'humanity transcends itself'.[1] What does this mean? On one plausible interpretation, Pascal is adverting to that strange *restlessness* of the human spirit which so many philosophers have pondered on, from Augustine before him, to Kierkegaard and many subsequent writers since.[2] To be human is to recognize that we are, in a certain sense, incomplete beings. We are on a journey to a horizon that always seems to recede from view. Unlike all the other animals, who need nothing further for their thriving and flourishing once the appropriate environmental conditions are provided, human beings, even when all their needs are catered for – physical, biological, social, cultural – and even when they enjoy a maximally secure and enriching environment, still have a certain resistance to resting content with existence defined within a given set of parameters. They still have the restless drive to reach forward to something more.

Human beings, in short, are possessed of what one might call 'transcendent urges'. Augustine and Kierkegaard, like Pascal, thought that these transcendent urges were urges for the Transcendent (with a capital 'T'). All three thought (though they expressed themselves in very different ways) that the restlessness and incompleteness of our nature derived from an inchoate longing for God. The notion of such a longing in these and other writers is often coupled with the idea that humans enjoy occasional glimpses into a deeper richer reality than is disclosed in our ordinary mundane experience of the world. William Wordsworth's famous ode on 'Intimations of Immortality' laments the fleetingness of these sporadic glimpses of the transcendent: he describes how, as we are ground down by the preoccupations of routine adult life,

---

[1] Blaise Pascal, *Pensées* [c. 1660], ed. L. Lafuma (Paris: Editions du Seuil, 1962), no 131.

[2] St Augustine of Hippo, *Confessions* [*Confessiones*, c. 398], Book I, Ch. 1; Søren Kierkegaard, *Sickness Unto Death* [*Sygdommen til Døden*, 1849].

doi:10.1017/S1358246112000124   © The Royal Institute of Philosophy and the contributors 2012
Royal Institute of Philosophy Supplement **70** 2012

John Cottingham

they 'die away and fade into the light of common day'. But he suggests that this mundane sense of flatness, of incompleteness, which surrounds much of our ordinary existence, itself bears witness to an innate longing for something that transcends it – an intimation that is an ineradicable part of what it is to be human. As Wordsworth puts it, drawing on religious language (with Platonic overtones) we are all born 'trailing clouds of glory … from God who is our home.'[3]

A nice poetic idea, perhaps; or possibly an irritating one, depending on your tastes. But either way, the hardnosed analytic philosopher (which I take it we all are, at least from time to time) may be very sceptical about the move from 'transcendent' longings to a transcendent *object* of those longings. May there not be other ways of explaining those longings, *immanentist* ways, as it were – ways that do not have to involve reference to anything other than the natural world we inhabit? For example, a Darwinian explanation might suggest that the restlessness of the human spirit is simply a by-product of a certain kind of open-ended energy and inquisitiveness that has proved an enormous advantage to our species in the struggle for survival. A tribe that constantly probes and reaches beyond the parameters defined by current conditions may be far better equipped to compete for scarce resources, especially in times of environmental crisis and change. So on this view the so-called urge to transcend could simply arise from a natural and highly advantageous drive to move one step beyond the present, and need not presuppose any ultimate Transcendent object, with a capital T.

The theist might take issue with this, on the grounds that the restlessness we are speaking of is a hunger not just to keep moving one step ahead, but a hunger for some ultimate answer, something entirely beyond the series of natural causes and conditions. But even if one grants that the hunger is of this uniquely transcendent kind, one might still be dubious that it must have an actual – or even a possible – transcendent *object*. Thomas Aquinas may have subscribed to the principle *nullum desiderium naturae inane* – no desire that is inherent in our human nature can be empty or vain – but the principle seems far from self-evident.[4] Even if most human urges have objects that can satisfy them – sexual longings have sexual objects, drives for

---

[3]   William Wordsworth, *The Prelude* 12, 208–218 [1805 edition].

[4]   'Inest enim homini naturale desiderium cognoscendi causam, cum intuetur effectum; et ex hoc admiratio in hominibus consurgit. Si igitur intellectus rationalis creaturae pertingere non possit ad primam causam rerum, remanebit inane desiderium naturae.' Thomas Aquinas, *Summa theologiae* [1266–73], Ia, q.12. a.1.

food have as their object actual or possible meals, and our yearning for affection reaches out towards possible companions and friends[5] – it does not seem to follow that all our natural aspirations must conform to this pattern. We may want there to be an ultimate answer that stills our human restlessness, but such an answer may simply not be available. We may want there to be an ultimate source of being and goodness, but there may not be one.[6]

Nevertheless, we may at least be prepared to agree with Aquinas that 'transcendent' longings in one form or another do seem to be 'natural' – they are a widespread feature of human experience. So without begging any questions about their object, one may at least conclude that they merit serious attention from any philosopher interested in understanding the human condition. I want in this paper to take a look at three aspects of the apparent human reaching after the transcendent, namely the cosmological, the aesthetic, and the moral. The general thrust of my argument will be that the demands of integrity, being sincere and true to the character of our own lived human experience, require us to reject deflationary or reductionist strategies for explaining away our transcendent urges; and as a result, that the field is very considerably narrowed, when it comes to understanding their significance.

2. The Cosmological Dimension

First, then, let me look briefly at the cosmological dimension – at how the human hunger for transcendence affects our conception of the

---

[5] A simplified version of the argument from the 'non-emptiness of natural desires' is canvassed by C. S. Lewis: 'Creatures are not born with desires unless satisfaction for these desires exists. A baby feels hunger; well, there is such a thing as food. A duckling wants to swim; well, there is such a thing as water. Men feel sexual desire; well, there is such a thing as sex. If I find in myself a desire which no experience in this world can satisfy, the most probable explanation is that I was made for another world.' C. S. Lewis, *Mere Christianity* [1952; based on radio talks of 1941–44] (London: Fontana, 1960), Bk. III, Ch. 10: 'Hope'. See further J. Haldane, 'Philosophy, the Restless Heart and the Meaning of Theism', *Ratio* **19:4** (December 2006), repr. in J. Cottingham (ed.), *The Meaning of Theism* (Oxford: Blackwell, 2007).

[6] Indeed some philosophers might be inclined to go further and question the very intelligibility of the idea of the transcendent – of a reality 'beyond' or 'behind' the natural world. Compare Bede Rundle, *Why is There Something Rather than Nothing?*, Oxford: Oxford University Press (2004).

John Cottingham

cosmos itself. In the Big Bang scenario, currently the best available account of what happened thirteen or fourteen billion years ago, a singularity of infinite energy produced everything there is: matter, space, time, all burst into existence out of nothing. Actually, you may think, this is uncannily like divine creation. But the increasingly prevalent naturalism of our times will not of course even entertain a theistic picture. Instead, the prevailing conception is of a *closed* cosmos, a universe shut in on itself – a universe that is, in the immortal words of Bertrand Russell, 'just *there*'. (In a radio debate with Frederick Copleston in 1948, Russell was challenged to say whether he could really accept that the universe was utterly contingent and gratuitous; he replied 'I should say that the universe is just there, and that's all.'[7]) So the naturalist or secularist holds that there is no reality beyond the total set of events and properties that emerged from the big bang, or have subsequently evolved from its debris.[8] That totality, pulsating, quivering, expanding until it finally cools down, simply *lies there*. All we have is brute facticity, as Jean-Paul Sartre might have put it – something that, as we contemplate it, produces a shudder or existential horror or nausea. Or as Albert Camus might have said, indeed did say, we inhabit a universe that is inherently *absurd*; we can, like Sisyphus, try to be defiant as we struggle with the meaninglessness of it all; but that queasiness, that shuddering sense of absurdity, always lurks beneath the surface. It was no accident that Camus, for all his defiance, proclaimed that the only serious philosophical problem left for us in such a world is whether to commit suicide.[9]

Now let me make it clear that I don't think we can *prove* philosophically that the universe we inhabit is not just such a brute, contingent universe. Here I follow the current philosophical consensus. Few people now suppose that anything like the cosmological argument, in any of its traditional forms, could provide a watertight demonstration of a transcendent divine cause of the world. My own view is that this is not so much a matter of this type of argument

---

[7]   'The Existence of God'. Debate with Fr Fredrick Copleston originally broadcast on the Third Programme of the BBC in 1948. Reprinted in Russell, *Why I am Not a Christian* (London: Allen & Unwin, 1957), Ch. 13, p. 152.

[8]   There are however, important distinctions between different kinds of naturalist; a point to which I shall return.

[9]   Albert Camus, *Le Mythe de Sisyphe* (Paris: Gallimard, 1942), final chapter.

being *invalid*, but rather of its failing to convince because it begs the question. The traditional cosmological argument starts by seeking a rational explanation of contingency, and finds it (as Aquinas put it) in 'something-we-call-God' – the ultimate, non-contingent being.[10] But this simply begs the question of why we should not, as the secularist apparently does, just accept the contingent in the first place. To acknowledge the brute universe as an ultimate dead-end may be horrible, scary, nauseating even: but that doesn't prove this isn't how things are.[11]

Nevertheless, cosmological type arguments do, I think, achieve this much. They show that the 'dead-end' assumption of secularism rides roughshod over something fundamental in our nature. We humans have a yearning for meaning and explanation: in no other area of our human lives do we accept brute facticity. The whole magnificent story of science is the story of human beings insisting, again and again, that there *is*, there *must be*, a reason for what seems initially to be utterly baffling and mysterious.[12] Amazingly (we do

[10] 'It is necessary to posit something which is necessary in its own right, and does not have the cause of its necessity from elsewhere but is itself the cause of necessity in other things; and this everyone calls "God".' Aquinas, *Summa theologiae*, Part I, question 2, article 3. There are complexities in Aquinas's 'third way', 'from the contingency of the world', which it is not part of my purpose to examine here. I am most grateful to Brian Davies for illuminating several aspects of the argument for me. I should add that he regards my reservations about the argument from contingency as misguided; though I am not so far convinced, it would not affect the argument of the rest of this paper were I to become so.

[11] In case of misunderstanding, these reservations about the argument from contingency should not be taken to imply any general denial of the possibility of natural theology, or of 'reason based' knowledge of God. Indeed, the considerations I shall be putting forward in the remaining sections of this paper do constitute, in my view, substantial rational support (though of a rather special kind) for theism. For a persuasive critique of the Kierkegaardian view that faith defies or overturns reason, see Brian Davies, 'Is God Beyond Reason?' *Philosophical Investigations* **32:4** (October 2009), pp. 338–359.

[12] The phrase 'there must be a reason' is perhaps ambiguous in this context (I owe this point to Peter Dennis). As interpreted by philosophers since the Enlightenment, science makes things intelligible only in the relatively thin sense of subsuming them under general causal principles, not in the sense of uncovering rational explanations. For more on this distinction, see John McDowell, *Mind and World* (Cambridge MA: Harvard University Press, 1994), pp. 70–71. I shall come on to discuss the 'Enlightenment' view of the limits of science in the next paragraph.

John Cottingham

not, I think, acknowledge as much as we should just how amazing it is), this supposedly brute, absurd universe turns out to conform to the most marvellous and intricate logical and mathematical patterns. That holds good even at the quantum level. For notwithstanding the implications of Heisenberg's Uncertainty Principle, or rather, in virtue of exploiting that very principle, quantum mechanics has managed to furnish us with laws of staggering accuracy and proven success, which enable us to bring even the micro world into the domain of mathematical understanding. The operation of the micro world, and especially its relationship to the laws of the macro world, may still elude our full grasp; but the fact remains that science, the greatest achievement of modern man, finds *logos*, intricate mathematical and logical order, at the very heart of reality, in the workings of the smallest particles and of the largest galaxies.[13] That all this rational intelligibility can emerge from a brute entity, a raw singularity whose existence defies explanation, could, perhaps, be the case. But I do not believe that it is in the nature of any human being to rest content with brute facticity, let alone with brute facticity that just happens, as a brute fact, to generate a cosmos of such extraordinary intelligibility. Cosmological secularism, the willed insistence on a closed world, impervious to anything beyond its own brute self, is an idea that comes near to self-destructing in the very act of its defiant proclamation.

You may object that what I have just suggested runs in the face of the secular revolution in philosophy that happened in the Enlightenment. Did not David Hume establish once for all that there is nothing wrong with an explanatory dead-end? As he put it in the First Enquiry, 'The utmost effort of human reason is to reduce the principles productive of natural phenomena to a greater simplicity ... But as to the causes of these general causes, we should in vain attempt their discovery ... The most perfect philosophy of the natural kind only staves off our ignorance.'[14] In other words,

---

[13]   The Kantian tradition would of course construe this order as a mere function of the grid imposed by the human mind. But even if one were to accept that view (which runs counter to the strong common-sense intuition that science discovers order in things rather than imposing it on things), it simply shifts the focus of wonder from the particles and the galaxies to the human beings made out of those materials: how can the marvel of *logos* in the human mind arise from brute facticity?

[14]   David Hume, *An Enquiry concerning Human Understanding* [1748], Sectn IV, part 1, penultimate paragraph.

no matter how far science progresses, it can never answer the ultimate question about the 'causes of the causes', the reasons for the ultimate laws: we had better just accept them as brute facts.

I think, however, that we have to be very careful how we read Hume here. It would in my view be a serious mistake to interpret cosmologically or ontologically a point that Hume merely intended to be taken epistemologically. Hume was talking (as indeed, in my view, were all the Enlightenment philosophers) about the limits of our *knowledge*, not about the limits of *reality*. This epistemological reading of Hume was persuasively advocated some years ago by John Wright in his book *The Sceptical Realism of David Hume*.[15] Take, for example, the case of causation. What Wright argued (later closely followed by Galen Strawson)[16] was that Hume is not denying the intelligibility or the possibility of underlying connections in nature, but is simply making the epistemic point that, since our knowledge is necessarily based on observation and experience, if such connections existed *we could never know anything about them*. This makes good sense of what Hume has to say in general about science and its limits. As a good empiricist, Hume would never go as far as the modern dogmatic secularist, and insist that science tells us the cosmos is closed. For how could science, if (as Hume thought) it is rooted in the phenomenal world, possibly tell us what does or does not like beyond the limits of that world? It is much better to think of Hume as a certain kind of sceptic – and sceptics characteristically suspend judgement; they do not lay down the law about ultimate reality. Hume the sceptic is in no position to pronounce, nor does he, on whether or not there are, as he puts it, some 'ultimate springs and principles' of reality. Admittedly he himself rejected the theistic belief in an ultimate principle – the mysterious first cause which, as Aquinas put it, 'all men call God'; but Hume's very empiricism and scepticism means that he cannot logically rule it out. His point is that if there is any such principle, then given the limits of our knowledge, it must remain (as he graphically put it) 'totally shut up from human curiosity and enquiry'.[17]

The upshot of this short digression on Hume (whom I take as a representative of the Enlightenment in general) is that nothing in

[15]   J. Wright, *The Sceptical Realism of David Hume* (Cambridge, Cambridge University Press, 1983).
[16]   G. Strawson, *The Secret Connexion: Causation, Realism and David Hume* (Oxford: Clarendon, 1989).
[17]   Hume, *Enquiry concerning Human Understanding*, loc. cit.

John Cottingham

Enlightenment philosophy supports the idea of the 'closed' cosmos. The limits of our knowledge *may* be the limits of the world, but reality may, for all we know, transcend our empirical knowledge. And one may add, to revert to my opening theme, that it remains an ineradicable part of our human nature never to rest content with any proposed limits, but always to yearn to reach beyond them. So if there is nothing beyond those limits, if the universe is simply 'there', then we are stuck in a blind cul-de-sac, a dead-end from which our deepest nature recoils in repugnance. Such repugnance does not logically refute the secularist, of course; but it does show, I think, that adopting the secularist outlook generates a certain internal dissonance or tension, which makes it harder than is generally realised to embrace that outlook wholeheartedly and consistently. This is even more apparent when we think about the moral and aesthetic aspects of our human drive to reach towards the transcendent, which will be my main focus in the remainder of this paper.

3. The Experiential Dimension

Let me consider first the aesthetic dimension of our transcendent urgings – though actually the word 'aesthetic', with its rather effete contemporary connotations can be very misleading here (our mind immediately goes to the art critic holding forth about the latest exhibition, or the wine-taster pronouncing on a vintage). What I have in mind rather is the kind of thing I alluded to at the start of the paper, the 'transcendent' moments that many people will from time to time have experienced, the times when the drab, mundane pattern of our ordinary routines gives way to something vivid and radiant, and we seem to glimpse something of the beauty and significance of the world we inhabit. Wordsworth expressed it as follows, in a famous passage in *The Prelude*:

> There are in our existence spots of time,
> That with distinct pre-eminence retain
> A renovating virtue, whence – depressed
> By false opinion and contentious thought,
> Or aught of heavier or more deadly weight,
> In trivial occupations, and the round
> Of ordinary intercourse – our minds
> Are nourished and invisibly repaired;
> A virtue, by which pleasure is enhanced,

That penetrates, enables us to mount,
When high, more high, and lifts us up when fallen.[18]

Do we classify what is being referred to here in terms of an aesthetic
or a moral or a mystical experience? None of these categories is quite
adequate, and the implied separation of our experience into such discrete components is in any case misleading. Certainly, great works of
art can occasion this kind of heightened awareness, but the experience
is not 'aesthetic' in the narrowly compartmentalised sense of that
term. For in such moments of 'lifting up', referred to here and in
many other passages in Wordsworth, and in the works of many
other poetic and religious writers, there is a kind of integrated
vision of the meaning of the whole. What 'lifts us up' is precisely
the sense that our lives are not just a disorganized concatenation of
contingent episodes, but that they are capable of fitting into a
pattern of meaning, where responses of joy and thankfulness and
compassion and love for our fellow creatures are intertwined; and
where they make sense because they reflect a splendour and a richness
that is not of our own making. Such a vision is patently at work in the
description of a transfigured reality set down by Thomas Traherne in
the seventeenth century:

> The Corn was Orient and Immortal Wheat, which never should
> be reaped nor was ever sown. I thought it had stood from ever-
> lasting to everlasting. The Dust and Stones of the Street were
> as Precious as GOLD ... And yong Men Glittering and
> Sparkling Angels, and Maids strange Seraphic Pieces of Life
> and Beauty! ... Eternity was Manifest in the Light of the Day,
> and som thing infinit Behind evry thing appeared: which
> talked with my Expectation and moved my Desire.[19]

Notice that this kind of 'transfiguration' is not a 'religious experience', if that latter term is understood in the rather narrow way that
has become common in our culture, when philosophers speak, for
example, of the 'argument from religious experience'. What is often
meant under this latter heading is some kind of revelation which is
taken to be evidence for, or to validate, the supposed truths of
some particular creed or cult – a vision of the Virgin Mary, for
example, or what William James calls 'a sense of presence', of some

[18] William Wordsworth, *The Prelude* **12**, 208–218 [1805 edition].
[19] Thomas Traherne, 'The Third Century' [*c.* 1670], § 3, in *Centuries,
Poems and Thanksgivings* ed. H.M. Margoliouth (Oxford: Oxford
University Press, 1958), vol. 1, p. 111. Quoted in J.V. Taylor, The
Christlike God (London: SCM, 1992), p. 33.

John Cottingham

mighty being. This kind of notion is I think uppermost in many people's mind when they insist that they have never had a 'religious experience'. By contrast, the kinds of 'transcendent' experience I've just been referring to – the kind described by Wordsworth or Traherne – involve not so much a revelation of supernatural entities, but rather a heightening, an intensification, that transforms the way in which we experience the world. Once one thinks in these terms, it is much harder for most of us, if we honestly interrogate ourselves, baldly to deny that our human experience has ever encompassed such moments. The term 'transcendent' seems appropriate not in the sense of that there is necessarily an explicit invocation of metaphysical objects that transcend ordinary experience, but rather because the categories of our mundane life undergo a radical shift: there is a sudden irradiation that discloses a beauty and goodness, a meaning, that was before occluded.

The domain of music provides another example, that in some ways is clearer, since we are not dealing with a pictorial medium and hence there is less temptation to suppose that transcendent experiences must involve a vision of a supernatural entity. Roger Scruton, writing of the work of Richard Wagner (for example in the Ring cycle) has put it as follows, inviting us to draw the lesson

> that you could subtract the gods and their stories ... and still the
> most important thing would remain. This thing has its primary
> reality not in myths but ... in moments that stand outside time,
> in which the deep loneliness and anxiety of the human individual
> is confronted and overcome. By calling these moments 'sacred'
> we recognize both their complex social meaning and also the
> respite that they offer from alienation. Forget theology, forget
> doctrine and belief, forget all the ideas about an after-life – for
> none of these have the importance ... that attaches to the
> moment ... when the human world is suddenly irradiated from
> a point beyond it.[20]

Depending on one's musical tastes, one may readily respond to the Wagner example, or prefer instead to invoke the work of some other composer. But I think it will be difficult for anyone who has had an overwhelming response to a great musical work not to acknowledge the force of Scruton's contention that what is offered thereby is a 'respite from alienation'. In using the label 'sacred' to

[20] Roger Scruton 'The Sacred and the Human' [2010] *http://www.st-andrews.ac.uk/gifford/2010/the-sacred-and-the-human/* accessed 30 March 2010.

describe the moments in which we have the relevant kinds of transcendent experience, he is referring in part to the way they take us far beyond the drab world of our ordinary transactions, and open up new layers of meaning.

But there is nevertheless one part of Scruton's account which may seem wholly problematic even to those who are sympathetic to the general notion of 'transfiguration' and 'irradiation' which I have been sketching out. The secularist may be fully alive to the deep human need for meaning and value in our lives, and wholly receptive to the transformative and transfiguring power of great artistic and musical creations that enables us to glimpse such meaning and value, but will nonetheless be strongly resistant to the suggestion that in such cases the human world is (in Scruton's phrase) 'suddenly irradiated from a point *beyond* it.' Can we not give an entirely immanentist account of the meaning and value disclosed in such experiences – an account that remains firmly within the confines of the human world? To tackle this question, which is crucial to my argument, it will be helpful to focus more closely on the phenomenology of our experience of value, both in the types of case we have been considering, but also in the domain of interpersonal morality, where the issues are thrown into sharper relief.

4. The Phenomenology of Value

I have spoken up till now of transcendent 'longings' or 'urges'; and the use of terms like these may give the impression of something entirely internal or endogenous, like an obsessive urge to scratch, or a wistful longing to become a television celebrity. Someone who confesses to restless yearnings of the latter kind may reasonably expect to be told 'get over it!' or 'grow out of it!'. But applying such a douche of cold water in every case simply will not work. To attempt to psychologize or subjectivize *all* our human longings would in many cases do violence to the phenomenology involved. In the case of the transfiguring experiences we have just been discussing, the disclosures of richness and beauty in works of art and of nature, what happens is irresistibly presented to the subject not merely as an endogenous occurrence, but as a *response*: it arises, to be sure, from something deep inside our nature, but it is also called forth and sustained by something outside of us, something that we in a certain sense seem constrained to submit to, in amazement or awe. René Descartes, often held up as the paradigm of the detached rational inquirer, described his encounter with the infinite source of goodness and truth in the *Meditations* in a way that can only be characterised in terms of submission: 'here let me pause for a while', he says at the end of the Third Meditation, 'and gaze at, wonder at and adore the beauty of this immense light, in so far as the eye of my darkened intellect can bear it.' Today's university lecturers tend to filter out such passages, perhaps from embarrassment, or because the texts do not fit their preferred image of Descartes as the detached academic epistemologist, but suggest instead something closer to the worshiper. But Descartes's account of the meditator's reaction is, I submit, meant quite seriously, and meant to do justice to the special phenomenology involved. The transcendent source that the meditator has groped towards in the course of his rational inquiries, turns out, once it is glimpsed even faintly, to call forth a passionate Cartesian response of wonder and admiration.

This kind of passivity or submission is very characteristic of what I have been calling transcendent experiences. It is manifestly to be found in our experience of sublime works of art. Martha Nussbaum, talking of our response to a great poem or other literary text, speaks of an awareness that involves a 'deliberate yielding'. The text in question

> *enlists us in ... a trusting and loving activity* ... we allow ourselves to be touched by the text, by the characters as they converse with us over time ... Before a [great] literary work ... we are *humble, open, active yet porous.*[21]

To any who reflect on the nature of transcendent experiences, Nussbaum's conjunction 'active yet porous' will I think seem particularly illuminating. There has to be activity on the part of the subject, a voluntary action of attentiveness, of willingness to be open to what is going on; yet there is also a passive receptivity to the power of something entirely other than oneself.

The same combination can I think also be seen in the exercise of our human moral faculties. The Danish philosopher Knud Løgstrup speaks of the 'ethical demand' in terms of trust and self-surrender that are a basic part of human life'.[22] His particular focus is the openness and responsiveness to another person which is

[21] Martha Nussbaum, *Love's Knowledge* (Oxford: Oxford University Press, 1990), pp. 281 and 282 (emphasis added).
[22] Knud E. Løgstrup, *The Ethical Demand* [*Den Etiske Fordring*, 1956] ed. H. Fink and A. MacIntyre (Notre Dame, Ill.: University of Notre Dame Press, 1997).

morally required in any human encounter or relationship. But a phenomenologically somewhat similar process occurs, it seems to me, in our responsiveness to central moral values. What philosophers have come to call 'normativity' is one way of referring to a remarkable feature of moral values like the wrongness of cruelty, for example, or the goodness of compassion: such values exert a demand upon us, they call forth our allegiance, irrespective of our inclinations and desires. When we contemplate such properties, with the required combination of attentiveness yet receptivity, we transcend ourselves, as Pascal might have put it: we are taken beyond our own inclinations or endogenous attitudes to something higher and more authoritative. No matter what you or I may feel about cruelty – even if we develop a taste for it – it remains wrong, wrong in all possible worlds. And no matter how disinclined you or I may be to show compassion, the goodness of compassion retains its authority over us and demands our admiration and our compliance, whether we like it or not.

These are truths that we cannot honestly deny, if we sincerely interrogate ourselves. Integrity is important here: we may pretend to question these truths, or may try to construct some philosophical argument against them as apart of an intellectual game; but if we retain our integrity, if we are 'active yet porous' in the way Nussbaum recommends, we cannot deny the authoritative power of these values (which of course, and unfortunately, does not mean that we always follow them, since we are self-evidently weak and conflicted beings).

The conflictedness of our nature is of more than incidental interest here, since it is connected with the 'moral gap', as the theologian and philosopher John Hare has called it – the gap between what we are and what we might be, or what we are called to be. This ties in closely with our theme of transcendence. In our transcendent moral impulses, as with the other areas we have been discussing, something appears to draw us forward and beyond ourselves, beyond the flux of our contingent and fluctuating inclinations, beyond the bundle of traits and characteristics we happen to have evolved to have, towards something more absolute and unchanging. This of course was what was expressed by the traditional notion of the 'eternal' verities – timeless and authoritative values of truth, beauty and goodness that seem immune to the vicissitudes of fashion, culture and inclination.

5. Eternal Values Versus Darwin and Nietzsche

Some may find this traditional notion of eternal values very implausible: since conditions change over time, it may be objected, then surely how we should act must correspondingly change (for example, tribal loyalty may have been at a premium in an earlier stage of our development, while environmental stewardship was largely irrelevant; whereas today the opposite is true).[23] Of course I would not deny that there are many rules for living that fluctuate, and rightly so, over time, as conditions change. But this does not at all show that there are not certain fundamental core moral values that do not and cannot change. Those who reject this, denying that our deepest and most central moral impulses give us a window onto the transcendent, are typically inclined to see the domain of moral value as ultimately dependent on certain structural features of human nature, as it has developed over time. But before we are tempted down this route, we should reflect on the hostages to moral anarchy that are offered in this capitulation to contingency. For what we are in the end faced with, if we go down this route, is a damagingly deflationist conception of morality. Once the historical and developmental contingency of moral values is allowed, then instead of providing us with insight into ultimate meaning and value, our faculty of moral judgement becomes simply a product, or by-product, of how our ancestors happened to have evolved in the struggle for survival. In the course of Chapters 4 and 5 of the *Descent of Man*, which are about the evolution of our moral sensibilities, Charles Darwin drops a highly significant phrase – the '*so-called* moral sense'.[24] His essentially reductionist approach sees conscience, and other so-called 'higher' impulses, as merely one or more of a plethora of natural feelings that have developed under selection pressure. Altruism and self-sacrifice, for instance (to take one example he discusses) may have arisen because tribes in which this trait is prominent 'would be victorious over most other tribes, and this would be natural selection'.[25]

But this approach in the end undermines everything that has traditionally been associated with the idea of eternal moral values – their objectivity, universality, necessity and (ultimately) their normativity. *Objectivity*: it is vital to the idea of morality that does not

[23] Cf. Alan Holland 'Darwin and the Meaning of Life' *Environmental Values* **18** (2009) pp. 503–18, and the response in J. Cottingham, 'The Meaning of Life and Darwinism', *Environmental Values* **20** (2011).

[24] Charles Darwin, *The Descent of Man and Selection in Relation to Sex* [1871; 2nd edn repr. 1879] (London: Penguin, 2004), Ch. 4, p. 143.

[25] Darwin, *Descent of Man*, Ch. 5, p. 157–8. Modern evolutionary theorists would see this apparent endorsement of group selection as problematic, but, with the aid of genetic theory, could easily adjust the story, rewriting in terms of the advantages of prevalence within a given population of an individual gene or genes linked to altruistic behaviour.

depend merely on our subjective drives and preferences (which may change, or be corrupted). *Universality*: conceptions of virtue do of course differ in different epochs and tribes – something that Darwin makes great play with– but there can still be core moral values that hold always and everywhere. The wrongness of slavery, for example, or the goodness of compassion, may not universally acknowledged in all lands or all historical periods, but that does not prevent their reflecting perfectly objective and universal truths about virtue and value. (Compare scientific laws, which hold universally, but are certainly not acknowledged everywhere and always.) *Necessity*: cruelty does not just *happen* to be wrong, but is wrong in all possible worlds. We may of course transgress such fundamental norms, and often do, but they are, as Gottlob Frege put it in a rather different connection (discussing the truths of logic and mathematics) rather like 'boundary stones which our thought can overflow but not dislodge'.[26] And finally *normativity*: moral principles (as I have stressed earlier) exert an authoritative demand or call upon us, whether we like it or not. Darwin tries to wriggle out of acknowledging this special kind of authority this when he speaks deflatingly of 'the imperious word *ought*'. 'The imperious word *ought*', he says in the *Descent*, seems merely to imply the consciousness of the existence of a rule of conduct, *however it may have originated.*'[27]

But notice the disturbing implications of this idea. If our ethical conceptions are a product of a purely contingent concatenation of events, if they might have been otherwise, then it begins to look as if they might be *overridable*. As Friedrich Nietzsche put it, in the *Genealogy of Morals* (published not too long after Darwin's *Descent*) once we start to think about the conditions under which man invented the value judgements good and evil, we can start to ask *what value to these value judgements themselves possess.*[28] It is no accident that Bernard Williams's conception of ethics, and his scepticism about what he called 'the morality system', was strongly influenced by Nietzsche, and his idea that, once we accept that ethics

---

[26] Frege was talking about the laws of logic, which he regarded as wholly objective, holding independently of contingent facts about human psychology. They are 'fixed and eternal … boundary stones set in an eternal foundation, which our thought can overflow, but not dislodge.' Gottlob Frege, *The Basic Laws of Arithmetic* [*Die Grundgesetze der Arithmetik*, Vol. I, 1893], transl. M. Furth (Berkeley: University of California Press, 1964), p. 13.

[27] Darwin, *The Descent of Man*, Ch. 4, p. 140.

[28] Friedrich Nietzsche, *On the Genealogy of Morals* [*Zur Genealogie der Moral*, 1887], Preface, § 3.

John Cottingham

has a genealogy, a contingent history, this frees us from acknowledging the authority of so called eternal moral values.[29] Williams in his later work was seriously occupied with this problem of the 'radical contingency' of the ethical, as he called it, and opinions differ about whether he succeeded in defusing it. But Nietzsche's sinister conclusion, at any rate, was that we can, if we are strong enough, decide to *invert* eternal moral values. In a godless universe, where God is 'dead', then we are not subject to any higher authority, and so questions of value become merely a function of the projects we autonomously decide to pursue. So (as Nietzsche frighteningly suggested in one of the most disturbed and disturbing passages in Western philosophy) there might be conclusive reasons to steel ourselves *against* impulses of love and mercy, to harden our hearts against compassion and forgiveness, since such sentiments might get in the way of our will to power, or our passion for self-realisation as a new and stronger kind of being.[30]

6. Some Qualified Concessions to the Naturalistic Framework

Before drawing the threads together to a conclusion, I want to make some qualified concessions to the naturalistic framework for understanding ourselves, which in my talk of eternal values I may seem to have been entirely rejecting. We human beings are, to be sure, creatures who belong within the natural world, and any plausible account of human nature needs to acknowledge this. The existentialists of the twentieth century of course went so far as to deny there was any such thing as human nature; instead there was just the existing subject, free to write any script he desired on the blank slate of his self-sufficient and autonomous life. But whatever his faults, Darwin was surely right to insist that we humans are part of nature, shaped and formed by the dynamic flux of the natural world. And although

[29] '[A] truthful historical account is likely to reveal a radical contingency in our current ethical conceptions. Not only might they have been different from what they are, but also the historical changes that brought them about are not obviously related to them a way that vindicates them against possible rivals.' Bernard Williams, *Truth and Truthfulness* (Princeton: Princeton University Press, 2002), Ch. 2, p. 20.

[30] See F. Nietzsche, *Beyond Good and Evil* [*Jenseits von Gut und Böse, 1886*], § 37, and (for 'inverting' eternal values) § 203. For further discussion of the issues raised in this paragraph, see J. Cottingham, 'The Good Life and the "Radical Contingency of the Ethical",' in D. Callcut (ed.), *Reading Bernard Williams* (London: Routledge, 2008), Ch. 2, pp. 25–43.

Darwinian ideas may seem to give comfort to the existentialist denial of a human essence, by putting pressure on the idea of fixed and immutable natures,[31] any plausible developmental account of our origins must surely allow there are stable features of the human condition that remain virtually unchanged across vast swathes of time. These stabilities are of course reflected in the ethical domain. For example, Aristotelian ethics aimed at specifying those excellences of character that enable us to flourish as the kind of creatures we are – possessed of drives and needs we share with other animals, yet also having the capacity for rational reflection; and it is striking how much of that ethics continues to speak to us today. Of course it is not entirely immutable: there may be room for dispute about which virtues need to be added to or subtracted from the list; but despite all the ways in which our lives diverge from those of Classical Greece, say, there is ample evidence from literature and history and biology to believe that our human nature has changed very little, if at all; indeed, in evolutionary and genetic terms, the whole human story since prehistoric times is the merest blink of an eye. So it is perfectly plausible to maintain that any account of human flourishing must be anchored in certain relatively stable, basic facts about human nature, and that, whatever the variations in these accounts from epoch to epoch, or culture to culture, there will necessarily be a vast amount in common.

---

[31]   There are complex philosophical issues involved in the move away from fixed essences, which I won't discuss here, except to say that they go way beyond the domain of pure natural science, and have important implications for ethics, and for our general conception of the human predicament. For example, if our human characteristics, including our deepest impulses, inclinations and intuitions, are not grounded in anything beyond the contingent flux of evolution, which itself is driven by blind and indifferent natural forces, then it becomes much harder to hold on to the kind of teleological framework for the guidance of life which informed so much philosophical writing on the good for humankind prior to the modern era. In the theistic worldview of Thomas Aquinas, or in the earlier Greek philosophical framework which strongly influenced him, the good for humankind consists in our following the *telos* or goal determined by our nature. By investigating the human nature, and our place in the overall scheme of things, we can see, in principle, the kinds of thing that are good for creatures like us to pursue. *En tô ergô to agathon*, as the Platonic and Aristotelian slogan has it: in the function lies the good. The function is related to the *telos*, and the telos is related to the essence. Ethical debate thus operates within a very stable metaphysical landscape.

John Cottingham

So our human nature is part of a relatively stable but slowly evolving story that gradually unfolds as part of the developing history of the natural world. Nothing I have said today should be taken as denying that: we human beings are indeed 'dust of the earth', as the book of Genesis puts it,[32] and we have to understand ourselves as part of the vast natural process of the cosmos. And yet, if what I have been arguing here has any force, we also, in some way that we cannot perhaps fully grasp, transcend that process. We have, as I began by suggesting, transcendent cosmological impulses: the idea of accepting the 'given', of tranquilly making our home within an entirely closed cosmos that is simply 'there' – this generates a fundamental sense of dissonance deep within us. And, as I went on to suggest, even within our ordinary human lives, as we endeavour to cope with the routine demands of living, we are gripped from time to time by powerful intimations of beauty and goodness that seem to take us beyond the domain of the contingent.

You may object to the last step. Why should not our ethical impulses simply reflect certain fundamental and relatively stable contingent facts about our biological and social nature as it has evolved over time? Here, I return to the argument from phenomenology. Go back to Descartes: the meditator described in the Third Meditation encounters something that calls forth responses of admiration and awe – something that he recognizes as exceeding his capacity to fully grasp. In somewhat analogous fashion, I am suggesting that our responses to value are of this kind: as we struggle through life, we seem compelled to acknowledge, sooner or later, the call to orient ourselves towards values that we did not create, and whose normativity cannot be explained merely as a function of a given subset of our natural impulses. Love, compassion, mercy, truth, justice, courage, endurance, fidelity – all belong to a core of key virtues that all the world's great religions (and the modern secular cultures that are their offspring) recognize, and which command our allegiance whether we like it or not. We may try to go against them, to live our lives without reference to them, but if we are honest we cannot gainsay their authority over us. And it's that authority which it seems to me is likely to prove the Achilles heel of all reductionist accounts of value, which relegate them to the status of merely natural phenomena.[33]

---

[32] Chapter 2, verse 7.

[33] There is no space here to discuss the various reductionist or deflationary accounts on offer, from those (like projectivism) that effectively deny the reality of objective moral properties), to more recent 'buck-passing' accounts

250

The 'enriched' naturalism of John McDowell might at first seem to offer a way out here. On McDowell's view, the term 'nature' is ambiguous: it can merely mean what I have called the brute facticity of the natural processes and events as described by physical science; but in a richer sense it can refer to the products of human culture, including our systems of morality. These are perfectly 'natural', in the sense that they were developed out of our ordinary contingent activities as biological and social creatures of a certain kind, and hence they do not require us to posit any transcendent or supernatural properties or entities. But they are nonetheless genuine realities, to which we

---

which make moral properties second order reason-providing properties based on natural properties. Some of these are discussed in J. Cottingham, *The Spiritual Dimension* (Cambridge: Cambridge University Press, 2005), Ch. 3, and *Why Believe* (London: Continuum, 2009), Ch. 2. It is interesting that many modern ethicists have moved away from naturalism altogether, but the resulting 'non-naturalism', in so far as it floats free from anything like a traditional theistic support, seems to me to reach a terminus of explanation rather too quickly for comfort. Thus Russ Shafer-Landau tells us that values are 'a brute fact about the way the world works'; or, in a later formulation, 'moral principles are as much a part of reality as ... the basic principles of physics'. *Moral Realism* (Oxford: Clarendon Press, 2003), p. 46; 'Ethics as Philosophy: A Defense of Ethical Non-naturalism', in Shafer Landau (ed.) *Ethical Theory*, Ch. 8. In fairness, Shafer-Landau concedes that his theory is one with 'very limited explanatory resources' (*Moral* Realism, p. 48). But in that case, the danger is that it will not come down to much more than the mere assertion that moral values really (mysteriously) exist. Another non-naturalist moral realist, Eric Wielenberg asserts that moral truths are 'part of the furniture of the universe', and indeed constitute the 'ethical background of every possible universe.' *Value and Virtue in a Godless Universe* (Cambridge: Cambridge University Press, 2005), p. 52. This latter phrase suggests that we should think of values as purely abstract objects, perhaps rather like triangles or prime numbers. So if we are prepared to accept that abstract mathematical entities exist (waiting to be discovered and investigated by mathematicians), could we not perhaps accept that abstract values exist (waiting to be investigated by moralists)? Yet this kind of approach seems to invoke one mystery (the existence in all possible worlds of objective mathematical realities) in order to explain another (the existence of moral realities). If eternal mathematical and logical and moral reality is somehow involved in the very existence of things, yet cannot be explained in naturalistic terms, then this is a remarkable fact (and, one might add, remarkably consistent with traditional theism); it seems the non-naturalist needs to *respond* to this, instead of just asserting that such realities are 'part of the universe'.

gain access by being inducted as children into a certain ethical culture; and in virtue of the access thereby gained, we do indeed become subject to moral requirements and demands. As McDowell puts it:

> the rational demands of ethics are not alien to the contingencies of our life as human beings ... Ordinary upbringing can shape the actions and thoughts of human beings in a way that brings these demands into view.[34]

It would take far more space than I have here to embark on a proper discussion of McDowell's rich and subtle position. But perhaps I have said enough already to indicate why I do not believe it will work. On the McDowell view, the 'reality' of the moral demands to which we are subject is in the end simply a function of a given human culture with a given biological and social history. There is no further, no more ultimate, moral reality to constrain it or measure it against. Yet that brings us right back into contact with the difficulty discussed in the previous section in connection with Nietzsche and Williams. The history of our ethical culture is a contingent one; it might have been otherwise, and if it had, then, it seems to follow, even on McDowell's enriched picture of nature, that the relevant ethical 'realities' and 'demands' might have been different. I see no way of escaping the subversive implications of this for what Bernard Williams (with a scathingness that was surely apt enough given his Nietzschean reflections on its contingency) called the 'peculiar institution' of morality.[35] Once the cat is out of the bag, once the idea is accepted that the authority and power of the moral demands which seem to call forth our allegiance is simply a function of the contingent culture into which we happen to have been inducted, then true normativity evaporates. The 'morality system' becomes one among other potential systems, a 'peculiar institution' whose shackles we may think, like Nietzsche, that we have reason to shake off in our quest for self-realisation. Yet my argument has been that, although we can try to think ourselves into this subversive frame of mind, to do so runs counter to the depth and richness of our human experience which we cannot in integrity gainsay.

[34] McDowell, *Mind and World*, p. 83.
[35] B. Williams, *Ethics and the Limits of Philosophy* (London: Collins, 1985), Ch. 10.

7. Conclusion

The human experiential facts I have been referring to in the paper seem to me, if we think about them, to be very striking and important ones. We are dependent and flawed creatures, yet possessed of impulses that awaken within us a powerful longing to orient ourselves towards certain enduring values. If we reflect on this, and couple it with an awareness of the obvious fact of our human weakness, and the notorious difficulty humans experience in steadfastly pursuing the good they aspire to, then one is struck by the extent to which religious belief offers a *home* for our aspirations. Theism, in its traditional form found in the three great Abrahamic faiths, involves the idea of a *match* between our aspirations and our ultimate destiny. On this picture, the creative power that ultimately shaped us is itself the source of the values we find ourselves constrained to acknowledge, and has made our nature such that we can find true fulfilment only in seeking those values. In the much-quoted words of St Augustine, 'you have made us for yourself and our heart is restless until it finds repose in you.'[36] The natural response to this – to acknowledge that creative source of goodness with joy, and to turn towards it for strength in our struggle – is so basic that it presents itself to the believer as a fundamental and necessary way of going through life. It is not a matter of intellectual hypotheses about the precise macro- or micro- mechanisms that formed our planet or our species, but rather a *necessary impulse of trust*.

I have called this an argument from phenomenology, but in one way that label may mislead because it may suggest that various aspects of our experience are supposed to provide evidential support for a form of theistic-based ethical objectivism. In a certain way I am saying just that, but it needs to be understood correctly. I have not here claimed to provide any sort of coercive argument, or indeed an probabilistic one, if probabilistic is interpreted in the normal way, in terms of impartially and impersonally accessible evidence. What I have tried to offer instead is a challenge, or appeal, to the integrity of the listener. Of course integrity is itself a moral category, and that indicates something important about the kind of 'evidence' we are speaking of. Just as the Cartesian 'encounter' of the finite mind with the infinite requires a certain kind of submission to the light, so the power exerted by the values of beauty and goodness may require a moral change in the subject if it is to be fully

[36] Augustine, *Confessions* Book I, Ch. 1: "fecisti nos ad te, et inquietum est cor nostrum donec requiescat in te."

John Cottingham

apprehended. Moral and aesthetic realities, like religious ones, may be among the set of truths which are subject to what I have elsewhere called 'accessibility conditions': they do not manifest themselves 'cold', as it were, but require a focused and sincere receptivity on the part of the subject.[37]

So the challenge, in conclusion, is to focus, clearly and sincerely, on the character of our transcendent impulses, and our intimations of compelling meaning and value which seem to call us forward to transcend our nature. And then to ask if we are really satisfied with deflationary attempts to classify those impulses away as no more than a given subset of the propensities humans happen to have evolved in the random process defined by genetic lottery and the struggle for survival. If we *are* satisfied with that, well and good. But we need to be very clear about what we would be giving up.[38]

Heythrop College, University of London
jgcottingham@me.com

[37] Cf. Cottingham, *Why Believe?*, Ch. 5, section 2.
[38] Earlier versions of this paper were given at the 2010 Royal Institute of Philosophy Conference on Human Nature, at Oxford Brookes University, at the 2010 Sullivan Lecture delivered at Fordham University, New York, and at the Philosophy Department seminar at Stirling University in May 2011; I should like to thank the participants at those events for helpful discussion. I am also most grateful to Peter Dennis for substantial improvements arising from his detailed and acute comments on the penultimate draft.

Being Human: Religion and Superstition in a Psychoanalytic Philosophy of Religion

BEVERLEY CLACK

1. Introduction

At one place in his collection of essays *The Crane Bag and Other Disputed Subjects*, the novelist and mythographer Robert Graves makes the following claim that might sound rather shocking to the ears of an analytic philosopher:

> I find myself far more at home with mildly superstitious people – sailors and miners, for instance – than with stark rationalists. They have more humanity.[1]

It is the connection Graves makes between superstition and the experience of being human that is explored in this paper. Considering the relationship between superstitious and religious forms of thought and behaviour is not an unusual thing for a philosopher of religion to do: much time and energy has been expended in showing the differences between superstition and religion by those concerned to establish the meaningfulness of religion.

My intention in addressing the relationship between religion and superstition is not, however, to distinguish religious ideas or practices from superstitious behaviours. Rather, I want to consider what discussion of possible connections between the two might reveal about some of the experiences that shape human experience. Analytic philosophy of religion works with the basic assumption that the human subject is primarily defined by the ability to reason. By considering psychoanalytic ideas, and particularly the notion of the unconscious, a rather different reading of superstition might be possible. Thinking differently about superstition allows for an approach to religion to emerge where it can be understood less as a rationally constructed system of belief and more as a phenomenon which arises as a response to the attitudes, fears and desires that shape the human individual.

---

[1]   Rupert Graves, *The Crane Bag and Other Disputed Subjects* (London: Cassell, 1969), 212.

doi:10.1017/S1358246112000136   © The Royal Institute of Philosophy and the contributors 2012
Royal Institute of Philosophy Supplement **70** 2012

Employing psychoanalytic ideas is far from uncontroversial: for many, psychoanalysis lacks as much credibility as religious frameworks. My concern in this paper is not to consider that critique but simply to suggest ways in which psychoanalytic theories might illuminate the fears and desires that shape religious beliefs, while also challenging the shape and concerns of analytic philosophy of religion.

2. Setting the Scene: Defining the Human in Anglo-American Philosophy of Religion

Philosophers of religion in the Anglo-American tradition have tended to focus their attention upon the analysis of religious belief.[2] Such an approach presupposes, firstly, that all aspects of human life – including the religious dimension – can be assessed according to rational criteria; and, secondly, that human beings are defined primarily by their ability to reason. Both assumptions lend themselves to an account of religion where its value is assessed in terms of its truth-claims.[3] Under this model, a properly philosophical investigation of religion must be aligned to – or at least informed by – the ideals of scientific method. As a result, the worth of religious beliefs is assessed according to their ability to reflect accurately the nature of reality.

---

[2]   Examples of this approach include Richard Swinburne's classic accounts (see *The Coherence of Theism* (Oxford: Clarendon Press, 1977); *The Existence of God* (Oxford: Clarendon Press, 1979)), and, more recently, Tim Mawson's restatement of this approach (*Belief in God* (Oxford: OUP, 2005). There are notable exceptions: most significantly perhaps the 'Wittgensteinian' approach developed by D Z Phillips whose ideas on the relationship between superstition and religion will be considered in more detail later in this paper.

[3]   For important examples of this approach in the development of analytic philosophy of religion, see *Roger Trigg, Rationality and Religion: Does Faith Need Reason?* (Oxford: Blackwell, 1998), and Antony Flew, 'Theology and Falsification' A. Flew (Ed.), *New Essays in Philosophical Theology* (New York, Macmillan, 1955).

For recent examples, see Yugin Nagasawa, 'A New Defence of Anselmian Theism', *Philosophical Quarterly* **58** (2008), 577–596; and Kevin Timpe, *Arguing about Religion* (London: Routledge, 2009). Timpe provides a clear statement of the dominant approach to religion in Anglo-American philosophy of religion when he introduces his collection thus: "philosophy of religion approaches religion with an eye to logical analysis and rational consistency" (Timpe, *Arguing about Religion*, p. 1).

Emphasising those aspects of religion most amenable to rational exposition inevitably prioritises belief with less attention paid to other aspects of religious life and experience. Recent interventions in the subject suggest a growing awareness of these limitations, with Amy Hollywood writing extensively on the need to take seriously the role of religious practice in any account of religion,[4] and Mark Wynn using a cognitive account of the emotions to support an argument for the emotive content of religion.[5]

A further, and possibly more radical, attempt to broaden the perspective of the philosophical engagement with religion is found in the work of Grace Jantzen. Jantzen's criticism of the primacy given to reason and rationality in analytic philosophy of religion is framed against a tacit acceptance of the psychoanalytic account of the 'dynamic unconscious.'[6] While her approach is not unprecedented,[7] it is distinguished by her concern to employ psychoanalytic ideas in order to enable a philosophical investigation of the desires and fears that inform religious narratives and images. In similar vein, I want to suggest that an analysis of the relationship between religion and superstition proves particularly enlightening as a way of considering the *nature* of those fears and desires. Like Jantzen, my approach necessitates challenging the model of human being that underpins mainstream analytic philosophy of religion. Emphasising the rational subject allows the embodied experience of human beings to be largely ignored. Subjectivity is primarily structured through the idea of the thinking self, rather than the experience of being a vulnerable, mortal creature in a physical, mutable world. More than that, by limiting the investigation of thought to an assessment of which ideas are rational, logical and well-grounded, means

---

[4]   Amy Hollywood, *Sensible Ecstasy: Mysticism, Sexual Difference and the Demands of History* (Chicago: University of Chicago Press, 2002); Amy Hollywood, 'Practice, Belief and Feminist Philosophy of Religion' in Pamela Sue Anderson and Beverley Clack (Eds.), *Feminist Philosophy of Religion: Critical Readings* (London: Routledge, 2004) 225–240.

[5]   Mark Wynn, *Emotional Experience and Religious Understanding: Integrating Perception, Conception and Feeling* (Cambridge: CUP, 2005).

[6]   Grace Jantzen, *Becoming Divine: Towards a Feminist Philosophy of Religion* (Manchester: Manchester University Press, 1998).

[7]   See Pamela Sue Anderson, *A Feminist Philosophy of Religion* (Oxford: Blackwell, 1998) 103–114; John Cottingham, *The Spiritual Dimension* (Cambridge: CUP 2005); Morny Joy *et al.*, *Religion in French Feminist Thought: Critical Perspectives* (London: Routledge, 2003); George Pattison, *A Short Introduction to Philosophy of Religion* (London: SCM, 2001); Graham Ward, *The Post-Modern God*, Oxford: Blackwell, 1997).

that the thoughts and feelings elicited by the anxieties attending to embodiment can go largely ignored. What I want to suggest is that placing the idea of the psychoanalytic subject at the heart of philosophical discussions of religion enables a deeper engagement with the vulnerabilities that shape human individuality – expressed through that which seems irrational – while also opening up the importance of religion as a way of engaging with human anxiety.

3. Identifying the Unconscious

When Freud places the idea of the dynamic unconscious at the heart of his theorising, he goes some way to undermining the claim that human nature can be equated primarily with the ability to reason. The claim for an unconscious aspect to human behaviour is not peculiar to Freud; it can also be traced in the work of Schopenhauer[8] and Nietzsche.[9] Freud's account is distinctive because it emerges from his clinical work. The claim that there is a dynamic unconscious that influences action arises from his attempt to understand the experiences of his neurotic patients, and particularly those suffering from hysteria.[10] In attempting to understand bodily symptoms for which there was no discernible physiological or biological source, Freud came to the conclusion that his patients were troubled by 'unacceptable ideas' that had been driven from consciousness but which still had the power to affect behaviour. In order to bring about a 'cure', Freud's therapeutic method acted as a means

[8] See Christopher Young and Andrew Brook, 'Schopenhauer and Freud,' *International Journal of Psychoanalysis* **75** (1994), 101–118.

[9] See Ronald Lehrer, *Nietzsche's Presence in Freud's Life and Thought* (New York: State University of New York Press, 1995).

[10] Hysteria is something of a contested illness (see Julia Borossa, *Hysteria* (Cambridge: Icon, 2001)). It has, for example, been subjected to feminist criticism (Charles Bernheimer and Claire Kahane, *In Dora's Case: Freud, Hysteria, Feminism* (London: Virago, 1985), and is no longer listed as a specific mental disorder in the DSM IV. However, according to Christopher Bollas, *Hysteria* (London: Routledge, 2000), since the 1990s "psychoanalysis not only rediscovered hysteria, [it] may well also have recovered from its own forgetting" (178). Recognising that the symptoms that led to its diagnosis still exist, albeit it under alternative labels – for example anorexia or bulimia – Bollas argues that it remains a useful way of understanding the nexus of symptoms that define the sufferer's experience. Indeed, he offers his own definition, writing that the hysteric's experience is marked by the attempt to "perpetuate a child innocent as the core self" (162).

of making that which was unconscious conscious. Through the practice of free-association, whatever sprang into the patient's mind during their conversation with the analyst was discussed, regardless of how irrelevant or shameful it might seem. This enabled the source of the symptoms, now outside of consciousness, to be recognised. When this happened, Freud claimed, the symptom disappeared.[11]

This 'clinical achievement' led Freud to wider conclusions for a more general anthropology. The unconscious may lie outside that which is immediately accessible to consciousness, but this does not mean that it is without influence over behaviour. In neurotics, this might take on extremely debilitating forms, but *all* human beings are similarly subject to unconscious forces. Not all human action is conscious. In some ways this might seem an obvious claim: after all, not all our actions are consciously chosen. For example, when walking, I do not have to consciously think about placing one foot in front of the other. But Freud's contention goes further than this: unconscious desires and fears also shape human behaviour. In order to underscore this claim he provides, in the aptly named *Psychopathology of Everyday Life*, examples of parapraxis. Once analysed, apparently meaningless actions – forgetting and losing things, miswritten or misspelled words, slips of the tongue – reveal unconscious fears and desires. For example, forgetting a place name associated with an estranged friend suggests a desire to forget that friend. Such ordinary, everyday examples supported his contention that the unconscious influenced not just the behaviour of the mentally ill, but also that of the fully-functioning individual.

The effect of Freud's project was to suggest a complex account of the human psyche where the rational faculty was only one part of the picture.[12] Factors lying outside the conscious, rational mind were equally significant for understanding the actions and beliefs of the individual. Particular emphasis was given to considering the

[11] Josef Breuer and Sigmund Freud, 'Studies in Hysteria' in *Standard Edition of the Complete Psychological Works of Sigmund Freud* (hereafter 'SE') (London: Virago, [1893–95] 2001) Vol. **2**, 101.

[12] Some contemporary analysts go further in expressing the radical effect of accepting the unconscious on the notion of human personhood. According to Andre Green "the idea of a totalising unitary structure remains inconceivable for psychoanalytic thought. Which is why I believe it is necessary to remain cautious in regard of the psychoanalytic conceptions of the *Self* or identity which are phenomenologically inspired" (Andre Green, 'Anxiety and Narcissism,' in A. Weller, *Life Narcissism, Death Narcissism* (London: Free Association Books 1979), 99; his emphasis.

Beverley Clack

fears and desires of earliest childhood, now long forgotten, that shape human psychosexual development.

Allowing the unconscious realm to take centre-stage in one's theorising can seem bizarre, even meaningless, as is evident from some of the most famous philosophical critiques of psychoanalysis.[13] There is, after all, something self-contradictory about allowing what is 'unconscious' to shape one's theorising: how can that which stands *outside* of consciousness be known or talked about at all? For Sartre, this was the major problem with the Freudian project, for 'bad faith' could only result from the postulation of this mysterious and unknown agency, as another person – the analyst – is required if the individual is to identify the unconscious forces that are (allegedly) influencing their behaviour.[14]

Freud recognised the difficulty of identifying the unconscious and suggested that knowledge of it can only ever be indirect. In order to get some sense of the concerns of the unconscious, it is necessary to take seriously phenomena which operate outside the scope of rationality and consciousness, and his early work was concerned to document such phenomena.[15] Alongside the investigation of dreams, jokes and parapraxis, he also considered art and creativity as activities which reveal long-forgotten fears and desires;[16] something to which we will return later in this paper.

If one becomes convinced that there is an unconscious, it is almost inevitable for the practice of philosophy to come under scrutiny.[17] The attempt to track the workings of the unconscious involves

---

[13] See for example Ludwig Wittgenstein, *Lectures and Conversations on Aesthetics, Psychology and Religious Belief* (Oxford: Blackwell, 1966), 22–27, 42–52; and T.R. Miles' *Eliminating the Unconscious* (Oxford: Pergamon Press, 1966).

[14] Jean-Paul Sartre, *Being and Nothingness* (London: Philosophical Library, 1957), 47–52.

[15] So Freud discusses the content of dreams (*The Interpretation of Dreams*, SE **4** and **5** (1900) and jokes (*Jokes and Their Relation to the Unconscious*, SE **8** (1905)), the symptoms manifested by people suffering from a variety of neurotic illnesses ('Studies in Hysteria'), as well as the examples of parapraxis that were noted earlier (*Psychopathology of Everyday Life* SE **6** (1901)).

[16] See Sigmund Freud, 'Delusions and Dreams in Jensen's Gradiva, SE **9** (1907), 1–95; 'Creative Writers and Day-Dreaming', SE **9** (1908), 141–153; 'Leonardo Da Vinci and a Memory of His Childhood, SE **11** (1910), 57–137.

[17] And largely this conviction has defined the way in which Continental philosophers have understood the scope and practice of philosophy (see

260

paying attention to those things which are often excluded from philosophical discussions on the grounds that they are irrelevant or
irrational. To include such features involves a different kind of analysis: in order to identify the unconscious at work it is necessary to consider not just what is present but what is absent; not just what is said
but what is not said; not simply that which is coherent, but also that
which is not. The benefit of such an approach is that it leads to more
complex and arguably more realistic accounts of human experience.
For my purposes, it also opens up a broader philosophical discussion
of what religion involves. The psychoanalytic self – because of the
emphasis on the unconscious – is defined by obscurity rather than
transparency, and this affects the investigation of religion. As Julia
Kristeva notes, 'we are strangers to ourselves', whose lives are
shaped by unconscious fears and desires of which our conscious
selves know little.[18] I might think I know who I am, why I do what
I do, but the apparently trivial actions to which Freud draws our attention – forgetting, slips of the tongue, dreams, jokes – reveal much
about myself of which I am not aware. In such a context, a philosophy
of religion that is primarily concerned with establishing the coherence of belief runs the risk of ignoring what religious strategies and
feelings might reveal about that which lies beneath the surface of
ratiocination.

Philosophers of mind such as Sebastian Gardner[19] and Marcia
Cavell[20] have accepted the importance of engaging philosophically
with that which is apparently irrational, not in order to show why
such ideas or actions are wrong-headed or false, but in order to understand what irrational thought and behaviour might tell us about the
nature of the mind and what it means to be a subject. In their respective explorations of the irrational, both Gardner and Cavell employ
psychoanalytic categories. In not dissimilar fashion, I want to
suggest that taking seriously that which is apparently irrational in religious formulations might lead to deeper, richer accounts of the
sources of religion than an approach which limits its attention to
establishing the coherence or otherwise of religious beliefs and

---

Grace Jantzen 'What's the Difference? Knowledge and Gender in
(Post)Modern Philosophy of Religion, *Religious Studies* **32** (1996), 431–48.

[18] Julia Kristeva, *Strangers to Ourselves* (New York: Columbia
University Press, 1991).

[19] Sebastian Gardner, *Irrationality and the Philosophy of Psychoanalysis*
(Cambridge: CUP, 1993).

[20] Marcia Cavell, *Becoming a Subject* (Oxford: OUP, 2006).

practices. At this point, the discussion of how the relationship between religion and superstition might be understood becomes particularly helpful.

4. Like or Unlike? Connecting Religion and Superstition

The attempt to discredit religion by exposing it as a form of superstitious practice has proved a popular strategy with its critics. While the meaning of what is considered 'superstitious' has changed over time, philosophers of the European Enlightenment came to view it as a form of 'bad science'.[21] In the struggle between science and religion, the religious, like the superstitious, could be seen as holding beliefs about the world which postulate false connections between disparate phenomena. Read thus, prayer is aligned with superstitious actions (like crossing one's fingers) as both seem to reflect the belief that blind universal forces can be controlled through employing the right form of words or actions. For the religious, such similarities are problematic. If religion is to be seen as a 'serious' endeavour, it is tempting to seek 'clear blue water' between what might be called 'genuine religion' and the erroneous practices of the superstitious.[22]

The most interesting exemplar of such an approach is D.Z. Phillips, not least because his philosophy of religion was defined by his trenchant criticism of the discipline's dominant analytic model. Challenging the attempt to offer *justifications* of religious beliefs, Phillips adopted a Wittgensteinian approach where the task of philosophy was to describe with utter clarity that which the religious do and say.[23] Such an approach entailed rejecting accounts of religion which he considered to be based upon philosophical 'misunderstandings' of

[21] See for example the contemporary criticisms of Richard Dawkins, *The God Delusion* (New York: Random House, 2006) and Daniel Dennett, *Breaking the Spell: Religion as a Natural Phenomenon* (New York: Allen Lane, 2006).

[22] The longevity of this approach is worth noting, not least in the struggle between different religious traditions. See the biblical ridicule of 'pagan' idols in contradistinction to the 'living God' of Israel; for example Isaiah 44: 6–23.

[23] Phillips' rendition of Wittgenstein is not uncontroversial; see for example Brian R. Clack, 'D.Z. Phillips, Wittgenstein and Religion,' *Religious Studies* **31** (1995), 111–120. For an alternative understanding of what consideration of Wittgenstein might bring to the philosophy of religion, see also Brian Clack's *An Introduction to Wittgenstein's Philosophy* (Edinburgh: Edinburgh University Press, 1999).

what the believer means when they perform certain actions or make certain claims. If we are to understand the nature of religion we should listen to what *the believer* says they are doing, rather than constructing a 'philosophers' myth' of religion that bears little relationship to what the believer understands their words or actions to mean.[24]

Phillips is particularly critical of the methods philosophers employ to abstract religious claims from their roots in the religious life. Religious beliefs are not abstract assertions which can be distilled from the patterns of a life, and to treat them thus leads to distortion. Instead, the philosopher should act more like an anthropologist, engaging directly with what the believer thinks they are doing.

An example of this approach is amply illustrated by his account of immortality. What does it mean for a believer in the Christian tradition to talk of 'eternal life'? The philosopher looking at such language might assume they know what this phrase means; presumably that death is not the end, that one can live 'forever'. But if attention is paid to the complexity of religious texts, and the understanding given to such words by the believer, a different conclusion may be reached about the meaning of 'eternal life' that does not necessitate considering the coherence or otherwise of its rendition as that contradictory notion 'surviving death'. Considered in their proper religious context, the commitment to eternal life reveals the religious experience of a new quality of life in the here-and-now, freed from the fear of meaninglessness. To understand 'eternal life' as 'immortal existence' reveals a philosophers' misunderstanding that ignores the way in which such phrases relate to particular forms of the religious life.[25]

Paying attention to the believer and what they think they are doing is undoubtedly important if one is to avoid the distortions that can arise in the academic theorising of religion: although it should be noted that Phillips ignores the fact that many of his opponents are themselves religious, and presumably their rather different accounts of the religious terms he considers suggest at the very least that there are a myriad ways of 'being religious' within any given tradition; but that's another story. My interest is in exploring Phillips' attempt to distinguish what he calls 'genuine religion' from superstition. This attempt reveals an anxiety about forms of religious practice that fail

---

[24]   D.Z. Phillips, 'Philosophy, Theology and the Reality of God,' in *Wittgenstein and Religion* (Basingstoke: Macmillan, [1963] 1993), 1–9.
[25]   D.Z. Phillips, *Death and Immortality* (Basingstoke: Macmillan, 1970), 41–60.

Beverley Clack

to cohere with rational criteria remarkably similar to that of the philosophers he criticises.

Phillips is aware of the troubling similarities between religious and superstitious practices, and in attempting to distinguish the one from the other he assesses the *intentions* which lie behind each. The results of this method are expressed most clearly in this discussion of what makes a prayer genuinely religious:

> A prayer which involves an overt action, such as lighting a candle, might be a genuine act of devotion, or it might be superstition in so far as one thinks that *something would go wrong* if one did not light it. Similarly, laying a garland of flowers on the statue of the Virgin Mary might be devotion: an act of thanksgiving at the birth of a child; or it might be superstition if it were thought that the action would *influence* the Virgin to aid one more powerfully.[26]

The nature of one's intentions, then, determines whether an act is religious or not. In coming to this conclusion, Phillips goes beyond an analysis of what *the believer* thinks they are doing, and brings into play his own views of what makes something 'religious'. And the distinction he employs revolves around the extent to which fear comprises the backdrop to any ritualistic practice. A prayer is superstitious if it arises from fear and involves the attempt to manipulate the powers of the universe. This distinction effectively aligns religious actions with scientific principles: a genuinely religious form of prayer cannot have at its heart the belief that it is possible to influence the processes of the universe through saying the right kind of words or performing the correct ritual.

Phillips' attempt to distinguish religion from superstition mirrors his more general approach to religion. Religion through his lens is defined as a coherent way of life involving a set of beliefs that shape one's attitude to the world and its processes. As a result, for an action or belief to be religious it must be placed in an appropriate framework of other beliefs: 'the importance of prayer, to a large extent, depends on the role it plays in the life of the person who offers it'.[27] In case we are not clear what this means, he offers a further example:

> There is a great deal of difference *in what is being said* between parents who ask God to save their child within the context of a

[26]   D.Z. Phillips, *The Concept of Prayer* (London: RKP, 1965), 118; my emphasis.
[27]   Op. cit. 115.

264

relationship with God, and parents who make the request where such a relationship is absent...When deep religious believers pray *for* something, they are not so much asking God to bring this about, but in a way telling Him of the strength of their desires. They realise that things may not go as they wish, but they are asking to go on living whatever happens.[28]

Phillips has no truck with the kind of 'crisis faith' and the superstitious practices that attend to it that the theologian Dietrich Bonhoeffer was similarly critical of.[29] But to neglect such practices and what they might reveal about the vulnerabilities inherent in human experience is, I think, unfortunate. By limiting philosophical discussion of religion to the claims of the seriously committed, we ignore its grounding in the more general attempt to engage with the fragility and transience of human life. We also ignore the way in which religious beliefs and images might allow us to engage with the fears that arise from the experience of being vulnerable beings in a mutable world that can destroy us.

Terrence Tilley's critique of Phillips' approach makes apparent something of its limitations. Tilley claims that by excluding practices designed to manipulate external forces or those which arise out of fear, Phillips limits his engagement to 'only a part of religion';[30] namely, that which is coherent and grounded in serious epistemic and existential commitments. By excluding that which he deems 'superstitious', despite their similarities to religious practice, Phillips ignores what such excluded practices might reveal about the nature of religion itself. Indeed, Tilley goes so far as to argue that 'in actual religious practice... "religious belief" and "superstition" are rarely, if ever, unmixed'.[31] What we have in Phillips'

---

[28]   Op. cit. 121; his emphasis. Phillips reiterates this point in a later paper: "the same form of words may be superstitious in one practical context, and not in another" (D.Z. Phillips, 'Religion in Wittgenstein's Mirror' in *Wittgenstein and Religion*, 237–255; 247).

[29]   For Phillips' comments on Bonhoeffer, see *The Concept of Prayer*, 115–116.

[30]   Terrence Tilley, 'The Philosophy of Religion and the Concept of Religion: D.Z. Phillips on Religion and Superstition', *Journal of the American Academy of Religion*, **68** (2000), 345–356.

[31]   Ibid, 350. A similar point is made by Sami Pihlström, albeit it to reach a different conclusion: see 'Religion and Pseudo-Religion: An Elusive Boundary,' *International Journal of Philosophy of Religion*, **62** (2007), 3–32. Pihlström argues that "it is difficult to draw the religion vs. pseudo-religion boundary" (29); such a line can, he argues, only be drawn

attempt to remove superstitious elements from religious belief and practice is evidence of 'the sort of philosopher's gloss on religion that Phillips otherwise would normally oppose.'[32]

Tilley suggests that an analysis of superstition might reveal much about the nexus of desires and beliefs that inform religious positions, and that the problem with Phillips' approach to this discussion is that it shuts down prematurely an investigation of this kind. This refusal to consider the common ground between religion and superstition seems strange, given that elsewhere Phillips notes the importance of re-cognising that religious concepts are not '*technical* concepts; they are not cut off from the common experiences of human life, joy and sorrow, hope and despair.'[33] If this is the case, why not consider the role that fear might play in the construction of both superstition *and* re-ligion? Tilley is right to suggest the fruit this might bear for the study of religion; and what follows pursues this line of enquiry. Exploring the connection between religion and superstition enables not just an illumi-nation of religious beliefs and practices; it also holds out the possibility of relating religious ideas and behaviours to the very patterns and experiences that establish human individuality in the first case.

5. Psychoanalysis and the Investigation of Religion

At first glance the application of psychoanalytic theory to such an en-deavour does not seem particularly promising. Despite William James' attempt to develop a philosophy of religion that takes seriously human psychology,[34] psychoanalysts have on the whole been loath to consider religion as anything other than a form of pathology. There are notable exceptions in the case of Carl Jung[35] and Donald Winnicott[36]; and we will return to Winnicott's ideas shortly. But

---

once one is 'inside' the religious life, grappling with all the experiences that life throws at us and the varying ways in which we seek to respond.

[32] Tilley, 'The Philosophy of Religion and the Concept of Religion', 350.

[33] Phillips, *The Concept of Prayer*, 40.

[34] William James, *The Varieties of Religious Experience: A Study in Human Nature* (Harmondsworth: Penguin, [1902] 1985).

[35] Although after his falling out with Freud he was not allowed to use the term 'psychoanalysis' for his school of thought and was instead to use the term 'analytical psychology'.

[36] For the use of Winnicott in philosophy of religion, see John Cottingham, *The Spiritual Dimension*.

until very recently,[37] Freud's account of religion as a form of sickness to be eradicated from human life and society limited the extent to which religion might be approached by analysts as something that might have a positive role to play in understanding the psychic processes forming the human individual.

Freud's rather simplistic dismissal of religion reflects aspects of his various models for the workings of the mind.[38] His early attempts to map the unconscious are matched by his later concern to devise ways of bolstering the ego against the unruly demands of the id.[39] The tension between id and ego is mirrored in his identification of two principles that shape the infant's engagement with their world and which influence the way in which Freud approaches religion. Freud argues that the primary engagement with external reality is through the 'pleasure-principle' which seeks to maximise pleasure by placing the infant's needs and desires at the heart of the world. Accompanying the desire to maximise pleasure is the need to manage the anxiety which arises from the mother's absence. The mechanism that he identifies in this process involves a form of hallucination where the mother is 'conjured up' in the child's thoughts. So, when the child sucks their thumb, they are in effect seeking to replicate the satisfaction of feeding. There are, of course, limits to the success of this activity. Thumb-sucking might allow for the phantasy[40] of the mother's presence, but it does not provide 'real' nutrition, and so, faced with the limits that reality places on the experience of pleasure, the child comes to develop a second principle for mental functioning: the

---

[37]   See David Black, *Psychoanalysis and Religion in the 21st Century: Competitors or Collaborators?* (London: Routledge, 2006); Janet Sayers, *Divine Therapy: Love, Mysticism and Psychoanalysis* (Oxford: OUP, 2003).

[38]   For discussion of the different foci of these attempts, see Joseph Sandler *et al.*, *Freud's Models of the Mind: An Introduction* (London: Karnac, 1997); Richard Wollheim, *Freud* (London: Fontana, 1971).

[39]   Sigmund Freud, 'The Ego and the Id', SE **19** (1923), 3–66.

[40]   This spelling reflects the distinction which is sometimes made by analysts between 'conscious fantasy' – day-dreaming and conscious creativity – and 'unconscious phantasy' – the fears and desires the child experiences as they engage with the external world, and which have, in adulthood, been long repressed. It should, however, be noted that some analysts challenge this distinction as too rigid – unconscious phantasy itself is seen as the root of conscious fantasising (see for example Jean Laplanche and J-B Pontalis, 'Fantasy and the Origins of Sexuality' in *Unconscious Phantasy*, edited by Riccardo Steiner (London: Karnac, 2003), 107–143.

Beverley Clack

'reality-principle' against which the pleasure-principle must be tested.[41]

The rule of the reality-principle shapes Freud's explicit discussions of religion.[42] Maturation involves adapting to the way the world is, rather than staying as a child trapped in illusions about the relationship between thought and the external world. This progressive development in the individual's mental functioning must be mirrored, Freud argues, in societal structures: as the scientific age emerges, so the death-knell is sounded for religion. Religion – grounded in the illusions of the child's earliest experience – works with a view of the universe that science reveals to be false. There is no kind benevolence at the heart of the universe; there is no providential care overseeing what happens to us. If we are not to remain children forever, we must put aside religious beliefs that reflect our experiences in the nursery and go bravely out into hostile life.[43]

There is something decidedly odd in these conclusions. In many ways, psychoanalysis suggests that we *do* remain children forever, our attitudes and lives shaped by those earliest experiences of childhood. Indeed, Freud's final comments on the extent to which it is possible to affect lasting change in the patient through analysis suggests the limitations of therapeutic interventions when confronted with patterns established in infancy.[44] It seems strange to dismiss the importance of religion on the grounds that it is a formation of the nursery when so much else in human life shares this categorisation.

Given this tension, it is worth pursuing an alternative approach grounded in the interests of the Freud who James DiCenso calls 'the other Freud'.[45] This is the Freud who is fascinated by the weirdness of human experience and who seeks to explore that which is not rational rather than eradicate it;[46] the Freud who allows the presence

[41] Sigmund Freud, 'Formulations on the Two Principles of Mental Functioning', SE **12** (1911), 213–226.
[42] Sigmund Freud, 'The Future of an Illusion', SE **21** (1927) 1–56; 'Civilization and Its Discontents,' SE **21** (1930) 57–145.
[43] Sigmund Freud, 'The Future of an Illusion', 49.
[44] Sigmund Freud, 'Analysis Terminable and Interminable', SE **23** (1937) 209–253.
[45] James DiCenso, *The Other Freud: Religion, Culture and Psychoanalysis* (London: Routledge, 1999).
[46] It might be noted that the recent reappraisal of Freud in the wake of the 150th anniversary of his birth led the psychologist Michael Billig to suggest that this is where Freud's importance lies: in providing the basis for a "psychology of the irrational" (Michael Billig, 'The Persistance of Freud' in *The Psychologist*, **19** (2006), 540–541; 541).

of the irrational to inform and shape his anthropology.[47] By considering that which is not coherent – that which is apparently irrational – we
might discover much about the forces that shape human life and
culture.

In particular, the path to be pursued here involves investigating
two important and interconnected features which, according to psychoanalytic theory, are particularly important for shaping human behaviour: the desire to make connections and the need to deal with the
anxiety that accompanies becoming an individual. Religious and
superstitious positions, I shall argue, both involve strategies for
achieving psychic reassurance and – far from undermining the significance of religious positions – recognising this connection gives some
sense of the importance of religious strategies for the human animal.

6. Only Connect: Superstition, Religion and Being Human

The frontispiece of E.M. Forster's *Howards End* declares 'only
connect'. For Forster, making connections between experiences
that appear, at first sight, to be disparate and unconnected has political significance, opening up the public world to challenge and
change. These words can be applied, albeit with a different intent,
to the psychoanalytic account of what it is to be human. When
Freud attempts to illuminate the sources of neurotic illness, he considers the fallacious connections his patients made between their
thoughts and the world. In the case of the Rat Man, a young man's
ability to function was severely restricted by a number of bizarre,
self-imposed rituals. Through his analysis, these apparently
incomprehensible rituals were shown to be connected to a series of
phantastical fears. For example, his conflicted sexuality was apparently structured by this belief: 'If I have a wish to see a woman
naked, my father will be bound to die'.[48] Far from being meaningless,
his rituals were attempts at influencing an external fate perceived to
be threatening his loved ones. And as Freud makes clear in his

[47] See also Rosine Perelberg, *Freud: A Modern Reader* (London:
Whurr, 2005) for examples of a not dissimilar approach. Perelberg is influenced by the kind of readings of Freud that shape French psychoanalysis and
which emphasise the so-called 'Metapsychological Papers' written in the
years around 1915.
[48] Sigmund Freud, 'Notes upon a Case of Obsessional Neurosis', SE **10**
(1909), 155–318; 163.

Psychopathology of Everyday Life, this need to connect is not something peculiar to the sick.

Here the analysis of superstitious beliefs becomes interesting. Superstitions are notable because they reveal explicitly the attempt to connect things that are not connected. Take the common superstition that seeing one magpie heralds bad luck: analysed rigorously (or not even that rigorously!), the causal link between 'one magpie' and 'sorrow' cannot be established. But the desire to make the processes of the world readable through postulating a fate responsible for what happens is a powerful one; so powerful, indeed, that even Freud was not immune to its spell. In an addition to *The Psychopathology of Everyday Life* made in 1907, he tells of an incident that followed the recovery of his eldest daughter from a serious illness in 1905. Passing through his study, 'I yielded to a sudden impulse and hurled one of my slippers from my foot at the wall, causing a beautiful little marble Venus to fall down from its bracket'.[49] As it breaks into pieces, Freud finds himself quoting "quite unmoved" a passage from Busch: "Oh! The Venus! Lost is she!" Freud sees "the wild conduct and my calm acceptance of the damage" in the following way:

> My attack of destructive fury served therefore to express a feeling of gratitude to fate and allowed me to perform a *'sacrificial act'* – rather as if I had made a vow to sacrifice something or other as a thank-offering if she recovered her health![50]

As Michael Palmer has shown, this is not an isolated example of Freud's superstitious inclinations.[51] At various times in his life Freud was convinced that he would die at the age of 51, 61 or 62, the last number being derived from the publication date of *The Interpretation of Dreams* and his own telephone number.[52] Similarly, he was fascinated by ideas of clairvoyance and telepathy. What drives all these connections is the same as the impulse that he identifies in religious theorising: attempts are being made to make connections where there are none; attempts which are all, in differing ways, designed to locate the individual's life in a broader, more

---

[49]   Freud, *Psychopathology of Everyday Life*, 169.
[50]   Op. cit. 169.
[51]   Michael Palmer, *Freud and Jung on Religion* (London: Routledge, 1997), 11.
[52]   Letter to Jung, 16 April 1909; Peter Gay, *Freud: A Life for Our Times* (London: Papermac, 1995), 58.

supportive context, where something – or someone – is in control of the seemingly chance events of one's life.

Now, when Freud explores the connections made by his patients he is, of course, aiming to help them establish coherent connections; connections that relate to the universe in an accurate and appropriate way. Thus his therapeutic method coheres with his scientific principles. He is not exposing such connections in order for them to remain a part of the individual's experience. Reality-testing lies at the heart of his clinical practice in order that the sick might find healing. And this method to a large extent forms the basis for his engagement with religion. The religious make false connections between self and world that are based upon infantile desires for security which must be put aside in order to live more healthy lives.[53]

His 'metapsychological' speculations, however, suggest the basis for a rather different approach. Here, the movement is away from the clinical towards the theoretical and, specifically, towards the attempt to understand the psychic processes that shape what it is to be human. When Freud criticises religion as a form of wishful illusion because it claims that the world has been set up with us in mind or that prayer can alter the outcome of events, he may be drawing attention to the lack of evidence for seeing the world in such terms, but he is also doing something else that arguably opens the way for a rather different discussion of religion. The kind of connections that Freud details the religious making can be related to the more general human attempt to deal with the anxieties that surround being human.

At this point, we need to return to that which prompts superstitious activity; namely, its emergence from the fears that attend to transient human life. Now, for D Z Phillips, if a supposedly religious action is grounded in a false sense of causality and arises from fear it cannot be deemed properly religious. My concern is that this kind of approach ignores the importance of engaging with the vulnerability that arises from being human in a troubling and changing world. Rather than avoid considering the role that fear might play in both religious and superstitious connections, we might be better advised to explore *why* we seek to make such connections and what they might tell us about the experience of being human.

One of Freud's favourite analogies for psychoanalytic practice was to describe it as a form of archaeology, where the task was to go 'beneath the surface' in order to discover the long-forgotten origins of our actions.[54]

---

[53]   Freud, *Future of an Illusion*, 30.
[54]   Sigmund Freud, 'Constructions in Analysis', SE **23** (1937), 255–269; 'Great is Diana of the Ephesians', SE **12** (1911), 342–344.

Beverley Clack

Employing psychoanalytic ideas about the process of individuation suggests some interesting possibilities about the origins of religion and the role that it plays in the attempt to manage anxiety.

7. Religion and Anxiety

It might appear that I am following the countless critics of religion who locate its development in fears of one kind or another and then proceed to reject it on that basis. In part, this neatly describes Freud's critique. Show religion to be based, like superstition, in the desire for psychic reassurance and you can reject it as a meaningful attempt to deal with life. This is not my intention. While it would be possible to consider the all-too-real fears that accompany being human in this world – fears of natural forces and so on – I want to consider the kind of fears that emerge from the stresses and strains that psychoanalysts associate with the processes that shape individual development. Consideration of such fears might reveal much about the usefulness of religion as well as its origins.

There are a number of different psychoanalytic descriptions of psychosexual development, but all suggest something of the precarious nature of that process. There is nothing sure or certain about how an individual will turn out, given the lengthy process of individuation and socialisation.[55] Much depends upon the nexus of early experiences and relationships as well as inherited traits from one or other parent. The precarious nature of this process suggests something of the anxiety that attends to being human in the world, and as R D Hinshelwood notes, "the history of psychoanalysis has been one of trying to understand the core anxiety of the human condition" (Hinshelwood 1991: 218). It is the notion of anxiety that will be

[55]   Some examples: Freud's stages of psychosexual development suggest significant shifts are needed between parts of the body which shape psychic attitudes (see 'Three Essays on the Theory of Sexuality', SE **7** (1905), 135–243); while Anna Freud develops these stages into her theory of 'developmental lines' – an approach which suggests considerable overlap between the stages through which a child passes on the path to individuality (see *Normality and Pathology in Childhood* (Hogarth Press, 1965), 59–82). Melanie Klein's theory focuses on the shifts between two positions - the 'paranoid-schizoid' and 'depressive' – which define the child's experience (and, indeed, continue to operate in adulthood) as it develops (see 'Notes on Some Schizoid Mechanisms' in *Envy and Gratitude and Other Works, 1946–1963* (London: Vintage) 1–24; 'On the Theory of Anxiety and Guilt' in *Envy and Gratitude*, 25–42).

pursued here, as it illuminates some of the fears that shape religious attempts to make sense of the change that defines human experience.

In the years after Freud's death, psychoanalysts paid particular attention to the role of the mother in managing the child's experience of the external world. In part, this shift in emphasis reflected the changing practice of psychoanalysts who were increasingly working with children, and mothers and babies.[56] For analysts such as Wilfred Bion and Donald Winnicott, for the world to be experienced as something supportive rather than overwhelming, the mother must be able to ameliorate the infant's potentially frightening experience of it.[57] According to Winnicott, if the child is to develop a sense of security, it needs a 'good enough mother'[58] who can provide an environment where the child is the sole focus of her attention. As the object of this 'primary maternal preoccupation,'[59] the child experiences itself as omnipotent. The mother's responsiveness to the child gives it 'the moment of illusion'[60] when it feels that its wish has created the object that it desires but which, in reality, has been produced by the mother. This 'experience of omnipotence'[61] enables the child to feel that its wishes can make things happen, and this illusion is necessary if the child is to develop a sense of the world as a safe rather than a threatening place. Confronted too soon with the realities of the external world, the child's psychological development will be stunted. For the discussion of anxiety, this is an important point. If the child does not experience a 'good-enough environment' where its needs are met and where it has this illusion of power, its psychic

[56] The most important analysts in the period following Freud's death – Melanie Klein and Anna Freud – worked with mothers and babies and contributed to the development of child-analysis (see Klein, *The Psycho-Analysis of Children* (London: Vintage, [1932] 1997); and Anna Freud, *Normality and Pathology in Childhood* (London: Hogarth Press, 1965).

[57] Wilfred Bion, 'A Theory of Thinking' in *Second Thoughts* (London: Heinemann, 1967), 100–120; D.W. Winnicott, *Playing and Reality* (Harmondsworth: Penguin, 1971).

[58] Winnicott, *Playing and Reality*, 13.

[59] D.W. Winnicott, 'Primary Maternal Preoccupation' in *Through Paediatrics to Psychoanalysis* (London: Hogarth Press, [1956]), 300–305.

[60] D.W. Winnicott, 'Primitive Emotional Development' in *Through Paediatrics to Psychoanalysis* (London: Hogarth Press [1945]), 145–156; 152.

[61] D.W. Winnicott, 'Communicating and Not Communicating Leading to a Study of Certain Opposites' in *Maturational Processes and the Facilitating Environment* (New York: International Universities Press [1963]), 179–192; 180.

health will be disturbed. The mother might be physically or emotionally absent, she might be too intrusive, or she might be incapable of responding to her child. For healthy development to take place, the experience of 'maternal failure' has to be *gradual* as the mother acts to disillusion the infant's sense of omnipotent control.[62] As the child comes to realise that its wishes are not omnipotent, it feels dependent for the first time. The feeling of dependence opens up a gap between what is desired and the satisfaction of that desire. Desire, as Lacan might say, is based upon a sense of what is lacked.[63]

Where might religion fit in this model? Winnicott's notion of the 'transitional object' lends itself to one possible account.[64] As the child develops, it needs to negotiate between inner and outer worlds. A transition must be made 'from a stage of being merged with the mother to a state of being in relation to the mother as something outside and separate,'[65] and this requires an object which exists between mother/world and child, and which shares aspects of each. This might take the form of a toy, a blanket, even a sound.[66] The chosen object shares features of both worlds and thus allows for connection between what is experienced as inside and what is outside the child. The object both 'is' and 'is not' the child. This transitional object between self and world must be resilient, capable of supporting the child's feelings, both good and bad.[67] Eventually, the child puts aside this object, but it is never totally rejected: rather, 'it loses meaning, and this is because the transitional phenomena have become diffused, have become spread out over the whole intermediate territory between 'inner psychic reality' and 'the external world as perceived by two persons in common', that is to say, over the whole cultural field.'[68]

This intermediate territory provides the space for play and creativity, and, interestingly, for religious feeling. In this space, it is possible to play with the relationship between what is inside and what is outside, and it is in this realm that Winnicott locates the importance

[62] Winnicott, *Playing and Reality*, 14, 15.
[63] For similarities between Winnicott and the kind of psychoanalytic theory informed by Lacan, see André Green, *Play and Reflection in Donald Winnicott's Writings* (London: Karnac, 2005).
[64] See Ann Belford Ulanov, *Finding Space: Winnicott, God and Psychic Reality* (Louisville: WJK Press, 2001) for one account of the way Winnicott's ideas might inform accounts of religion.
[65] Winnicott, *Playing and Reality*, 20.
[66] Op.cit. 5
[67] Op.cit. 7.
[68] Op. cit.

of religion, not least because the establishment of the relationship between what is inside and what is outside is never finally complete:

> It is assumed here that the task of reality-acceptance is never completed, that no human being is free from *the strain* of relating inner and outer reality, and that relief from this strain is provided by an intermediate area of experience...which is not challenged (arts, religion, etc).[69]

Religion, it would seem, provides a safe space where self and world are in some sense felt as one; where it is possible to retain that first illusory sense of connection between thought and the world. And this need for connection suggests something of the vulnerability of human psychic experience; not least because the process of individuation in psychoanalytic theory is precarious. Much may happen in the child's early years that can lead to varying degrees of instability and insecurity. Even the most stable of beginnings has to confront the vulnerabilities inherent in transient human experience. The transitional space identified by Winnicott provides a safe place to play with experience. While Freud emphasised play as the child's attempt to master the external world,[70] Winnicott develops a more subtle account of the purposes of play. Play is not simply about mastering reality; indeed, it is not something that is limited to the experience of the child. When practised in the analytic setting it enables fresh perspectives on the past to be developed.[71] Out of this playful engagement, healing can occur.

---

[69] Op.cit. 18; my emphasis.

[70] In 'Beyond the Pleasure Principle', SE **18** (1920) 1–64, Freud comments on the game his grandson play's when his mother is absent. Taking a cotton reel on a piece of thread he throws it away from himself, saying 'fort' ('gone'), and brings it back, saying 'da' ('there') (14–17). Freud interprets the 'fort/da' game as an attempt to master the absence of his mother. The child is creating "a world of his own" where the absence of the mother is under his control.

[71] For examples from Winnicott's practice see D W Winnicott, *The Piggle: An Account of the Psychoanalytic Treatment of a Little Girl* (Harmondsworth: Penguin, 1977) and Sayers, *Divine Therapy*. Freud sounds similar when reflecting on the transference, although he tended to think that the playing out of past emotions into the analytic situation and onto the analyst was more likely to have negative consequences. Comments on the compulsion to repeat, however, suggest an approach closer to Winnicott's: "We render the compulsion harmless, and indeed useful, by giving it the right to assert itself in a definite field. We admit it into the transference as a *playground* in which it is allowed to expand in

The religious space can be thought of in similar terms. Religious art, read against this backdrop, provides a space where the fears and desires that arise in childhood and that continue as we negotiate our way through the adult world might be played with. For Freud, art and creativity allowed a glimpse of the unconscious at work, and Julia Kristeva extends this view, reading religious stories as forms of psychodrama which illuminate aspects of individual experience. Kristeva's analysis of Holbein's painting of 'the Dead Christ' thus employs a religious theme – the body of Christ taken down from the cross – to explore the experience of depression and loneliness. Here, a religious image is connected to the stuff of ordinary human life.[72] Following this method, discussion of the anxieties accompanying the move into the world beyond the nursery might be illuminated by some of the disturbing images that have haunted the religious imagination.

As Piero Camporesi has documented, the fear of hell has plagued the western religious imagination,[73] and perhaps it is in this doctrine that the merger between 'religion' and 'superstition' is most keenly felt. Read literally as metaphysical claims, they might easily be dismissed as baseless fears that have no logical support. We might, for example, challenge the belief on the grounds that it defies the laws of physics for such a place to exist, or that eternal torture would be impossible. But the tenacity of this belief may have little to do with metaphysical claims and much more to do with the ordinary experience of life in this world and the attempt to engage with our deepest fears concerning our vulnerability.

Arguably the most famous images of hell are to be found in Hieronymous Bosch's graphic paintings. Bosch's depictions of the fate of the damned retain their power to repulse *and* fascinate not just the religious. For Freud, emotional responses of this kind

---

almost complete freedom and in which it is expected to display to us everything in the way of pathogenic instincts that are hidden in the patient's mind" (Freud, 'Remembering, repeating and working through', SE **12** (1914), 145–156; 154; my emphasis).

[72] Julia Kristeva, *Black Sun: Depression and Melancholia* (New York: Columbia University of Press, 1986), 106–138. A similar method is employed in her essay 'Stabat Mater' in Toril Moi, *A Kristeva Reader* (New York: Columbia University Press, 1986), 160–186, where the figure of Mary the Mother of Child is used to provide a mirror for reflecting on her own experience of motherhood.

[73] Piero Camporesi, *The Fear of Hell: Images of Damnation and Salvation in Early Modern Europe* (Cambridge: Polity Press, 1991).

herald 'the return of the repressed'[74] when the desires and fears of infancy, now long forgotten, are reawakened. If viewed in this way, Bosch's strange and disquieting paintings might be read as providing insights into the tensions that defined the infant's formative experiences. Following Winnicott, his paintings might also be viewed as providing safe spaces for playing with the anxieties that attend to human life.

Consider 'The Haywain' (1485–1490), a picture that might be read as representing the anxieties attending to the child's move from mother to world.[75] The left-hand panel details the events of Eden: Eve is created, the first couple fall from grace and are expelled from the garden. The central panel depicts the dangers of the fallen world; earth is portrayed as a seething mass of humanity fighting over a loaded hay cart, which is being pulled, inexorably, towards the right-hand panel, and its depiction of the torments of hell. Hell itself is chaotic, a place where the body is fragmented or threatened with destruction, consumed by monsters, destroyed by fire. The lost paradise is a distant memory, with the only hope in the presence of an angel astride the cart, who is pleading with God for help. God's presence offers at least the possibility of safety, although His ability to save seems limited, Bosch's God being a rather weak and distant figure.

Such a painting opens up space for engaging with the anxieties that attend to the experience of entering the world that lies outside the relationship with the mother. Freud claimed that the task facing human beings was to find some way of feeling at home in a world that has not been set up with human happiness as its goal.[76] Adults, like children, retain that sense that the world is not always a supportive place for human growth. In a telling phrase, Freud describes the human task as the attempt to find ways of being 'at home in the uncanny.'[77] The uncanny (or the 'unheimlich') is defined by Freud as the experience of the familiar in the unfamiliar that, if analysed, leads back to the formative experiences of infancy. Translated literally, this process could be rendered as the attempt to feel 'at home in the unhomely'.[78] The world is not an easy place

---

[74]   Sigmund Freud, 'Repression', SE **14** (1915), 141–158.

[75]   For Freud's own sustained reflections on pieces of art, see 'Delusions and Dreams in Jensen's Gradiva', SE **9** (1907), 1–95 and 'The Moses of Michelangelo', SE **13** (1914), 209–238.

[76]   Freud, *Civilization and Its Discontents*, 140.

[77]   Freud, *Future of an Illusion*, 17.

[78]   'The German word "*unheimlich*" is obviously the opposite of "*Heimlich*" [homely], "*heimisch*" ["native"] – the opposite of familiar; and

for human beings and the possibility of unresolved emotions from earliest childhood make safe passage through it even more difficult.

It is here that religion is of particular importance, offering stories, pictures and rituals which aid the attempt to engage with the struggles inherent in the continuing process of individuation. So in Bosch's images of the fears that attend to embodiment, we are confronted with ways of coming to terms with the vulnerabilities of life in this world. By refusing to accept fear as an appropriate factor in the shaping of the religious response to the world, philosophers of religion like Phillips miss something important. In addressing the importance of establishing psychic security, psychoanalysts suggest the importance of addressing our fears and desires.

Considering the connections between religion and superstition offers the possibility of exploring the unconscious pressures that attend to being human in a world like this. In religious stories and beliefs we find reflective spaces for the continuing struggle to cope with the anxieties of being human. By seeing religious pictures as ways of making the unconscious conscious, we might be able to find some kind of psychic security in a changing and troubling world.

8. Conclusion

It could, of course, be argued that what I have presented is not a philosophy of religion but something entirely different. After all, I have not dealt with the attempt to prove or disprove the truth-claims of religion; I have not sought ways of showing how religious ideas might reflect the fundamental nature of the cosmos. Such criticisms are entirely correct. My concern has not been to distinguish religious ideas or practices from superstitious behaviours, but instead has been to consider what discussion of possible connections between the two might tell us about the processes that, according to psychoanalytic theory, define individual psychic development.

There is undoubtedly much to be gained from the attempt to determine the truth or otherwise of religious positions. Claims to absolute truth in the religious domain can lead to oppressive ways of living or destructive acts. Through the application of critical methodologies, such ideas can be challenged. But to only stress reality-testing

---

we are tempted to conclude that what is "uncanny" is frightening precisely because it is *not* known and familiar' (Freud, 'The Uncanny', SE **17** (1919), 217–256; 220).

avoids deeper engagement with the emotional scars that drive religious theorising and that, given the experiences that forge the individual, can never completely be eradicated.

Towards the end of his life, Freud made a not dissimilar point as he pondered the continued belief in superstitious practices. 'One feels inclined to doubt sometimes,' he writes, 'whether the dragons of primaeval days are really extinct.'[79] Perhaps this is because the attempt to eradicate superstition (or, for that matter, religion) does not destroy the anxieties that contribute to such constructions. The poet Thomas Blackburn suggests something similar in his poem 'The Citizens: A Chorus from a Play':

> After the marsh was drained and its vast monsters
> Had gasped their lives out in the well-rinsed air,
> Our city corporation cleaned the fosse up
> And charged us sixpence to see Grendell's lair.
> We thought that with the Great Panjandrum banished
> An era of sweet dreams was sure to start;
> But gracious no, only his cave has vanished;
> Don't look now, but he's walking in your heart.[80]

The fears and desires which give rise to religion remain, regardless of philosophical attempts to neutralise them. Alongside the application of reality-testing, a method which seeks to examine the connections the religious make allows for a deeper grappling with it as a phenomenon that enables exploration of the fears and anxieties that shape our humanity. Such an approach allows for a rediscovery of the humanity that Robert Graves sought to celebrate in his account of superstition. It is in the attempts at connection that we are at our most human, and if we acknowledge that, more interesting accounts of the meaning of religion might emerge.

Oxford Brookes University
bclack@brookes.ac.uk

---

[79]   Freud, 'Analysis Terminable and Interminable', 229.
[80]   Thomas Blackburn, *Selected Poems* (Manchester: Carcenet Press, 2001), 39.